Working with Windows

Michael A. Henry

REGENTS/PRENTICE HALL
Englewood Cliffs, New Jersey 07632

Library of Congress Cataloging-in-Publication Data

Henry, Michael A.
    Working with Windows / Michael A. Henry.
        p. cm.
    Includes index.
    ISBN 0-13-952748-6
    1. Windows (Computer programs)   2. Microsoft Windows (Computer
file)   I. Title.
    QA76.76.W56H46   1993
    005.4'3--dc20   92-32001
                                          CIP

Editorial/production supervision: *Julie Boddorf*
Cover design: *Bruce Kenselaar*
Interior illustrations: *Michael A. Henry*
Prepress buyer: *Ilene Levy*
Manufacturing buyer: *Ed O'Dougherty*
Acquisitions editor: *Liz Kendall*
Editorial assistant: *Jane Baumann*
Book design: *Daniel Will-Harris, TYPEStyle Ink.*
Typesetting/production: *Toni Will-Harris*

> Dedication:
> For Carla.
> *Thank you for believing in me.*

Adobe Type Manager, ATM, the ATM logo, and Adobe are trademarks of Adobe Systems Incorporated. Hayes and Smartcom are registered trademarks of Hayes Microcomputer Products, Inc. Icondraw, Icondraw Plus, Libview, and Autolaunch are registered trademarks of Winsoft Corporation. Lotus, Lotus 1-2-3, and Lotus for Windows are registered trademarks of Lotus Development Corp. Microsoft is a registered trademark and Windows is a trademark of Microsoft Corporation. Tiffany Plus is a registered trademark of Anderson Consulting and Software. Tiffany Plus was used for all Windows screen captures in this book. Winpost is a registered trademark of Eastern Mountain Software. WordPerfect is a registered trademark of WordPerfect Corporation.

 © 1993 by REGENTS/PRENTICE HALL
A Division of Simon & Schuster
Englewood Cliffs, New Jersey 07632

Printed in the United States of America
10 9 8 7 6 5 4 3 2 1

ISBN   0-13-952748-6

PRENTICE-HALL INTERNATIONAL (UK) LIMITED, London
PRENTICE-HALL OF AUSTRALIA PTY. LIMITED, Sydney
PRENTICE-HALL CANADA INC., Toronto
PRENTICE-HALL HISPANOAMERICANA, S.A., Mexico
PRENTICE-HALL OF INDIA PRIVATE LIMITED, New Delhi
PRENTICE-HALL OF JAPAN, INC., Tokyo
PRENTICE-HALL OF SOUTHEAST ASIA PTE. LTD., Singapore
EDITORA PRENTICE-HALL DO BRASIL, LTDA., Rio de Janeiro

Contents

Preface

This book differs from most other books about Windows in at least two important ways. First, this book remembers that DOS still exists. In other words, Windows does not make DOS disappear in a puff of smoke. At best, Windows only covers DOS with a fresh coat of paint because DOS still establishes the ground rules. A user who is comfortable with the basics of DOS (and with computer operations in general) will make a better Windows user.

Second, the information in this book was compiled (and tested) in a wide variety of actual work situations. Every objective, every set of performance skills, and every project was taken from real life experiences without neglecting the details of the underlying theory. These two features (along with some practice and experience) should help to create many new competent computer users.

Outstanding Features

Working with Windows has several outstanding features compared to other Windows books on the market. For example:

1. The book describes the workings of Windows version 3.1 but does not overlook the thousands of people that are still using version 3.0.

2. Each chapter begins with an overview of the material to be covered and a list of new terms that the student will need.

3. The Learning objectives and the Performance objectives are stated at the beginning of each chapter.

4. General descriptions of each task are provided in a informal, non-intimidating manner.

5. If a detailed operation is necessary, it is described in short, easy to understand step-by-step manner.

6. Every practice project was taken from real life situations and the details of the underlying theory are never ignored.

7. At the end of each chapter all important concepts are summarized, point by point.

8. Comprehension questions are provided to evaluate the student's grasp of the concepts behind each chapter.

9. When necessary, completion and matching questions are provided to reenforce the student's use of new terms and the application of those terms.

10. Many helpful hints and information about undocumented features of Windows are provided at useful points throughout the book.

Where This Book Can Be Used

This book can be successfully used in a wide variety of instructional settings. It can be used as a textbook for a complete Windows class that includes both lecture and computer laboratory work, as a reference for an short professional training seminar, as a supplement to many other types of microcomputer courses or even as a self-paced independent learning tool.

Highlights of Each Part

Part One

Part One contains four chapters and they provide an overview of Windows as it compares to DOS. Chapter One includes a summary of Windows' features and how to do things the old way, that is, without Windows. This leads into Chapter Two and it contains a short course in computer fundamentals. Chapter Three details a basic explanation of the essential DOS commands (as used from the command line prompt) and coordinates with Chapter Four where the student learns how to perform the same operations the easy way, with Windows.

Part Two

The second part of this book is concerned with the operation of the Program Manager and actually using Windows to do your

---

job. It includes chapters on Starting the Program Manager (Chapter Five), Launching Applications (Chapter Six) and Program Group Management (Chapter Seven) while Chapter Eight provides information about the Windows Accessories that are an important part of Windows. Finally, Chapter Nine concentrates on the Write word processing application and Chapter Ten provides details about the Paintbrush drawing application.

Part Three   The File Manager is the theme of Part Three. Here the student will obtain information about using File Manager to manipulate and maintain files and subdirectories. Chapters Eleven and Twelve are concerned with starting File Manager and General File Manager Operations and Chapters Thirteen and Fourteen provide information about basic disk and file operations. Chapters Fourteen and Fifteen teach the student how to create, maintain, and utilize the subdirectory structure and Chapter Seventeen allows the student to work with (launch) applications from File Manager. The last chapter in Part Three (Chapter Eighteen) supplies other miscellaneous, but important, information about File Manager that does not clearly fall into any of the other chapters.

Part Four   Part Four contains instructions for using the Print Manager. Chapter Nineteen is about the Print Manager in general and Chapter Twenty talks about installing a printer in Windows. This chapter also includes checklists that can be used to troubleshoot printer problems. Chapter Twenty-one discusses how Windows uses and displays fonts on the screen and printer.

Part Five   The last part of the book provides information about making Windows work the way the user wants it to work. Chapter Twenty-two discusses methods used to control Windows' appearance, and Chapter Twenty-three details other aspects of Windows that can be modified by the user. Chapter Twenty-four is about the PIF editor and optimizing DOS applications running under Windows. Finally, Chapter Twenty-five covers the Recorder and how to produce macros that automate repetitive Windows tasks.

Instructor's Manual

An instructor's manual is available. It contains answers to all of the questions, additional information about the practice projects, unit tests, and a comprehensive test (or final exam) and transparency masters.

Call the Author

If you have any questions, problems, or difficulties, feel free to write or call the author directly:

Michael A. Henry
PO Box 386
St. Charles, MO 63302

314-946-9765
CompuServe address:
72740,1532

Acknowledgments

It has been said before but it is worth repeating. A finished book is the result of much hard work by many people. First I want to thank Regan Caruthers for getting this project off the ground and for her work as liaison to Prentice Hall. While I am on the subject, I want to thank Liz Kendall, Senior Editor for the Office Technology division of Prentice Hall, for her incredible patience and helpfulness.

Thanks for constructive criticism and content evaluation to Carla Henry, Andy Liss, John O'Riley, Phil Tiller and all of my students in the Working With Windows Classes at Lewis and Clark Adult Education. Thanks also to Don Busche, Saddleback College; Marie Flatley, San Diego State University; Marilyn J. Landers, Herzing Institute; and Donna M. Matherly, Tallahassee Community College, who reviewed the manuscript, as well as Meredith Flynn and James Trick, who keystroke tested the manuscript.

Thanks to Tom Jorgenson, John Thro, Jim O'Neil and Mark Ward for technical and hardware support.

A special thanks to my cats, Ming and Jade, for their indispensable work as paperweights during the production of the manuscript.

Finally, I must thank the office staff in the Lewis & Clark Adult Education office. The director, Kathy Spaulding, and all of her staff, Judi Sitner, Shelly Fischer, Sandi Barrett, Cheri Amsler, and Sharon Colbert were subjected to all manner of Windows experiments while this book was being written. Perhaps now the office (and the rest of my life) can get back to "normal."

Michael A. Henry
August 1992

1

An Overview
of Windows

Learning Objectives

1. Define a window.

2. Define multi-tasking.

3. List the four different types of windows.

4. Identify each of the elements of a window.

Performance Objectives

1. Start the Windows program.

2. Open a window.

3. Use a Mouse to point, drag, and select window elements.

4. Start an application program from Windows.

5. Close a window.

Chapter Terms

Application When you are using Windows, the programs that you use are called Applications.

Application Window Programs that are written specifically for Windows will display in an Application window. An Application window will always have a menu bar just below the title bar.

Click If you press a mouse button one time, that is called a Click.

Command Line When you first turn on your computer, the screen will probably display a prompt that looks something like this: **C:\>**. When you type a command, it will appear on your screen to the right of this prompt. The area that displays this command as you type is called the Command line.

Control Button The upper left hand corner of every window will display a small box with a dash inside. This box is the Control button.

Desktop When Windows is active, the Desktop covers your entire computer screen. Everything that you do in Windows takes place on the Desktop.

Dialog Box A Dialog box will be displayed any time it is necessary to select from a group of options or if the system needs additional information.

Document Window Document windows are found inside many application windows. Once an application is running, it may be necessary to view data from two (or more) different files. Each file in an application will display in its own Document window.

DOS DOS is an acronym that stands for Disk Operating System. DOS is the program that actually controls all of the input and output operations of your computer.

Double-Click If you press a mouse button twice, quickly, that is a Double-click.

Dragging To drag an object, position the mouse pointer over the object to be moved, press *and hold* the mouse button and the object will follow the mouse pointer to a new location on the screen.

Drop-Down Menu At the top of many windows you will find a menu bar. If you click the mouse on one of the words in the menu bar a Drop-down menu will appear.

Icon An Icon is a little picture that represents an application, a group, or a function that is available when you are using Windows.

Message Box A Message box is another type of window and will appear any time an unexpected error occurs. Usually, a Message box will contain one or more buttons that must be "pressed" before the system can continue.

Multitasking This is the ability to do more than one job at the same time. For example, if you are writing a letter while your computer is printing an expense report, you are Multitasking.

Scroll Bar If the information in a window is too tall (or too wide) to fit in the area allowed, a Scroll bar will appear at the right (or bottom) of the window.

Window A Window is simply a subdivision of your computer screen. All of the work that you do while using the Windows program will take place inside these subdivisions.

Work Area The area *inside* the borders of a window is called the Work area. Do not confuse the Work area with the desktop. The Work area is inside a window and the desktop is outside.

Chapter Overview

Until very recently learning to use a computer meant memorizing many new terms and commands. It was necessary to type these commands into the computer and hope that the computer understood what you needed to do. If you typed something incorrectly, the computer would display an error message or do something very unexpected.

The program that is actually in control of your computer is called DOS (Disk Operating System). To use DOS, you must first learn its language and then you use this language to control the computer environment. Commands are typed at the command line and if everything is spelled correctly, all the punctuation is in the right place, and enough information is provided, it works. DOS has a very limited vocabulary (less than 100 words) and if anything happens that DOS does not understand, well, that's where the error messages come from.

Windows is a program that makes it easier to use your computer. Windows does not replace DOS, it just acts as an interpreter that "translates" your intentions into commands for DOS. Rather than remembering complex command statements (and typing them in correctly), you just select an object or point to a picture (called an icon), and Windows does the rest. It's almost like magic.

What is a Window?

A window is, very simply, a subdivision of your computer screen. Normally, a different program or operation takes place in each window. The individual windows can be sized, arranged, opened, and closed to meet your needs. Windows places these items on your desktop and just like the surface of a real desk, if it is not arranged conveniently, you can change it.

To start a Windows session, DOS must be running and Windows must be installed. At the DOS prompt, type WIN and press [Enter←]. After a few seconds you will see a screen similar to Figure 1.1.

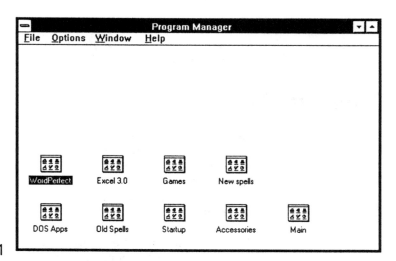

Figure 1.1

The opening screen for Windows

Multitasking with Windows

Windows insulates you from DOS, but that's not all. Windows also helps you to organize your work, transfer information between jobs, and in general, work smarter. Windows also allows you to do more than one job at the same time. This is called multitasking and before Windows, multitasking was difficult and often unreliable. The screen in Figure 1.2 shows three active applications: Paintbrush, Calculator, and a Card game.

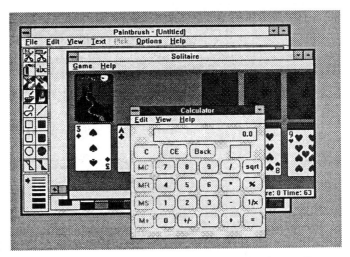

Figure 1.2

Windows will let you run more than one application at the same time.

Multitasking can be compared to a telephone with several incoming lines. When a second call comes in, the operator can put the first call "on hold" and deal with the second (or even third) caller.

When you multitask on the computer, there are several important differences. When a second computer operation starts, the first operation does not get put on hold. It continues, under the computer's control, in the background. Unless the computer needs your input, the task will run until it is completed. Your computer can perform as many tasks as the computer's resources will permit. Unlike a telephone, it is not limited to three or four incoming lines. Windows will create (and release) work areas based on the demands of your work session.

For example, it might be necessary to write a letter that contains product price information. With Windows it is very easy to run your word-processing program and your spreadsheet program at the same time. You write the letter with the word processor and refer to the spreadsheet (where the price information is stored) as necessary. In fact, Windows will let you take information from one program and transfer it directly to another program, eliminating errors and any need to retype.

Different Windows – Different Uses

Just as different jobs require different tools, Windows provides four types of windows. Applications (programs) run in application windows, data is displayed in document windows, important messages are displayed in message boxes, and if the system needs more information, you will see a dialog box.

Most of the time you spend using Windows will be in one or more application windows. Application windows are defined by a border, have a title bar at the top, and can be sized or moved as necessary. Programs written specifically for Windows (and sometimes programs written for DOS) will run in application windows (see Figure 1.3).

Figure 1.3

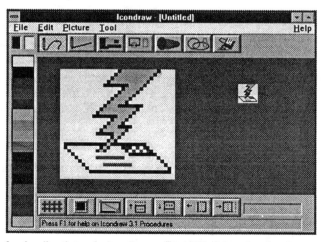

An Application window in a typical Windows Application

Document windows are found inside of many application windows. Once an application is running, it may be necessary to view data from two (or more) different files. For example, if you are writing a paper, it may be convenient to place your outline in one document window and your finished text in another. Both documents can now be examined and, if necessary, you can copy (or move) information from one window to the other (see Figure 1.4).

■ **Note**   Not all applications have document windows.

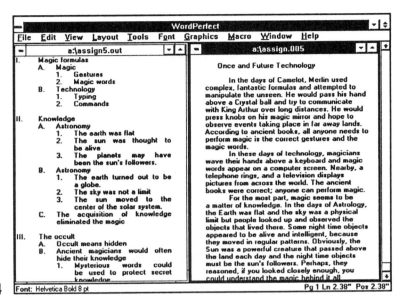

Figure 1.4

There are two Document windows open inside this Application window.

A message box will appear any time an "executive decision" is required. If a disk read or other unexpected error occurs, Windows will display a message box and ask for additional instructions. As shown in Figure 1.5, a message box will often contain one or more buttons that must be "pressed" before the system can continue. Message boxes can usually be moved but cannot be resized.

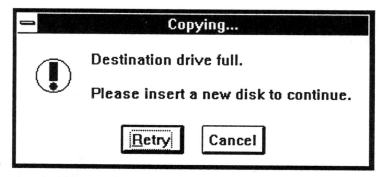

Figure 1.5

A typical Message box

Many of the specific instructions that you give to Windows will be placed in dialog boxes. A dialog box is displayed any time it is necessary to select from a group of options or if the system needs additional information. For example, to rename a file the system needs to know the current and the new name of that file (see Figure 1.6). The user would fill in the blanks and give the system permission to continue. Like message boxes, dialog boxes can usually be moved but not resized.

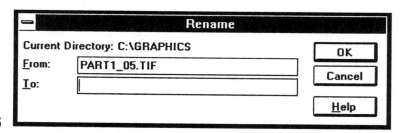

Figure 1.6

A typical Dialog box

Opening Windows

Once the Windows program is installed and running, you will see one or more little pictures on your screen. These little pictures are called Icons. To open an icon, move the mouse until the pointer is sitting on top of the icon you need and press the left mouse button twice.

■ **Note**   There are several mouse skills that must be learned before you can use Windows. The action described above is called a double-click. To double-click, press the left button twice quickly. If you press too fast,

Windows will accept only a single-click. If you press too slowly, Windows will accept two single-clicks. With a little practice, double-clicking (and single-clicking) will not be a problem.

The Elements of a Window

The main part inside a window is called the Work area. The work area will contain any icons, subwindows, or dialog boxes needed to do your work. The size of the work area is controlled by the position of the movable window borders. If the material in the window is too wide, a horizontal scroll bar (and control arrows) will appear at the bottom of the window. If the material is too tall, as in Figure 1.7, a scroll bar will appear on the right.

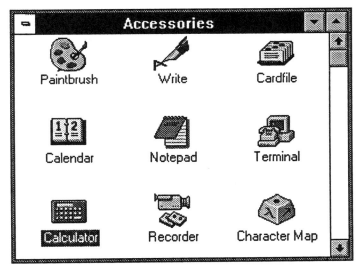

Figure 1.7

A window with a scroll bar on the right side

To view information that is outside of the current work area, you can do several things. If you want to move the data one element at a time, position the pointer on one of the arrows and press the left mouse button. The information will move each time you click.

■ Note

Pressing the left mouse button one time is called a single-click.

Between the arrows on the scroll bars you will find a little box called the Scroll box. The scroll box allows you to move quickly to material that is a long way off the screen. To use the scroll box, place the pointer on the box, and then press *and hold* the left mouse button. Continue to hold the button and move the box to a new location. (A faint outline of the box will follow the pointer as you move.) Release the button and the new material will be displayed. Moving the scroll box is not as accurate as using the arrow buttons, but it is much faster.

■ **Note** To move an item inside a window, you must master a mouse skill known as dragging. Whenever you need to drag, position the mouse pointer, press *and hold* the left mouse button, and move the item to a new location. When the mouse button is released, the change is made. Dragging is used to move scroll boxes, reposition the borders of a window, and rearrange items on your desktop.

At the top of each Application window you will find a Title bar that identifies each application by displaying its name. The title bar also contains the Maximize/Minimize buttons (little arrows pointing up and down) and the Control-Menu button (a box containing a horizontal bar). The title bar is also used to drag the entire window to a new location.

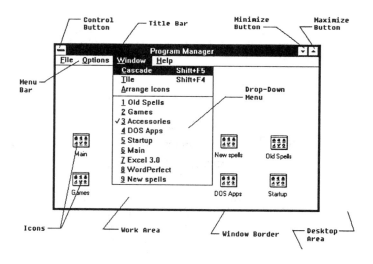

Figure 1.8

A window with a Drop-down menu open

Below the title bar you will find the menu bar. (Note: Not all windows will have a menu bar.) The menu bar is used to access any drop-down menus that are available. All you need to do is move the pointer to the correct word on the menu bar and single-click. When the drop-down menu displays, move to your choice and click again (see Figure 1.8).

▲ Hint   Save a keystroke. You can also select an item from a drop-down menu if you move to the item, press *and hold* the left mouse button, "slide" down the menu to the correct choice and then release the mouse button. When you release the mouse button, the selection is made. ▲

Running an Application Under Windows

To run an application under Windows all you need to do is open a window for that application. Move the pointer to the icon that represents the application and double-click. The window will open automatically.

Closing Windows

To close an application window, just exit from the application. The Exit command is found under the File drop-down menu. Open the File menu, select Exit and the window will close. You may also press the Control button in the upper left hand corner of the Title bar. When the Control menu appears, select Close or Exit and the window will disappear.

Dialog boxes and message boxes will close when the Continue or OK button is pressed. (Note: You can also use the Control button to close message and dialog boxes).

▲ Hint   If you double-click on the Control button, the system will bypass the Control menu and close the window immediately. ▲

Summary Points

1. Windows does not replace DOS; it just makes it easier to use. DOS is actually in control of your computer.

2. A window is a subdivision of your computer screen.

3. Windows helps you to organize your work, transfer information between applications, and provides multitasking functions.

4. Windows provides four type of windows including application windows, document windows, message boxes, and dialog boxes.

5. The main part of a window is called the work area.

6. If the data to be displayed is larger than the work area scroll bars will appear at the right and/or at the bottom of the window.

7. To use a mouse (when running Windows) you must know how to point, single-click, double-click, and drag.

8. To run an application under Windows, move the mouse pointer so that it is on top of the icon that represents that application and double-click.

9. To close a window, open the File menu and select Exit or double-click on the Control button.

Practice Exercises

At your computer, perform the following practice exercises.

1. Start the Windows program by typing WIN at the DOS prompt. Open the Accessories Group and list, on paper, the names of the items you find there. When you are finished, close the Accessories Window.

2. Open the Program Manager (if it is not already open) and rearrange the icons you find there for your convenience. Drag the icons to new locations as desired.

3. Open the Accessories Group from Program Manager. Find the icon for the Clock and double-click. When the Clock opens, place the mouse pointer over its title bar and drag the entire window to the lower left hand corner of the display screen.

Experiment with the menu bar and the various buttons. For example, try changing the clock from an analog display to digital and back. When you are finished, close the application and do *not* save your work.

Comprehension Questions

1. What is the name of the program that is actually in control of your computer?

2. What does multitasking mean?

3. Name four different types of windows.

4. When using Windows, what is the maximum number of tasks that can be performed at one time?

5. Applications run in application windows. In what type of window is data normally displayed?

6. What are the "little pictures" called?

7. If the material in a window is too tall or too wide to fit in the window, what will happen?

8. In addition to the title of the application, what else is found in the title bar?

9. What is a drop-down menu?

10. List two ways to close a window.

Completion Questions

1. A window is a _____ of your computer screen.

2. If a disk read or other unexpected error occurs a _____ will be displayed.

3. A _____ is displayed any time it is necessary to select from a group of options or if the system needs additional information.

4. To open an application, position the pointer on top of the correct icon and _____ the left mouse button.

5. To drag an item, you must _____ the left mouse button.

6. To open a drop-down menu, move the pointer to the correct word on the _____.

7. The Exit command is always found in the _____ drop-down menu.

Identify each of the items in the picture below.

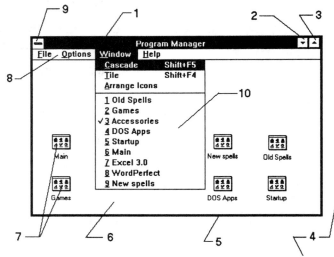

Figure 1.8A

1 _____

2 _____

3 _____

4 _____

5 _____

6 _____

7 _____

8 _____

9 _____

10 _____

2

Computer
Fundamentals

Learning Objectives

1. Define hardware and software.

2. List three major divisions of a computer.

3. Define the magic formula for using a computer.

Performance Objectives

1. Boot the computer.

2. Load the Windows program.

Application Software
This is just another name for a program. When you are using Windows, all programs are called Applications.

Boot
To Boot your computer means that you have turned on the computer's power or pressed its reset switch.

Hardware
The computer itself. In general, Hardware is anything that has a wire attached to it.

Input
Instructions or unprocessed information that is going *in* to your computer. You can get information into your computer from the keyboard, a disk drive, or even from a mouse.

Microprocessor
The Microprocessor is the actual device that performs all of the processing tasks and is sometimes called a CPU or Central Processing Unit. The Microprocessor in your computer is identified by a model number such as 8088, 80286, 80386, or 80486.

Output
When the computer is finished processing information it often becomes Output. Output could be in the form of a printout, characters displayed on your monitor screen, or a beep from the computer's speaker.

Processing
Between Input and Output there is Processing. When the computer processes information, it is changed in some way. For example, you could tell the computer to calculate all the formulas in a spreadsheet and while the computer is performing the calculations, it is in the act of Processing.

Software
Software is any program that you use to make your computer perform actual work. Some examples of Software would be a game, a word processing program, or even Windows itself.

System Software
System software is a program (or set of programs) that teaches the computer how to be a computer. In general, the computer uses System software to perform basic input and output operations. DOS is an example of System software.

Chapter Overview

If you could take a computer back to the days of King Arthur, Merlin would be dismissed from his position as Court Magician. By waving your fingers above the keyboard (and pressing keys, of course) you could create more magic than Merlin ever imagined. You enter the "magic words" and lights flash, messages appear mysteriously. King Arthur would be impressed and Merlin would be unemployed.

To perform "computer magic" you need two things: hardware and software. In general, hardware is any part of the computer that has a wire attached to it, and the programs that you run on the computer are called software. The system unit, the monitor, the keyboard, and the mouse are all hardware. A word processing program, a spreadsheet, a poker game, or even a flight simulator are software. The hardware needs instructions from the software before it can do anything. Computer hardware without computer software is nothing but a large, expensive paperweight.

The Hardware

The computer's hardware can be divided, by function, into three general groups: input, processing, and output. To put it very simply, a computer accepts data from input devices, processes that information, and then sends it back to you through the output devices.

First, you need to get data into the system through Input devices such as the keyboard, the disk drives, and the mouse. Input devices translate the data into a form that the computer can use. When you think of Input, you may think of the keyboard first. Most of the information and instructions that come directly from you is entered through the keyboard. There are, however, many ways to get information into your machine. For example, when you are using Windows, the mouse is very important. Rather than typing commands, you select functions or programs by positioning the mouse pointer on the screen and clicking the mouse buttons. The computer doesn't care where the input comes from as long as it is entered in a way that the computer understands.

Figure 2.1

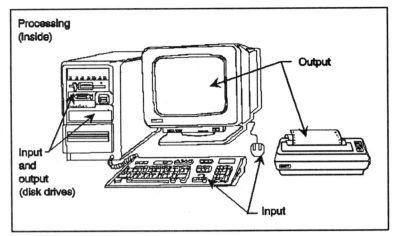

The Hardware (identified by function)

The core of the computer's hardware is the microprocessor. As the name implies, the microprocessor (along with the memory) form the Processing part of the hardware. The microprocessor is usually located in the same case that holds the disk drives. PC compatible computers use one of several different types of microprocessors. Other than speed, the type of microprocessor does not make much difference as far as DOS is concerned.

Finally, when the microprocessor finishes its work, the data will be sent to the monitor, the printer, a disk drive, or other Output device. The output devices translate the data back into a form that people can use. The Output data may end up as mysterious messages on the screen, as finished text on the printer, or as files tucked safely away in a disk drive.

■ **Note**   Disk drives are a special type of computer device. They can perform both Input and Output functions. What they do depends on the instructions they receive from the software (or from commands entered at the keyboard). The important thing to remember is that even though they are usually in the same container as the microprocessor and memory, they are *not* part of the Processing equipment. Do not confuse disk drives with memory.

A Short Overview of Software

There are two very broad categories of software. The first is called system software and it provides the instructions that the computer needs to perform very basic computer tasks such as saving and retrieving files. When the computer is first turned on, the system software must be loaded into memory or the computer will stop and display an error message.

■ **Note**   The system software that we will be concerned with is called DOS. It comes in several versions (3.1, 3.2, 4.0, 5.0, etc.) and in several types (PC-DOS, MS-DOS, and others), but we won't worry about the minor differences here. To run Windows, DOS must be loaded first and it must be version 3.1 or higher. (Remember, DOS stands for Disk Operating System.)

The second category is called application software. This is a very general name for the software that is used to do actual work on your computer. A word-processing program, spreadsheet, or a database program are all applications.

If a CD player, amplifier, and speakers are the hardware for a music system, then the CDs could be called the software. The "data" on your CDs is Input through the CD player, is Processed through the Amplifier, and the Output can be heard through the speakers. The type of CD that is played controls the output. If you play a classical CD, the output is classical music. In the same manner, the output from a computer is controlled by the type of application software.

Applications are usually written in one of two forms: for DOS or for Windows. A DOS application is designed to run directly from the C:\> prompt. Just type the name of the DOS application and press ⌈Enter◄─⌉.

■ **Note**   Every DOS program you use will probably require completely different commands. When a DOS program loads, it completely takes over control of your computer. Every time you learn how to use a DOS program you need to learn its language. When it comes to DOS programs, there are no standard commands.

Figure 2.2

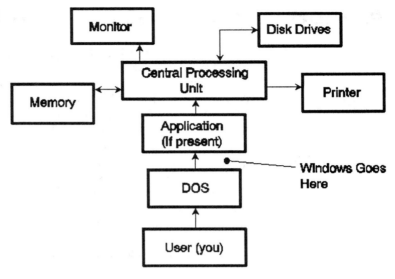

How your computer system is arranged

If an application is written to run under Windows, first, load Windows. Then, double-click the correct icon on the Windows' desktop. If you try to run a Windows application from the C:\> prompt, you will receive a message that says, "This program requires Microsoft Windows."

Programs written for Windows usually meet very specific standards. They will always have a title bar and a menu bar at the top of the screen. The work area will be surrounded by a movable border and the standard commands (such as Save, Exit, and Print) will always be in the same place in the File menu. Once you have learned the basic commands for one Windows application you know the basic commands for almost all Windows programs.

■ **Note**   Windows will let you run both DOS applications and applications written specifically for Windows. If you run a DOS application from Windows, Windows will "get out of the way" while the DOS program is active. A DOS application will run under Windows the same way it runs from the DOS prompt—you still need to learn the commands that program understands.

The Secret to Using a Computer

You have to remember that a computer is not intelligent. It cannot do anything without very specific instructions. These instructions could come from DOS, from an application, or from you, the user. The computer does not care where the instructions come from, but they must be in a form that the computer understands.

If there is a secret to using a computer, this is it. It could be called your magic formula.

> The Magic Formula...
> PROCESS -> INPUT -> OUTPUT

The PROCESS: Tell the computer what to do. From DOS, just type the command in at the C:\> prompt. This could be in the form of a specific command such as DISKCOPY or FORMAT. In Windows, you usually select a function from a menu or a dialog box. In any case, the first thing that you must do is tell the computer what to do.

The INPUT: Next, tell the computer where the source (original) information is stored. In a DOS command, the Input is separated from the Process by a space. In the magic formula the arrows actually represent spaces. (When using Windows, spaces and other punctuation are handled automatically.)

The OUTPUT: Finally, tell the computer where to put the information after it has been processed. Again, when typing a DOS statement, the Output is separated from the Input by a space.

■ **Note** DOS commands almost always follow the general format of the magic formula. For example, to copy a floppy diskette, you would type a command that reads:
DISKCOPY A: A:.
The word DISKCOPY is the Process, the first A: is the Input and the second A: is the Output. Each element of the statement is separated from the next by a space. In a DOS command, *no other spaces are allowed.*

Starting Your Computer

If your computer is set up correctly, all you need to do is to turn on the power. DOS is usually stored on the hard disk and the computer will find it and load it automatically.

Technically, Windows is a DOS application program. To start Windows, first load DOS. Then type WIN at the C:\> prompt.

Windows' function (as an application) is to make other applications easier to run. (Applications of this type are sometimes called a Shell). As shown in Figure 2.2, Windows places itself between DOS and your application programs. Remember, Windows does not replace DOS, it just "hides" it.

When the Windows desktop appears, you are ready to go to work.

Summary Points

1. A computer system needs two things to operate: hardware and software.

2. Hardware is the computer itself. In general, hardware is anything that has a wire attached.

3. Software is a set of instructions that tells the computer exactly what to do.

4. Software is divided into two very general categories: system software and application software.

5. DOS falls into the category of system software.

6. Technically, Windows falls into the category of application software. Its function is to make other applications easier to run. Applications of this type are sometimes called a Shell.

7. Every time you need to learn the commands for a DOS program, it can be like learning a new language. There is no standard for commands in DOS programs.

8. A DOS application will run inside Windows the same way it runs from the DOS prompt.

9. Once you have learned the standard commands for one Windows application, you know the standard commands for almost all Windows applications.

10. The secret to using a computer could be called the magic formula. The commands must always be entered in the form: Process, Input, Output. Each element of the command is separated from the next by a space. *No other spaces are allowed.*

11. To start Windows, type WIN and press [Enter←]. When the desktop appears, you are ready to go to work.

Comprehension Questions

1. In general, what is computer hardware?

2. What is computer software?

3. What are the two very broad categories of software?

4. What are the three parts of a DOS command? (Hint: The magic formula.)

5. When using a DOS command, what is used to separate each of the parts?

6. How will a DOS application act when it is run under Windows (as opposed to running it from the DOS prompt)?

7. What will happen when you run a Windows application from the DOS prompt?

8. What are the major advantages of a program written specifically for Windows compared to a program written for DOS?

9. What do the initials DOS stand for?

Completion Questions

1. DOS falls into the category of _____ software.

2. Technically, Windows is considered to be _____ software.

3. Along with the memory, the core of a computer's PROCESS-ING section is the _____.

4. A disk drive is both an _____ and _____ device.

5. The monitor is an _____ device.

6. The mouse is an _____ device.

7. The general form of a DOS command is: _____ _____ _____.

8. In order to run Windows, you must use version _____ of DOS or higher.

9. Windows is sometimes referred to as a _____ program.

3

Using DOS
Doing it the Hard Way

Learning Objectives

1. Identify the disk drives.

2. List the rules for naming a file.

3. List and define the DOS wildcards.

4. List the two general types of files.

5. List the four types of executable programs.

6. Define *Subdirectory* and *Path*.

Performance Objectives

1. Display a list of files from a specific disk.

2. Name a file according to DOS rules.

3. Format a floppy disk.

4. Make a backup copy of a floppy disk.

5. Copy a file or a group of files.

6. Create, activate, and remove a subdirectory from the tree structure.

7. Run a DOS application from the DOS prompt.

Application File
An Application file is a file that stores a program. You can easily identify an Application file by looking at its extension. If a file ends with .EXE, .COM, .BAT, or .PIF, then that file is probably an Application file.

Data File
If a file is not an application file then it must be a Data file. A Data file is used to store the work that you do while using the computer.

Default Drive
If you store a computer file and do not tell the computer which drive to use, the computer will use the Default drive. Normally, the hard disk (drive C:) will be the Default drive.

Disk Drive
A Disk drive is a piece of computer hardware that contains a Disk. All of the work that you perform at the computer will be stored, on disks, in the form of files.

Extension
An Extension is one to three additional characters added to the end of a filename. The extension is separated from the filename by a period.

File
A file is an organized collection of related data. When you are using a computer, your files are stored magnetically on Disks.

Filename
A Filename is used to identify your data when it is stored on a disk. A Filename cannot contain more than eight characters.

Floppy Disk
A Floppy disk is placed in a floppy disk drive and used to store files. Floppy disks are normally 5-1/4" or 3-1/2" in size. To use a Floppy Disk you place it in a floppy-disk drive and close the drive door (if necessary).

Hard Disk
A Hard disk is permanently built into a hard-disk drive. Often a hard disk drive is built into the computer system unit and cannot be easily removed.

Path
A Path is the name of a disk and the names of all the subdirectories that lead to the location of your files.

Subdirectory
A Subdirectory is a division of a disk that is used to keep related groups of files together.

Wildcard A Wildcard is a special character that can be used to represent any other filename character when you are searching for files. You could compare Wildcard characters to the joker in a deck of playing cards. The two Wildcard characters are: The asterisk (*) and the question mark (?).

Chapter Overview

There is an essential connection between DOS and Windows. The guidelines for naming files, the method used to select disk drives, and the general rules that control disk structure are functions of DOS, not Windows.

In this section, we will learn three essential computer skills: formatting a disk, copying a disk, and copying a file. That sounds pretty simple and, actually, it is. However, before you perform these tasks, you must know a little bit about disk drives, disk structure, and the rules for naming files. Windows hides DOS very well but the more you know about DOS, the easier it is to use Windows.

Disks and Disk Drives

IBM-PC compatible microcomputers identify disk drives with a letter followed by a colon. The first drive is called drive A:, the second is B:, and so on. In most systems, drives A: and B: are floppy drives and drive C: is a hard drive. (Note: Your system may have a slightly different disk drive arrangement.) As far as DOS is concerned, the only difference between a floppy drive and a hard drive is its capacity. That means almost all of the commands that work on a floppy drive will also work on a hard drive.

When you start your computer it will display an indicator, called a prompt, that tells you which drive is active. The active drive is called the default drive. If your computer has a hard disk, the default drive will probably be drive C:. The prompt will say C:\> or perhaps just C>. The letter C inside the prompt tells you that DOS is going to use drive C: for all operations unless *you* tell it otherwise.

■ Note When you tell the computer which drive to use, the colon that follows the drive letter must be included. It is part of the drive name.

If you want to change the default drive, simply type the name of the drive that you want to use and press [Enter←]. For example, to make drive A: the default drive, place a disk in the drive, type A: at the prompt and press [Enter←]. If everything is OK, (that is, if the disk in the drive is readable), your screen will look something like Figure 3.1.

Figure 3.1

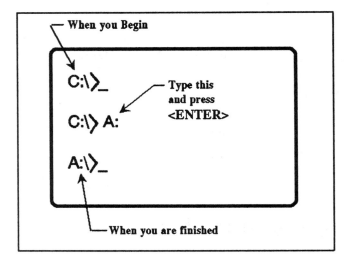

How to change the default drive

You can also access other drives by just referring to them as part of a command. For example, to copy a disk in drive A: to drive B:, you would enter the command DISKCOPY A: B: at the prompt. (Remember, DOS commands almost always follow the format of the magic formula: Process, Input, Output.) DOS will ignore the default drive and copy the contents of drive A: to drive B:.

Files and Filenames

When it comes to files, they are not very mysterious. A file is nothing more than an organized collection of related information. Any time you place some papers in a file folder, write a name on the tab, and place the folder in a filing cabinet, you create (and save) a file. Later, when you need to use the information stored in a file, you check the names on the tabs until you find the file you need.

Computer files are very similar to paper files (see Figure 3.2). After a computer file has been created and named, you can store it in a "filing cabinet" called a disk drive. Later, to retrieve your files, all you need to know is the file's name and its location on your disk. That name is the key that unlocks the file's contents.

Figure 3.2

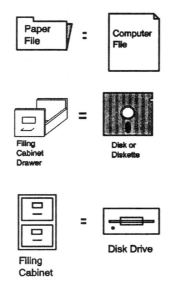

Paper File = Computer File

Filing Cabinet Drawer = Disk or Diskette

Filing Cabinet = Disk Drive

Computer files as compared to paper files

A complete filename has three parts: the drive indicator, the filename, and the extension.

The actual filename cannot be any longer than eight characters and cannot contain any spaces. All the letters, all the numbers, and all of the special characters (except for those in the following list) can be used in any combination.

■ **Note**   The special characters shown here *cannot* be used in a filename.

>	Greater than sign	?	Question mark
<	Less than sign	*	Asterisk
|	Vertical bar (pipe)	+	Plus sign
/	Slash	=	Equal sign

\ Backslash	: Colon
; Semi-colon	, Comma
[Left square bracket	] Right square bracket
. Period (except at the beginning of an extension)	

Most of the time, if you try to use one of these characters as part of a filename, DOS will display some sort of error message. However, some of these characters can be "dangerous." That is, if you try to use them as part of a filename, your file could be damaged or completely lost.

The last part of a filename is called the extension. An extension starts with a period and can be up to three characters long. Traditionally, the extension is used to identify the type of file (as shown in Figure 3.3) and many programs will automatically assign an extension for you.

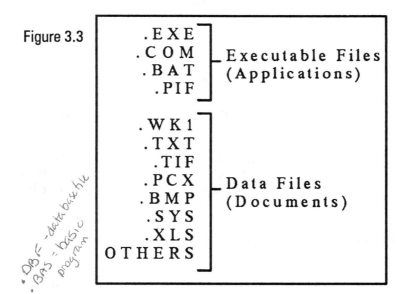

Figure 3.3

Caption: Some common file extensions

The remaining part of a filename is called the drive indicator. A drive indicator is simply the name of the drive that contains the file and is placed in front of the filename as shown in Figure 3.4. If the file is located on the default drive, the drive indicator is not required.

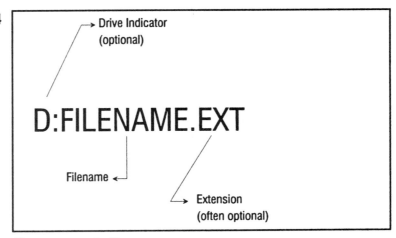

Figure 3.4

The structure of a filename

With an eight-character filename and a three-character extension you shouldn't have any trouble coming up with meaningful names for your files. However, there are several names that DOS reserves for its own use. These combinations of characters are used by DOS to identify various devices that may be attached to your computer. If you try to use a device name as a filename, DOS will get confused.

Here is a list of DOS reserved device names. *Do not* try to use these names as filenames.

PRN	LPT1	LPT2	LPT3
NUL	COM1	COM2	COM3
COM4	AUX	CON	CLOCK$

How to Display a List of Files

DIR is the DOS command that will display a list of files. The general form of the command is DIR d:. If you apply the magic formula to this command it looks like this:

PROCESS	INPUT	OUTPUT
DIR	d:	(screen)

Replace the drive letter (d:) with name of the drive you want to access. For example, if you want to use drive A:, enter DIR A:. To view drive C:, type DIR C:, and so on.

By default, the list of files will display on the screen, so in this case you do not have to provide the OUTPUT section of the command.

When you type DIR and press [Enter←], a list of files will scroll up the screen as shown in Figure 3.5. If the list contains more lines than the screen allows, it will scroll off the top. If you want to examine any of the filenames at the beginning of the list, you need to be a fast reader.

Figure 3.5

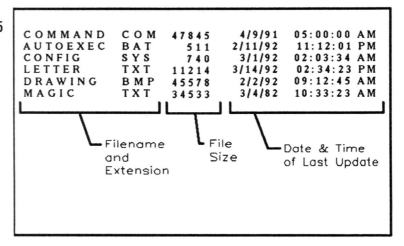

A typical directory listing as displayed by DOS

Actually, DOS provides some controls that can be used to modify the way a file listing will display. These controls are called switches. A switch starts with a forward slash and contains one or more additional characters. To use a switch, just add it to the end of the command.

If you type /P at the end of a DIR command, the screen will pause each time it fills with data. At the bottom of the screen, it will say, **Press any key to continue**.

The /W switch cause the file list to display in a "wide" format. Only the name of the file and the extension will be visible and the files will list in five columns across rather than down the screen. (Figure 3.6 shows a typical "/W" display.) If the list of files is exceptionally long, the /P and the /W switches can be used together.

Figure 3.6

```
Volume in Drive C is HENRY_003
Directory of C:\

    FILE1     FILE2     FILE3     FILE4     FILE5
    FILE6     FILE7     FILE8     FILE9     FILE10
    FILE11    FILE12    FILE13    FILE14    FILE15
    FILE16    FILE17    FILE18    FILE19    FILE20
    FILE21    FILE22    FILE23
```

A Wide (or /W) directory display

■ **Note**   DOS provides several other switches that can be used with the DIR command. For more information, check your DOS reference manual.

How to Use the DIR Command to View a List of Files on Drive A:

What to Do	**What Happens**
1. Place the disk in drive A:.	Nothing
2. Enter the command: DIR A: (Press [Enter⏎])	The list of files will be displayed on the screen.
3. If the list of files is too long, reenter the command with the /P or the /W switch. DIR A:/p or DIR A:/W	If the /P switch is used, the screen will pause each time it fills. If the /W switch is used, the list of files will display in five columns across the screen.

Preparing a Floppy Disk for Use

If you have ever played a blank video tape in a video recorder, you have a general idea of what an unformatted disk looks like to your computer. When you format a disk, the computer will place invisible magnetic circles, called tracks, on the disk surface. These tracks are subdivided into nine or eighteen wedge-shaped sectors. The formatting process also checks the disk for any physical damage and sets aside some disk space to store the directory information.

> The basic form of the FORMAT command is:
> FORMAT d:

Replace the drive letter (d:) with the name of the drive that contains the disk to be formatted. For example, to format a disk in drive A:, enter the command: FORMAT A:. The FORMAT process takes about 45 seconds, but it always seems to take longer if you are in a hurry.

▲ **Hint**
When you open a new box of disks it is a good idea to format the entire box. That way you always have a good supply of disks ready to be used.

If you have a disk that has been used before, you can format it again. All data that was on the disk will be completely erased. ▲

One more thing to remember: The FORMAT command is extremely dangerous. If you do not tell the computer which drive to format, it will format the default drive, which is usually your hard disk. Remember, as far as the computer is concerned, the only difference between a hard disk and a floppy disk is its capacity. You can destroy all the data on your hard disk just as easily as on a floppy disk.

■ **Note**
When using the FORMAT command *always* include the name of the drive that contains the disk to be formatted.

How to Format a Floppy Disk

■ **Note**
Actually, there are two types of floppy diskettes: high density and double density. In order to format your

disks correctly, you need to know what type of diskettes your computer can use. Not all computers can use both types of disks.

What to Do	**What Happens**
1. Place the disk that is to be formatted in the disk drive and close the door.	Nothing.
2. Enter the command FORMAT A: and press [Enter←]. **Don't forget to include the A: part of the command!**	The screen will say, **Insert new diskette for drive A: and strike [Enter←] when ready.**
3. **READ THE SCREEN.** Make sure that the computer is going to format the disk that you want to format. If everything is correct, press [Enter←] again.	The system will begin to format the disk. A counter will appear on the screen.
4. Assign a volume name if desired.	The computer will assign the volume name and display a message about the capacity of the disk. It will also ask if you want to format any more disks.

■ **Note**   On some versions of DOS, you must specifically tell DOS that you want to assign a volume name while other versions will always ask for a volume name.

5. If you are done formatting disks, type N and press `Enter←`.
If you have more disks to format, type Y and press `Enter←`.
(Go to step 3).

If you type Y, the process will repeat. If you type N, the DOS prompt will return.

Making a Backup of a Floppy Disk

Most of the work that you do on the computer will be stored on floppy disks. However, disks often fail to operate correctly and your work could be lost. Disks are the weak link in a computer system. The best way to deal with this problem is to prevent it, and the best way to prevent it is to have more than one copy of your valuable disks.

The tool that DOS provides to copy your disks is the DISKCOPY command. It is convenient to think of DISKCOPY as your computer "photo copy" machine. The DISKCOPY command will make an exact duplicate of your existing diskette.

Place the original disk (called the Source diskette) into your disk drive, type the DISKCOPY command and press `Enter←`. Now all you have to do is read (and respond to) the prompts. After a few seconds, the computer will tell you to remove the Source diskette and replace it with another disk (called the TARGET disk). Depending on the type of disk being copied, you may have to swap the Source and the Target disks two (or more) times.

■ **Note** It is a good idea to format your target disk before using it. The FORMAT process will identify all defects (if any) on the disk. Do not use a disk that has defects as the Target of a DISKCOPY operation.

If the Target disk is not formatted, DISKCOPY will format it for you, but it will ignore any defects and may write data on top of a damaged area. If this happens your Target diskette will not be usable.

How to make a Backup Disk

What to Do	**What Happens**
1. Write-protect the disk that is to be copied.	On 5-1/4" disks, place a piece of write-protect tape over the notch on the side of the disk. On 3-1/2" disks slide the little switch to the "open" position.
2. Place the disk to be copied (called the Source disk) into the disk drive and close the door.	Nothing.
3. Type the command: DISKCOPY A: A: and press [Enter←].	The screen will say, **Insert Source diskette in drive A: Press any key when ready**.
4. Press any key and the system will read the data from the disk into memory.	The disk-drive indicator light will come on as the computer reads the data.
5. When the indicator light goes out, remove the Source disk from the drive and place the Target disk in its place.	The screen will say, **Insert TARGET diskette in drive A: Press any key when ready**.
6. Press any key and the process will continue.	The disk-drive indicator light will come on.

■ **Note**   Caution: The screen will not display any additional messages until the copying process is completed. Don't worry, if the drive indicator light is on, everything is proceeding correctly.

7. When the process is complete, the drive indicator
light will go out and the system will ask:

Copy another? (y/n)
If you press Y, the process
will repeat.

8. If you want to copy more
disks, press Y.
If you are finished copying
disks, press N.

If you press N the DOS
prompt will redisplay.

Using the COPY Command

The DISKCOPY command is used to copy the entire contents of
one disk to a second identical disk. That means that you cannot
use DISKCOPY to move information from a 5-1/4" disk to a
3-1/2" disk or from a 5-1/4" double-density disk to a 5-1/4"
high-density disk. To move data between disks that are different
sizes or capacities, you must use the COPY or XCOPY command.

The COPY command can be used any time you need additional
copies of your files. For example, if you need to send the same
letter to twenty different people, you have two choices. You
could type the letter twenty times (changing the name and address for each letter) or you could type a single master letter
and make nineteen copies.

■ **Note** Beginning with DOS version 3.3, a new command,
called XCOPY, was added to the DOS toolbox. XCOPY
is an enhanced version of the COPY command. There
are several important differences between COPY and
XCOPY. See your DOS manual for more information.

To use the COPY command, you must know the name of the
file that is to be copied and its location (that is, what disk is it
stored on) and where you want the copy to end up. Then just
enter the COPY command, the name (and location) of the
original (source) file and the desired new location. Figure 3.7
displays the process required to copy a file named CHARMS.TXT
from drive A: to drive B:.

Figure 3.7

The MAGIC FORMULA is:

| PROCESS | INPUT | OUTPUT |

When the MAGIC FORMULA is applied
to the COPY command it becomes:

| COPY   A:CHARMS.TXT   B: |

The MAGIC FORMULA

Wildcards   Many card games have wildcards. A wildcard can represent anything. DOS uses two symbols as wildcards to allow you to work with groups of files.

The first wildcard is the asterisk (*). The asterisk is used to represent anything. For example, if you enter the command COPY A:*.* B:, every file on drive A: will be copied to drive B:. The command, COPY A:*.EXE B: will copy every file on drive A: that has an extension of .EXE, to drive B:. Any file on drive A: that has a different extension will be ignored.

The other DOS wildcard is the question mark (?). The question mark is used to represent any one character. For example, if you enter the command COPY A:L?TTER.TXT B:, all files that start with the letter L and end with the letters TTER will be copied. The character in the position of the question mark can be anything. LETTER, LITTER, or even L$TTER will be copied (if the files exist.)

If necessary, you can use more than one wildcard in a single filename search. If you enter the command COPY A:L?TT??.* B:, all files that begin with the letter L and that have the letter combination TT in the third and fourth character position will be copied. The asterisk (as an extension) can represent anything.

■ Note   If you enter the command COPY A:L*TTER.EXE B:, all files that begin with the letter L and have an extension of .EXE will be copied. DOS will ignore the TTER. To solve the problem, use the question mark (as in L?TTER), rather than the asterisk.

How to Copy a File

In this example we will copy the AUTOEXEC.BAT file from your hard disk to a floppy disk.

What to Do	**What Happens**
1. Place a formatted disk in drive A: and close the door.	Nothing.
2. Type the command: COPY C:AUTOEXEC.BAT A: and press Enter↵.	The file will be copied from drive C: to drive A:. When the process is finished, the screen will say, **1 file(s) copied**.

Subdirectories and the Disk-Tree Structure

Disk drives are very similar to a filing cabinet. When you are using a filing cabinet, you can place a number of paper file folders in each drawer. Often, it is desirable to keep groups of related files together. In a filing cabinet, you could place a group of related files into an expanding folder and then put it in the drawer. DOS provides a tool that is very similar to an expanding folder. This tool is called a subdirectory. As shown in Figure 3.8, groups of related files can be stored together by placing them in a subdirectory.

To create a new subdirectory use the command MD (for Make Directory) followed by a name for the new subdirectory. For example, the command MD HERBS will create a subdirectory named HERBS on the default disk drive. If everything is OK, you will receive no message. If you examine the list of files on the default disk, you will see a new entry that says HERBS followed by <DIR>.

■ **Note** The separator that is used with subdirectories is the backslash, not the regular slash. The backslash leans to the left (\) and the regular slash leans to the right (/).

The regular slash is usually on the same key as the Question mark (?) character.

Figure 3.8

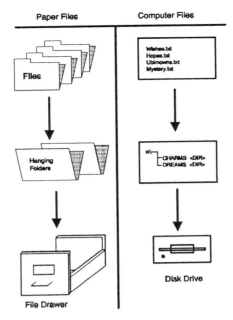

Subdirectories: Paper file and Computer files

Once the subdirectory is created you can open it and place files inside. To open a subdirectory, the CD (for Change Directory) command is used. For example, to open the subdirectory created previously, type the command, CD HERBS (or CD\HERBS.) Basically, to use the CD command, you just need to know the name and location of the subdirectory that you want to open.

■ **Note**   To display a list of subdirectory names, you can enter the command:

DIR *.

and press [Enter←]. All subdirectories (and any files that do not have an extension) will display.

It is possible (and often desirable) to create subdirectories inside of subdirectories. For example, you may have data about several types of plants. Start by creating a subdirectory called HERBS (type MD HERBS). Next, open that subdirectory (CD HERBS or CD\HERBS) and inside, create a series of sub-subdirectories for each plant. For example, to create a series of sub-subdirectories named THYME, BASIL, and OREGANO the commands would be MD THYME, MD BASIL, and MD OREGANO. The subdirectory structure would now look like Figure 3.9.

Figure 3.9

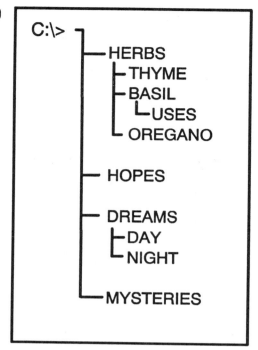

A typical Subdirectory structure or TREE

Subdirectories within subdirectories are quite common. (However, if you find it necessary to create a subdirectory structure more than three or four levels deep, you should probably look for a better way to arrange your files.) To access data inside subdirectories and sub-subdirectories you need to know the name of every subdirectory along the way that leads to your file. This list is called a path.

For example, to access a data file called USES.TXT that is stored in the BASIL sub-subdirectory, you would need to type C:\HERBS\BASIL\USES.TXT at the prompt. (Note: Do not place a backslash at the end of the command or the computer will expect you to type another sub-subdirectory name.) In other words, the path is the combination of subdirectories and sub-subdirectories that ends with the name of the file you need to use.

■ **Note**   A single path cannot exceed 127 characters. That is the maximum number of characters that DOS will let you type in a single command. You can, however, move through an exceptionally long path with a series of short commands.

The last command used to manage subdirectories is the RD command (RD stands for Remove Directory). The RD command is used to eliminate subdirectories that are no longer needed. For example, to get rid of the OREGANO subdirectory, you would type RD OREGANO.

■ **Note**   If any files or sub-subdirectories are inside a subdirectory that you are trying to remove, DOS will not allow you to remove it. When using DOS, you can only remove empty subdirectories.

Files and File Types

There are (as far as we are concerned) only two types of files: application files and data files. The general rule is simple: Application files create data files.

Application files are programs and are often referred to as executable files. Windows refers to all programs as *applications* so we will stick to that description. Normally, applications can be identified by their extension. If a file has an extension of .COM (for Command), .EXE (for Executable), or .BAT (for Batch file), then the file is probably an application file.

■ **Note**   Windows adds a fourth type of executable file called a .PIF or Program Information File. Technically, a .PIF is information that Windows uses when it launches a DOS application, but when using Windows, a file that ends with .PIF is treated like an application.

Data files are where you store your computer work. For example, a letter written using your favorite word-processing program is stored in a data file. The application (your word-processing program) will create a data file to store your letter.

How to Run a DOS Application from the DOS Prompt   To run a DOS application from the DOS prompt, you need to know two things: the name of the application, and where the application lives. For example, to run an application that has a filename of CHARMS.EXE, type the name of the file CHARMS at the DOS prompt and press [Enter←]. If the file is stored in a subdirectory on drive C: called SPELLS, you would type C:\SPELLS\CHARMS.

▲ Hint   When running an application from the DOS prompt, the extension is usually optional. ▲

Actually there are two types of application files: Windows applications and DOS (or non-windows) applications. If you try to run an application written for Windows from the DOS prompt you will receive a message that says, **This program requires Microsoft Windows.** A DOS application will run directly from the DOS prompt, but to run a program written for Windows, Windows must be loaded and running properly before the Windows application can be used.

■ Note   When using Windows, DOS applications are often called non-Windows applications.

Summary Points

1. There is an essential connection between DOS and Windows.

2. The three essential computer skills are formatting a disk, copying a disk, and copying a file.

3. IBM-PC compatible microcomputers identify disk drives with a letter followed by a colon. The first drive is drive A:, the second is B:, and so on.

4. As far as DOS is concerned, the only difference between a floppy disk drive and a hard drive is capacity.

5. When you start the computer the prompt will display the name of the default drive. To change the default drive, type the name of the drive and press [Enter←].

6. A file is nothing more than an organized collection of related data.

7. A complete filename has three parts: the drive indicator, the filename itself, and the extension. The actual filename cannot be any longer than eight characters and cannot contain any spaces. The extension begins with a period and can be up to three additional characters.

8. The DIR command is used to display a list of files.

9. Before a disk can be used to store data, it must be formatted. To format a disk, use the FORMAT command.

10. To make a backup of a floppy disk use the DISKCOPY command. DISKCOPY will copy the entire contents of one disk to another identical disk.

11. The COPY (or XCOPY) command is used to copy a single file or a group of files to a second location.

12. DOS uses two wildcards to work with groups of files. The asterisk (*) represents anything and the question mark (?) can represent any one character.

13. To keep a group of related files together, they may be placed in a subdirectory.

14. To make a new subdirectory, use the MD (Make Directory) command.

15. To open a subdirectory, use the CD (Change Directory) command.

16. To remove an unwanted subdirectory from your disk, use the RD (Remove Directory) command.

17. There are (as far as we are concerned) only two types of files: application files and data files. The general rule is that application files create data files.

18. When using Windows, there are four types of application files: .EXE, .COM, .BAT, and .PIF. All other files are considered to be data files.

19. The location of a file, including all the names of all the required subdirectories, is called the path.

20. To run a DOS application from the DOS prompt, type the name of the application (and its path, if necessary) and press $\boxed{\text{Enter}\leftarrow}$.

Practice Exercises

At your computer, perform the following practice exercises:

1. Obtain a new disk and use the FORMAT command to prepare it for use.

2. Use the COPY command to copy the AUTOEXEC.BAT file from your hard disk to a floppy disk.

3. On your hard disk, open your WINDOWS subdirectory with the command: CD\WINDOWS. Now, use the COPY command and wildcards to copy all of the files with the extension .EXE from the WINDOWS subdirectory to your floppy disk. (Note: There will probably be twenty or more .EXE files on your hard disk. If you receive a message that says, "Insufficient disk space," just ignore it.)

4. Use the DIR command to display the list of files on that disk. If the file list is longer than one screen, use the /P or the /W switch to control the display.

5. Obtain another blank disk and make a backup of your disk using the DISKCOPY command.

Comprehension Questions

1. Basic computer operations, such as guidelines for naming files and the general rules that control disk structure, are functions of what?

2. When you first turn the computer on, it will display an indicator. What is this indicator called?

3. As far as DOS is concerned, what is the difference between a hard disk and a floppy disk?

4. What is the name of the first drive in your system?

5. How do you select a new default drive?

6. What is a file?

7. How many characters are allowed in a filename?

8. An extension begins with a period and can be a maximum of how many characters?

9. What command is used to prepare a floppy disk so that it can be used to store files?

10. If you type in a command and do not tell the computer which drive to use, in general, what will happen?

11. What command is used to make a backup copy of a floppy diskette?

12. What command is used to make a new subdirectory on a disk?

13. What is a path?

14. What do you need to do to run an application from the DOS prompt?

Completion Questions

1. The three essential computer skills are
_____ a disk,
_____ a disk, and
_____ a file.

2. A filename has three parts: the
_____, the
_____, and the
_____.

3. When making a backup of a floppy disk, the original disk is called the _____ disk and the copy is called the _____.

4. IBM-PC compatible microcomputers identify disk drives with_____ followed by a
_____.

5. To use the COPY command, you must know the
_____ of the file to be copied and its
_____.

6. A disk drive can be compared to a filing cabinet and a sub-directory can be compared to a _____ inside a drawer of the filing cabinet.

7. A single path cannot exceed _____ characters in length.

8. There are, in general, only two types of files:
_____ files and _____ files.

9. In Windows, executable files end with the extensions
_____, _____, _____, or
_____.

Matching Exercises

Match the following terms to their definitions

___ **DISKCOPY**   A. This command will display a list of files in five columns across the screen.

___ **COPY**   B. When making a backup copy of a diskette, this is the original disk.

___ **DIR/P**   C. This command will remove an unwanted subdirectory from your disk.

___ **DIR/W**   D. Use this command to access a subdirectory on your disk.

___ **FORMAT**   E. When you first turn the computer on, this will appear. It usually displays the name of the default drive inside.

___ **source disk**   F. This command displays a list of files on the screen. If the screen fills up, the listing will pause.

___ **target disk**   G. This command is used to prepare a disk for use.

___ **CD command**   H. In general, these are created by applications to store the work that you do on the computer.

___ **MD command**   I. Use this command to move one or more individual files from one disk (of any type) to another (of any type).

___ **RD command**   J. When making a backup copy of a disk, this is the disk that will receive the information being copied.

___ **DOS prompt**   K. This command will make an exact copy of the entire contents of one floppy disk on another, identical floppy disk.

___ **data files**   L. If you need to make a new subdirectory on your disk, use this command.

4

Windows to the Rescue

Learning Objectives

1. List the two major parts of Windows.

Performance Objectives

1. Start Windows and access the Program Manager.

2. Launch a Windows application from the Program Manager.

Drive Bar   The File Manager window contains an area that displays an icon to represent each of the disk drives attached to your computer. This area is called the Drive bar.

File Manager   The File Manager is the second major part of Windows. It is primarily used to perform file and disk operations that would normally be entered as commands on the DOS command line.

Group Window   When a group is opened it will display as a Group window inside the Program Manager window.

Group   A Group is created to store a collection of related applications or data files. For example, when you install Windows a special group is automatically created that is used to store some of the applications that are shipped as part of the Windows package.

GUI   GUI is an acronym that means Graphic User Interface. Windows is often called a GUI program.

Non-Windows Applications   If a program can be run directly from the DOS prompt, then Windows refers to that program as a Non-windows application. However, a Non-windows application can also be launched from inside Windows.

Program Manager   The Program Manager is the main part of Windows. It is used primarily for managing and launching applications. When you exit Program Manager, you exit Windows.

Windows Applications   If a program is written specifically to run under Windows, then that program is called a Windows application. A Windows application cannot be run from the DOS command line.

Chapter Overview

As you have seen, using DOS to perform computer operations can be difficult, error prone, and irritating. For maximum DOS efficiency, you must memorize a long list of commands, remember where to place spaces, and know exactly where your files are located. Everything must be typed in character-by-character and if you are not a fast typist, this can be time consuming.

DOS has been around since the first PCs were released. It has improved, but not much. The basic operational requirements are the same now as they were when DOS first appeared. Fortunately, Windows can do virtually everything DOS can do, but Windows uses pictures (icons) and drop-down menus rather than a command-line prompt.

Windows Simplifies Computer Operations

Windows is often called a GUI or Graphic User Interface. That means, instead of typing in long, error-prone commands, a Windows user selects from a number of little pictures or from a list of commands displayed in a menu. To use Windows, all you have to do is move the mouse pointer and click. Typing is kept to a minimum; you do not need to memorize any complicated commands, and all computer operations are simplified.

Much of the time you will spend using your computer will be doing two things: using applications and managing files. That is why Windows is divided into two major parts: the Program Manager and File Manager. Program Manager is primarily used to manage and launch applications, and File Manager is designed to help you deal with file and disk operations.

The Program Manager

Program Manager is used to organize your applications (and data files) into convenient, logical groups by creating new groups (or removing old groups) as your needs change. For example, if you want to store all of your word-processing files in one group and your spreadsheet information in another, just create the new groups and place the files inside.

Figure 4.1

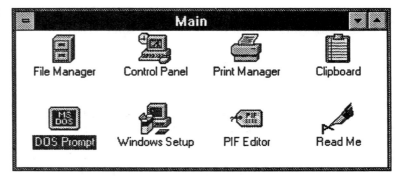

By default, the Main Group will contain the items shown here.

When Windows is first installed, one of the groups it will create is the Main Group. This group will contain six application icons as shown in Figure 4.1. By default, you will find the File Manager, the Print Manager, DOS Prompt, the Clipboard, Windows Setup, and the Windows Control Panel. (Note: Your system may have additional items installed.) These items are placed here for your convenience but you can move or duplicate them in other groups as needed.

The Accessories Group is also created by Windows during installation. This group is used to store the default Windows Utilities as shown in Figure 4.2. These applications include Paintbrush, Terminal, Notepad, Recorder, Cardfile, Calendar, Calculator, Clock, and the PIF Editor. Each of the icons you find here represents a complete application. In many cases an entire book (or at least an entire chapter) could be written about how to use each of these programs. For more information you should consult the Microsoft Windows User's Guide.

Figure 4.2

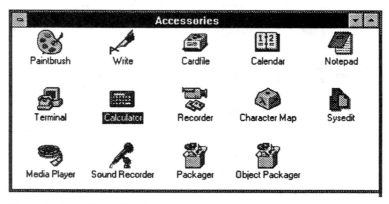

The default ACCESSORIES group

The Games Group will contain Solitaire and Minesweeper. These two games are supplied by Microsoft when you purchase Windows. If you obtain any other games for your system, this would be a good place to store them.

The last group that is created when you install Windows is the Applications Group.

■ **Note**   If Windows cannot locate any applications on your hard disk, this group may not be appear.

The Applications Group will be used to store icons for all of your applications that Windows is able to locate. You can, of course, add (or remove) applications in this group to meet your needs.

To open a group, move the mouse pointer to its icon and double-click. The program group window will open. Each icon inside the group window represents an application or file. To launch an application, move the mouse pointer to the correct icon and double-click again.

File Manager

It is possible to use Windows and not use Program Manager at all. The File Manager is designed to simplify computer operations (such as formatting disks and copying files) but it also can be used to launch applications. If you are using Program Manager to launch an application, locate its icon and double-click. To launch an application from File Manager, locate its filename and double-click. It doesn't really matter if you run applications from Program Manager or from File Manager. Often, the correct tool to use is the one that you happen to have in your hand.

Figure 4.3

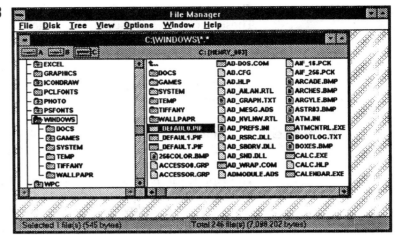

The main screen for the FILE MANAGER

When you first see File Manager you will notice it displays more text and fewer icons than Program Manager (see Figure 4.3). Almost all operations in Windows are performed by moving the mouse pointer and clicking, but File Manager is designed to deal primarily with files and file names.

One of the most important parts of File Manager is the drive bar. On the drive bar, you will find an icon that represents each of your disk drives. (Note: The default drive will be highlighted. To change the default drive, just move the mouse pointer and click.)

Near the top of the File Manager window you will see the menu bar. The first two items here are the File and Disk menus. All of the important DOS functions can be found here.

Figure 4.4

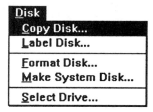

The FILE and DISK drop-down menus

As you can see in Figure 4.4, the File menu allows you to copy or delete a file. You may also run an application just as if it were entered at the DOS prompt. Creating new directories is simplified and renaming files is easy. In fact, the File menu helps you to perform some actions that are very difficult (or even impossible) when you are only using DOS.

The Disk menu contains the remaining essential computer commands. Here you will find the commands that are used to Format and Copy a disk.

When you are finished using File Manager, open the File menu and select Exit to return to Program Manager. To end your Windows session, open the File menu (in Program Manager) and select Exit again. After a few seconds the DOS prompt will return to the screen.

1. Windows is divided into two major parts: Program Manager and File Manager.

2. Program Manager is primarily used to manage and launch applications.

3. Inside Program Manager, the Main Group contains File Manager, Print Manager, the DOS Prompt, the Clipboard, Windows Setup, and the Windows Control Panel.

4. By default, the Accessories Group will store Paintbrush, Terminal, Notepad, Recorder, Cardfile, Calendar, Calculator, Clock, and the PIF Editor.

5. The Non-Windows Applications Group will contain all of the DOS applications that Windows is able to locate.

6. The Windows Applications Group will store an icon to represent each of the Windows applications on your system.

7. File Manager simplifies DOS and other computer operations.

8. File Manager can also be used to launch applications. It is, in fact, possible to use Windows without ever using Program Manager.

9. The drive bar contains one icon to represent each drive available to your system.

10. The Files menu displays the commands used to manipulate a single file or a group of files.

11. The Disk menu contains the commands that relate to disk-based operations such as FORMAT and DISKCOPY.

Practice Exercises

1. Start the Windows program and open Program Manager (if it is not already open). Locate the Games Group and open it.

2. Inside the Games Group, you should find an icon that represents the Solitaire game. Double-click and have fun.

Comprehension Questions

1. What are the two major divisions of Windows?

2. Much of your computer time will be spent performing what two operations?

3. What six applications will you normally find inside the Main group?

4. By default, where will your Windows applications be stored?

5. How can you identify the default drive on the drive bar?

6. Where (in File Manager) are the FORMAT and DISKCOPY commands found?

Completion Questions

1. Windows is often referred to as a GUI. GUI stands for

_____ _____

_____.

2. File Manager is used primarily to simplify file and _____ operations.

3. Program Manager is used to _____ and _____ applications.

4. By default, DOS applications are stored in a group called _____ Applications.

5. The File Manager display contains more _____ and fewer types of _____ than Program Manager.

5

Starting Program Manager

Learning Objectives

1. Define Program Manager.

2. Describe the two Windows 3.1 modes.

3. Identify a program group.

Performance Objectives

1. Start Program Manager in Standard mode.

2. Start Program Manager in Enhanced mode.

3. Control the size of a window.

4. Move a window to a new location.

5. Cascade all open windows.

6. Arrange windows as tiles.

7. Move and arrange icons as necessary.

AUTOEXEC.BAT After the CONFIG.SYS file is loaded, DOS will automatically run the AUTOEXEC.BAT program. This file usually contains a PATH and a PROMPT instruction and any other commands needed to set up your computer's working environment. Often, the last line of an AUTOEXEC.BAT file will automatically launch Windows.

Cascade The Cascade command resizes all open windows and places them in layers so that each title bar is visible.

CONFIG.SYS When you boot your computer, DOS will automatically load the CONFIG.SYS file. This file usually contains information that the computer needs to load memory management programs, device drivers and other data that your computer needs to operate properly.

Enhanced Mode If you have an 80386 (or higher) computer with two megabytes (or more) of memory, Windows will run in Enhanced Mode. Enhanced Mode allows true multitasking of both Windows and non-Windows applications.

Program Group Program groups are used to organize your applications and data in the Program Manager. A Program Group icon looks like a little window that contains six tiny icons.

RAM RAM is an acronym for Random Access Memory. RAM is where all of your applications and all of your data are stored while you are working. If you turn your computer off, and do not save your work on a disk, all of the information in RAM is lost.

Setup Program This program is part of the Windows package and is used to automatically install Windows on your computer system.

Standard Mode If your computer is an 80286 or has less than two megabytes of memory, Windows will start in the Standard Mode. While the computer is in Standard Mode, only programs written specifically for Windows can be multitasked.

Tile The Tile command resizes all open windows into small windows of similar sizes. They will not overlap.

Chapter Overview

At the core of Windows is a tool called Program Manager. The first time you launch Windows, it will dominate the screen. Its continuing mission is to maintain your system's resources, seek out your applications, and make your work easier than it has ever been before. Its primary function, as its name implies, is to help you manage your programs and data.

Figure 5.1

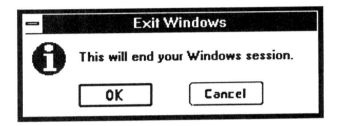

The Exit Windows dialog box

Inside the Program Manager window, you will see several program group icons and inside the program groups, you will find icons for your applications. Whenever you launch an application, Program Manager moves to the background but it continues to run. When the application is closed, Program Manager will return to the foreground. Everything in Windows eventually comes back to Program Manager. In fact, if you exit Program Manager you, exit Windows (see Figure 5.1).

▲ **Hint** If necessary, you can load Windows and automatically launch an application directly from the DOS prompt. For example, to start Windows and launch the Cardfile program, type WIN CARDFILE.

If the application to be launched is stored in a subdirectory, you may need to specify the entire path. For example, if Lotus 1-2-3 for Windows is stored in a subdirectory named Lotus, you would need to type: WIN C:\LOTUS\123. ▲

Windows and Its Modes

Before you can use Windows it must be installed. A program that comes with Windows, called Setup, makes this task simple.

Unpack the Windows disks and place the first disk in your disk drive. Then, at the DOS prompt, type SETUP.

As the Setup program runs you will need to make a few decisions about the specific configuration you want, but for the most part, Setup does everything automatically. It examines your hardware, searches your disks for any software stored there, and automatically creates several program groups that you will need later.

If necessary, the Setup program will change your AUTOEXEC.BAT and CONFIG.SYS files. The changes will depend on the type of computer you are using and the amount of memory installed. After the changes are made, type WIN at the DOS prompt and Windows will automatically try to start in the way that is best for your computer.

■ **Note**   For more information about the different types of computers and memory, check your Windows User's Guide and DOS manuals.

Windows version 3.1 can be run in one of two modes: Standard or Enhanced. If your computer is an 80286 or has less than two megabytes of memory, Windows will start in the Standard mode. While the computer is in Standard mode, only programs written for Windows can be multitasked. If a DOS application is loaded while you are in Standard mode, all other operations will be suspended as long as it is active.

■ **Note**   The Real mode (that was available in version 3.0) has been eliminated in version 3.1. If your computer is an 8088, 8086, or if it has less than 1 megabyte of memory, then you cannot use Windows version 3.1.

Windows can take full advantage of your computer's extended memory while in Standard mode. In other words, if you have two megabytes of memory installed, Windows can multitask as many programs as will fit in two megabytes.

▲ **Hint**   If you have an 80386 or 80486 computer with three or more megabytes of memory, you can force your computer to start in Standard mode by typing WIN/S (or WIN/2). If you do not use any DOS applications, Standard mode can sometimes run faster than Enhanced mode. ▲

If you have an 80386 (or higher) computer with two megabytes (or more) of memory, Windows will run in 386 Enhanced mode. In addition to all of the features provided by the Standard mode, the 386 Enhanced mode provides two additional and very powerful features. First, 386 Enhanced mode will allow true multitasking of both Windows and non-Windows applications. This means that when a DOS application is loaded, all other operations are *not* suspended. It is even possible to display Windows and non-Windows applications on the screen at the same time. Effectively, each application will be placed in its own little computer called a virtual machine. Each virtual machine will chug along, independently doing the job assigned to it.

Second, 386 Enhanced mode converts hard disk space into virtual memory. You could think of virtual memory as artificial RAM (Random Access Memory.) If your system runs out of actual RAM, portions of an application running in the background may temporarily be moved to the hard disk. That means, in the 386 Enhanced mode, the amount of "memory" available is limited only by the amount of hard disk space available.

■ **Note**   If you have an 80386 (or higher) with less than two megabytes of memory you can still run in 386 Enhanced mode. All of the benefits of 386 Enhanced mode will be available, but Windows will run more slowly.

To force Windows to start in 386 Enhanced mode, enter the command WIN/3.

Windows and Program Compatibility   If you have any programs that were written for older versions of Windows, that is, for Windows prior to version 3.0, you may not be able to use them with version 3.1. Windows version 3.0 had a third mode, called Real mode, that could be used to run Windows software that was written for versions prior to 3.0, but the Real mode is not available in version 3.1. If possible, you should contact the manufacturer of older software and obtain an updated copy. If this is not possible (or practical) you may need to continue using Windows version 3.0 or stop using your older programs completely (see Figure 5.2).

Figure 5.2

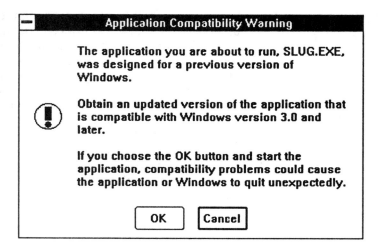

This is the warning box that will be displayed if you attempt to run an application that is written for a version of Windows prior to version 3.x.

Program Manager and Program Groups

When the Program Manager window is open, you will see several program group icons. These icons look like a tiny window that contain six tiny icons. When you open a program group, you will find actual application icons inside. In Figure 5.3, you can see the application icons inside a typical Accessories group. At the bottom of Program Manager you will see program group icons for the Games Group and Main Group among others.

Program groups are used to organize your applications and data inside Program Manager. The Setup program automatically creates several groups, but you can create additional groups as you need them. For example, if you have a group of related programs, such as a collection of utilities, you could create a Utilities group. If you need to write a newsletter for an amateur magicians club, you could create a group called Magic and use it to store all of the necessary applications and documents. Use your imagination. Arrange your Windows workspace as conveniently as possible.

Figure 5.3

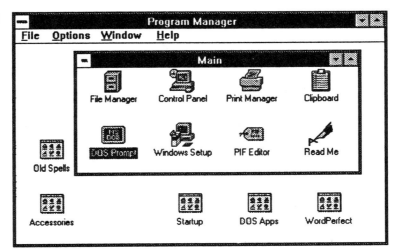

The main Program Manager window displaying several open groups

▲ **Hint**   If you need to move an icon, place the mouse pointer over the icon, press and hold the left mouse button, and drag the icon to a new location. ▲

Arranging Windows

Often it will be necessary to have more than one window open at the same time. Before long, windows will cover parts of other windows and your neat, easy-to-use workspace will begin to look like a table at a garage sale.

Fortunately, this is not a big problem. You control the horizontal borders—you control the vertical borders. You can reduce a window to a small icon or enlarge it to cover the entire screen. For as long as your Windows session lasts, the dimensions of your desktop are the only limits.

How to Change the Size of a Window

What to Do	**What Happens**
1. Position the mouse pointer over the border to be moved.	The pointer will change to a double arrow.

2. Press and hold the left mouse button and drag the border to the new location.

The window size will be changed.

▲ Hint If you place the mouse pointer over one of the corner "hot spots," the pointer will change to a double arrow that leans diagonally left or right. The "hot spot" will allow you to drag two adjacent borders to a new location simultaneously. ▲

How to Move a Window

What to Do   **What Happens**

3. Place the mouse pointer over the title bar.

Nothing.

4. Press and hold the left mouse button and drag the window to a new location.

The window will be moved.

How to Arrange Windows Automatically

There are two additional tools that you can use to arrange your open windows. If you open the Window menu (see Figure 5.4), you will find the Cascade and the Tile command. These commands arrange the windows so that at least some part of every window is visible.

Figure 5.4

Window	Help	
Cascade	Shift+F5
Tile	Shift+F4
Arrange Icons	
1 Accessories	
2 Main	
3 Startup	
4 DOS Apps	
5 WordPerfect	
6 Old Spells	
√ 7 New spells	
8 Games	
9 Excel 3.0	

The Window menu

Figure 5.5

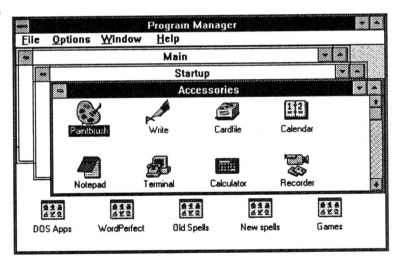

This shows several windows arranged in the Cascade pattern.

The Cascade command resizes all open windows and places them in layers so that each title bar is visible. Figure 5.5 shows several windows in a Cascade arrangement.

Figure 5.6

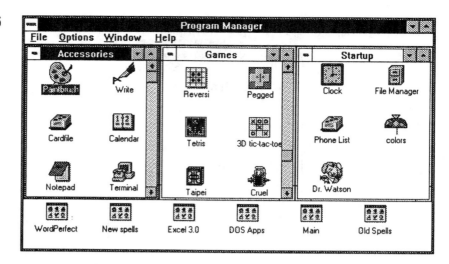

Several windows arranged as Tiles

If you select Tile from the Window menu, the space available in Program manager will be divided into smaller windows of similar sizes as shown in Figure 5.6. Some of the icons may not be visible, but each window will have a horizontal or vertical scroll bar if necessary.

▲ Hint   You can automatically straighten up all of the icons inside a window by selecting the Arrange Icons feature from the Window menu. ▲

Summary Points

1. Program Manager is the core of Windows.

2. Inside Program Manager you will see a number of group icons or open group windows.

3. If your computer is an 8088, 8086, or has less than 1 megabyte of memory you cannot use Windows version 3.1.

4. An 80286 computer or a computer with less than two megabytes of memory will run Windows in Standard mode. If you enter WIN/S or WIN/2, your system will be forced to run in Standard mode.

5. If your computer has two or more megabytes of memory and has an 80386 (or higher) microprocessor, Windows will run in 386 Enhanced mode. To force a system to run in 386 Enhanced mode, enter WIN/3.

6. A program group is used to organize your applications and data in Program Manager. Program group icons look like a little window that contain six tiny icons.

7. You can change the size of an open window by moving its borders to a new location.

8. To move an entire window, place the pointer on the title bar and drag.

9. Windows can be arranged automatically if you open the Window menu and select Cascade or Tile. Cascade arranges the windows so that all title bars can be viewed and Tile arranges the windows in a mosaic pattern.

Practice Exercises

1. Start Windows and open Program Manager (if necessary).

2. Open the Main, Accessories, and the Games window. Now, open the Window menu, select the Cascade command, and observe the results.

3. Open the Window menu again, select the Tile command, and watch what happens.

4. Finally, move, size, and rearrange the windows (and group icons) as necessary until you are satisfied with their location. Remember, it is up to you to make your Windows work environment as convenient as possible.

Comprehension Questions

1. What is the primary function of Program Manager?

2. What criteria does the Setup program use to make changes to your AUTOEXEC.BAT and CONFIG.SYS file?

3. What happens if you exit Program Manager?

4. If an application was written for an older version of Windows, that is, prior to version 3.0, what must you do?

5. If your computer is an 80286 and you want to run Windows in Standard mode, how much memory is needed?

6. What are the differences between Standard mode and 386 Enhanced mode?

7. What does a program group icon look like?

8. What are program groups used for?

9. How can you move two borders at the same time?

10. If you choose Cascade from the Window menu, how will your desktop be affected?

11. What does the Tile command do to your window arrangement?

Completion Questions

1. An _____, _____, or any computer with less than one megabyte of memory cannot run Windows version 3.1.

2. If you enter_____ or _____, Windows will be forced to run in Standard mode.

3. On an 80386 computer you must have at least _____ megabytes of available memory to run Windows in 386 Enhanced mode.

4. To force a system to run in 386 Enhanced mode, start Windows by typing _____.

5. You can change the size of a window by moving its _____.

6. To move a window, place the mouse pointer over the _____ _____ and drag the window to a new location.

6

Launching Applications
[from Program Manager]

Learning Objectives

1. Identify a program group window.
2. Identify a program group icon.
3. Identify an application icon.
4. Identify Task Manager.

Performance Objectives

1. Launch one or more applications from Program Manager.
2. Launch an application "automatically."
3. Move between program group windows.
4. Open the Task Manager window.
5. Switch between active applications with Task Manager.
6. Close an active Windows application from Task Manager.
7. Perform basic desktop "housekeeping" chores from Task Manager.

Active Window

Any time you have more than one program group open in Program Manager, the one that you are currently using is called the Active window. The title bar and borders of the Active window will be the same color as the main window.

Application Icon

Application icons are stored inside program group windows. Each Application icon represents a program or a document.

Program Group Window

A Program group window is a document window that is located in the Program Manager's work area. Each Program group window has its own Control, Maximize, and Minimize buttons but does not have a menu bar.

Program Group Icon

A Program group icon is a minimized program group window. Program group icons are found in the Program Manager work area.

Task Manager

Task Manager allows you to open, close, arrange, and select your applications directly.

Chapter Overview

As you will remember, the Setup program automatically creates several program groups. These default groups will contain the major Windows tools, several programs that come with Windows (including a couple of games), and any applications that Windows manages to locate on your disks. In any case, the Setup program will always at least create a Main Group, an Accessories Group, a Startup Group, and a Games Group (see Figure 6.1).

Figure 6.1

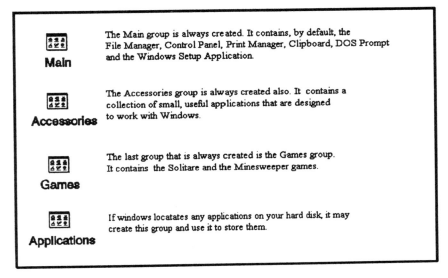

Main
The Main group is always created. It contains, by default, the File Manager, Control Panel, Print Manager, Clipboard, DOS Prompt and the Windows Setup Application.

Accessories
The Accessories group is always created also. It contains a collection of small, useful applications that are designed to work with Windows.

Games
The last group that is always created is the Games group. It contains the Solitare and the Minesweeper games.

Applications
If windows locatates any applications on your hard disk, it may create this group and use it to store them.

The SETUP program usually creates these default groups.

The Setup program assumes that everyone who uses Windows is going to need this particular arrangement, but in reality, nobody is an "average" Windows user. The arrangement that Setup establishes is a starting point at best. After you use Windows for a while, you will want to change things. Make any changes that you want to—Windows doesn't mind.

Understanding Program Groups

The program group is the basic unit of storage in Program Manager. These groups can be created, deleted, and moved as necessary. Each group will be displayed inside Program Manager as either a program group window or a program group icon.

A program group window is a document window that is located in the Program Manager's work area. Each program group window has its own Control, Maximize, and Minimize buttons, but does not have a menu bar because program group windows are affected by the commands in the Program Manager's menu bar. A program group window cannot be moved outside of the Program Manager, but if you press its maximize button, it will expand to fill the entire Program Manager work area.

A program group icon is nothing more than a minimized program group window. They are usually located at the bottom edge of the Program Manager work area. Like program group windows, program group icons can be moved around inside the Program Manager area but not outside of it. Unlike program group windows, program group icons all look alike. The only way to tell one program group icon from another is to look at their labels.

Figure 6.2

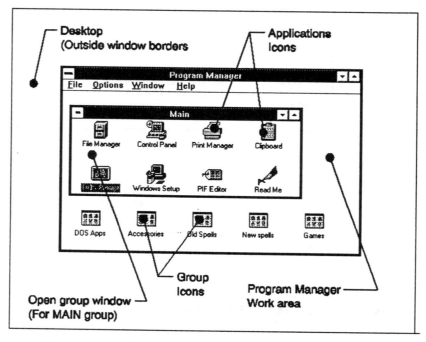

The parts of the Program manager window

Program item icons (or application icons) are stored inside the program group windows. Each icon represents an application or a document. Running applications from a program group window couldn't be easier. All you need to do is locate the correct icon and double-click. Application icons can be copied or moved from one program group window to another, but cannot be moved onto or outside of the Program Manager's work area.

Launching Applications from the Program Manager

What to do	**What Happens**
1. Place the mouse pointer over the program group icon that contains the application that you need and double- click.	The program group window will open.
2. Select the icon for your application, position the pointer, and double-click again.	The application will run.

■ **Note** When you are finished, you may want to clean up your desktop and close any program group windows that were left open.

Launching Applications Automatically

When you start a Windows session, and you know the name of the application that you need to use, you can load Windows and your application in one step. All you need to do is type the name of the application at the end of the WIN startup command. For example, to automatically run the Cardfile program, type WIN CARDFILE and as soon as Windows is finished loading, Cardfile will run.

You can also automatically run an application and load a data file for that application in one step if you add the name of the data file to the end of the command line. In other words, to run Cardfile and load a data file PHONE.CRD, the command line would read WIN CARDFILE PHONE.CRD.

■ **Note** If the application to be run is stored in a subdirectory, you will need to include the entire path name in the startup command. For example, if Excel is stored in a subdirectory on your hard disk called Excel, the startup command would be WIN C:\EXCEL\EXCEL.

Moving Between Windows

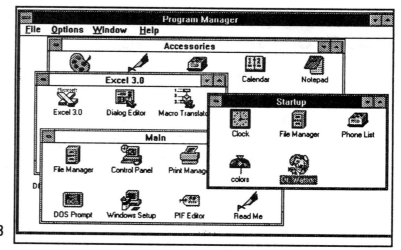

Figure 6.3

Only the group that is currently active will have colored borders

If you have more than one program group open in Program Manager, the one that you are currently using is called the active window. The active window will have a title bar and borders that are the same color as the main window. All other open windows will be the same color as the background. You can open as many windows as your systems resources will allow, but only one of them can be active (see Figure 6.3).

The easiest way to access an inactive window is to move the pointer anywhere inside its border and click. However, if the window you need is covered by other windows, you have to use another method.

You can display a list of all of the groups in Program Manager if you open the Window menu. Select the group you need from the list and it will open. (There will be a check mark by the name of the group that is currently active.)

▲ **Hint**
You can avoid using the mouse and just press [Alt]+[W] to open the Window menu. When the list of program groups is displayed, there will be a number in front of each one. To select and open a group, enter its number.

You can also cycle through all the program group windows by pressing [Ctrl]+[Tab]. Each time you press a key, the next window in line will be selected. ▲

Using Task Manager

As you know, Windows is a multitasking system. That means that you might have two or three (or even more) applications running at the same time. You can move back and forth between these applications, sharing data, performing different tasks, doing whatever is necessary to get your work done.

Figure 6.4

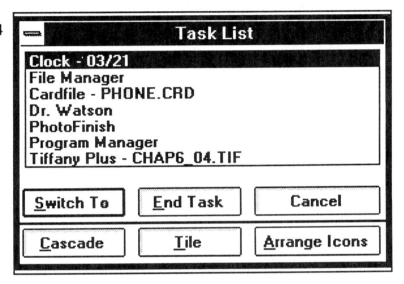

Task Manager window

Task Manager is a command center that allows you to open, close, arrange, and select your applications. To open Task Manager, click the Control button in the upper left corner of the Program Manager or of any application window. When the menu appears, select SWITCH TO and the Task Manager window will open (see Figure 6.4).

▲ Hint You can also open Task Manager by double-clicking anywhere on your desktop that is outside the borders of any open windows. ▲

When the Task Manager window appears, you can use it to switch to a different application, close an application, or clean up your desktop. When it is finished, the Task Manager window will close automatically. You can close Task Manager without telling it to perform an action by pressing [Esc], selecting the

Cancel button from Task Manager, or by clicking any spot outside the Task Manager window.

▲ **Hint**   You can open the Task Manager from the keyboard by pressing [Ctrl]+[End]. In fact, if you are running a full screen DOS application, this is the only way to access Task Manager. ▲

Using Task Manager to Switch from One Application to Another

What to do	**What Happens**
1. Open the Task Manager window in one of the following ways:	The Task Manager window will display a list of the currently active applications.
A) Press [Ctrl]+[End].	
B) Press the Control button in the upper left hand corner of any application window.	
C) Double-click on the desktop outside of any window areas.	
2. Select the application you want in one of the following ways:	The application you select will move to the foreground.
A) Double-click on its name from the list.	
B) Single-click on its name (to select it) and press the Switch To button at the bottom of the Task Manager window.	

▲ **Hint** When the Task Manager window is open, you can use the Up and Down arrow keys to move through the list. When the highlight bar is positioned over the task you need, press ⌨Alt⌨+⌨S⌨. ▲

Closing Applications from Task Manager

Normally, when you are finished with an application, you close it by double-clicking the Control button or opening the File menu and selecting the Exit command. However, if the application that needs to be closed is not in the foreground, it can be closed using the Task Manager.

All you need to do is open Task Manager, select the application to be closed, and press the End Task button. The application will react just as it does when it is closed normally. For example, if you try to close the Paintbrush application, and have not saved your work, Windows will display a dialog box that asks you to save (or not save) your file before the application actually ends.

■ **Note** You cannot close DOS applications from Task Manager. To close a DOS application, you must first switch to that application and close it in the regular way.

Arranging Your Desktop

As shown in Figure 6.5 (on the next page), the icons on your desktop can be easily moved and before long, your desktop can get to be quite messy. Remember, to move an icon, place the mouse pointer on top of the icon to be moved, press and hold the left mouse button, and drag it to a new location. If you are careful, the icons can be manually arranged, one at a time, in a neat row at the bottom of your screen as shown in Figure 6.6. This operation will only take a couple of minutes and everything will be much easier to find. However, if you use Task Manager, this operation only takes a second or two.

Figure 6.5

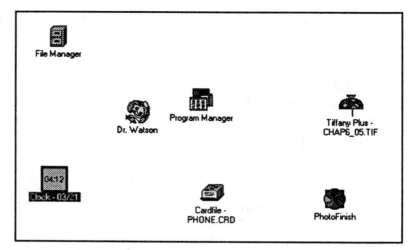

Figure 6.5: Before using the Arrange Icons command from the Task Manager

Figure 6.6

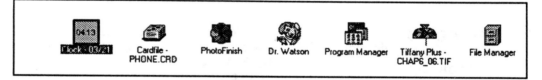

Figure 6.6: After using the Arrange Icons command

Open Task Manager again and you will notice that the button in the lower right corner is labeled Arrange Icons. All you have to do is press this button and the icons will arrange themselves automatically.

■ **Note**   Task Manager can also be used to arrange the applications on your desktop into cascaded or tiled windows.

If necessary, all of these "housekeeping" operations can be selected directly from the keyboard (without using the mouse).

■ *To Cascade windows* press [Ctrl]+[End] to open Task Manager and then press [Alt]+[C].

■ *To arrange the windows as Tiles* open Task Manager (by pressing [Ctrl]+[End]) and then press [Alt]+[T].

- *To arrange the icons* in a neat row at the bottom of your screen, open Task Manager and press ⌨Alt⌨+⌨A⌨.

Summary Points

1. The Setup program automatically creates several program groups. These groups include the Accessories Group, the Main Group, the Startup Group, the Games Group, and additional groups based on the applications that the Setup program finds on your hard disks.

2. The program group is the basic unit of storage in Program Manager.

3. A program group window is a document window that is located in the Program Manager's work area. Each program group window has its own Control, Maximize, and Minimize buttons, but does not have a menu bar.

4. A program group icon is a program group window that has been minimized.

5. To launch an application from Program Manager, move the mouse pointer to its icon and double-click.

6. To start a Windows session and launch an application at the same time, type the name of the application at the end of the WIN startup command.

7. The title bar and the border of the active window will be the same color as the title bar and border of the Program Manager window. The title bar and borders of all inactive windows will be the same color as the Program Manager background.

8. The easiest way to move from one window to another is to move the mouse pointer inside the borders of the new window and click.

9. To display a list of all active windows, open the Window menu from the Program Manager's menu bar.

10. Task Manager is used to open, close, arrange, or select your applications.

11. To open Task Manager, click the Control button in the upper left corner of any application window, or double-click in an open area of your desktop.

12. To switch to a new application from the Task Manager, double-click on the name of the application you need, or select it and press the Switch To button.

13. To close an application from Task Manager, select it and press the End Task button, or select it and press ⌷Alt⌷+⌷E⌷.

14. Task Manager can also be used to Cascade or Tile open windows and to arrange the icons neatly at the bottom of your desktop. Simply, open Task Manager and press the appropriate button.

Practice Exercises

At your computer, perform the following practice tasks:

1. Open the Paintbrush application. (Note: The Paintbrush program is probably stored in the Accessories Group.) Once it starts, click its Minimize button. Repeat this operation with the Cardfile and the Calculator programs. Finally, minimize Program Manager.

2. Practice dragging the minimized applications to new locations on the desktop.

3. Open Task Manager by double-clicking in a open area of the desktop. When the Task Manager window opens, press the Arrange Icons button. All of the icons should arrange themselves in a neat row across the bottom of the screen.

4. Open Task Manager again and switch to the Paintbrush application. Press the Maximize button and Paintbrush will fill the available screen area.

5. Press the Control button of the Paintbrush program and select SWITCH TO to open Task Manager again. Use Task Manager to switch to the Calculator program. Finally, use Task Manager to switch to the Cardfile program.

6. Open Task Manager and close the calculator application. Repeat with the Cardfile and Paintbrush programs.

Comprehension Questions

1. In the spaces next to the letters A - E, write the names of the parts of the Program Manager window.

Figure 6.2a

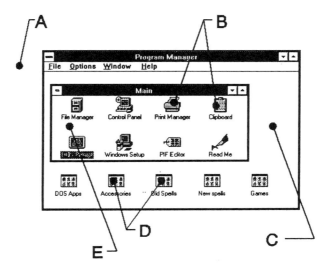

A _____

B _____

C _____

D _____

E _____

2. When you use the Setup program to install Windows, what four groups are always created?

3. What is the difference between a program group window and a program group icon?

4. Where are the program (application) icons stored?

5. List the steps necessary to launch an application from Program Manager if Program Manager is displayed as an icon on the desktop.

6. What command would you enter (at the DOS prompt) to launch Windows, automatically run an application named Cardfile, and load a data file named PHONE.CRD in one step?

7. How do you identify the active window when more than one window is open on your desktop?

8. List three ways to display the Task Manager window.

9. If you open Task Manager accidently, there are three ways to close it without performing a Task Manager action. What are they?

10. How do you open Task Manager if a full-screen DOS application is running?

11. List the three "housekeeping" tasks that can be performed from Task Manager.

12. In the Task Manager window, what is the difference between the Cancel button and the End Task button?

Completion Questions

1. The _____ is the basic unit of storage in Program Manager.

2. A _____ _____ is a document window that is located inside Program Manager.

3. A program group window _____ be moved outside of the Program Manager window.

4. You can display a list of all of the groups that you have in your Program Manager by opening the _____ menu.

5. You cannot close a _____ application from Task Manager.

6. Task Manager can also be used to arrange windows as _____ or in a _____ pattern.

7

Program Group Management

Learning Objectives

1. List the steps to create a new program group.

2. List the steps to create a new program item.

3. Define Control Panel.

Performance Objectives

1. Create a new program group.

2. Add applications to existing program group.

3. Copy and move program items between groups.

4. Remove an application from a program group.

5. Delete a program group.

6. Create an item that launches an application and automatically loads a data file.

7. Change the default icon for a program item.

8. Use the Arrange Icon and Auto Arrange features.

9. Use Control Panel to change the icon spacing.

Control Panel   Control Panel is an application that lets you change the way that your system is configured while you are running Windows.

Default Icon   When you add an item to a group, Windows will automatically choose an icon. The icon that Windows chooses is called the Default icon.

Group Description   The Group description is a line of text that is displayed as the label on a program group icon.

Group Filename   Windows uses the Group filename to store data about a program group. Whenever a group is created, Windows will automatically assign a group filename. There is rarely any reason to override the choice that Windows makes.

Chapter Overview

Your computer system is capable of storing billions and billions of bytes of data. If you do not apply some kind of organizational structure to your data, searching for a particular file can be like searching for a particular star on a cloudy night.

The basic unit of storage in Windows is the program group. Once a group is created, you can fill it with any collection of files that you find useful or convenient. For example, you might want to create a Utilities Group or a Graphics Group. If you need to create a monthly newsletter you could have a January Group, a February Group, and so on. The items placed in a program group can be applications or data files that are "attached" to applications. As usual, use your imagination and don't be afraid to make changes.

Program Group Management   When Windows is installed, it always creates the Main, Accessories, and Games groups. As discussed earlier, inside these groups you will find icons that represent the applications that are shipped as part of the Windows package.

In addition, the Setup program will search your hard disk and try to locate any applications already stored there. Then, with your permission, it will create an additional groups and place appropriate icons inside. When Setup has finished its job Windows is *ready* to use, but it is up to you to make Windows *convenient* to use.

Figure 7.1

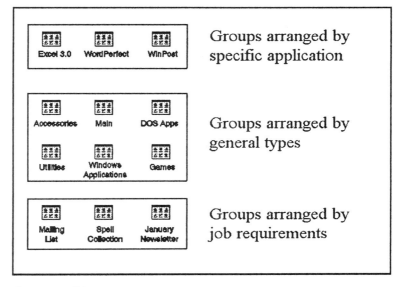

Groups arranged by specific application

Groups arranged by general types

Groups arranged by job requirements

Some possible program group arrangements

Creating a New Program Group

What to Do	**What Happens**
1. Open the File menu and select New	See Figure 7.2, below.

Figure 7.2

2. Make sure that the radio button is set to New Program Group.

The Program Group dialog box will appear (See Figure 7.3, below).

Figure 7.3

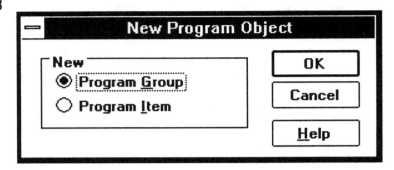

3. Enter a description for the new group. Hint: Keep it short because this will be the label for the program icon.

See Figure 7.4, below

Figure 7.4

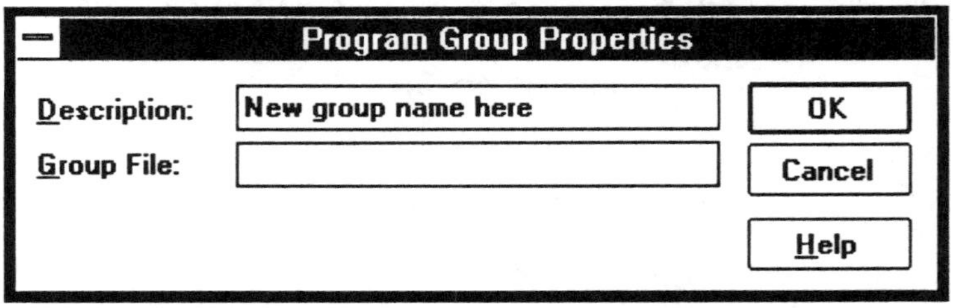

4. Enter a group filename if desired. If you do not assign a group filename, Windows will choose one for you. Select OK to finish.

The new program group window will appear as shown in Figure 7.5.

Figure 7.5

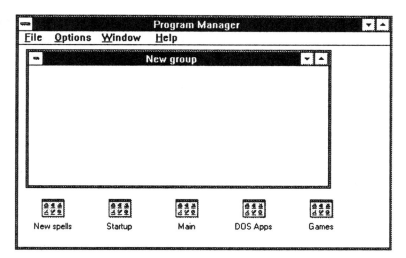

This is what a new, empty program group will look like.

■ **Note**   Windows uses the group filename to store data about the group itself. Do not confuse the group filename with the group description. The group description will be displayed as the label on the group icon and the group filename is used internally by Windows. Whenever a group is created, Windows will automatically assign a group filename. In general, there is rarely any reason to override the choice that Windows makes.

Adding Items to an Existing Group

Before you can add a new item to an existing program group, you might need to do a little research. When you add an item to a group, all you are really doing is telling Windows where the item is stored. Needless to say, if you don't know where the item is, you might have trouble telling Windows where to look.

Begin by opening the group window that is to receive the new item. Next, open the File menu and select New. When the dialog box appears, make sure that the New Program Item button is selected as shown in Figure 7.6. Click OK to continue.

Figure 7.6

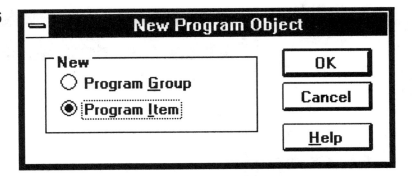

▲ Hint   You can also add an item to a group if you hold the [Alt] key and double-click in a clear area of the open group window. ▲

Type a description for the item into the next dialog box. This description will be used to label the group icon, so keep it short. If you have done your research, and know the complete path-name that leads to your new item, press [Tab]. Enter the path into the command line text box and press OK (See Figure 7.7).

Figure 7.7

Program Item Properties		
Description:		OK
Command Line:		Cancel
Working Directory:		Browse...
Shortcut Key:	None	Change Icon...
	☐ **Run** Minimized	Help

If your research is "incomplete," press the Browse button. A new dialog box will appear as shown in Figure 7.8.

At the top of the Browse box, you will see a filename and the name of the current subdirectory. By default, Windows will display a list of all files in the Windows subdirectory that have an extension of .EXE. If the list is too big to fit in the box, a scroll box will appear.

Figure 7.8

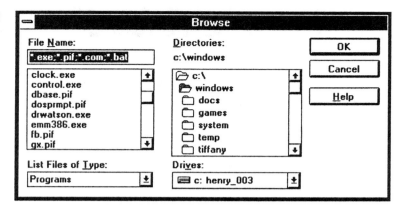

If necessary, type in the correct extension, press [Enter◄─┘]. If the name of your application still is not in the list, then you must continue to browse.

Next, look at the list of subdirectories displayed in the other box. If the name of the subdirectory containing your file is listed, double-click on it. If necessary, continue to examine the other subdirectories until you locate your file.

When the name of your application appears in the file list, double-click on it and press the OK button to finish.

Step-by-Step Example

Assignment: Add the SYSEDIT file to the Accessories Group. SYSEDIT is located in the C:\WINDOWS\SYSTEM sub-subdirectory.

What to Do   **What Happens**

1. Open the Accessories Group   See Figure 7.9.
and select the File menu
from the Program Manager
menu bar. When the drop-
down menu opens, select
New. Make certain that the
New Program Item button
is checked and press OK.

Figure 7.9

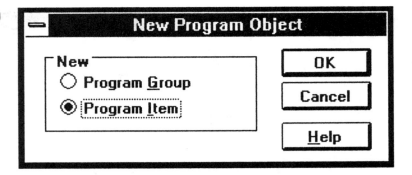

2. Enter a description into the top text box. For this example type SYSEDIT. Leave the second text box blank and press the Browse button.

See Figure 7.10, below.

Figure 7.10

Program Item Properties

Description: | Sys Edit |
Command Line: | |
Working Directory: | |
Shortcut Key: | None |
☐ Run Minimized

OK
Cancel
Browse...
Change Icon...
Help

3. In the Directories box, you will see the name of a subdirectory called SYSTEM. Double-click on it.

The Directory line will change to show the new path. See Figure 7.11.

Figure 7.11

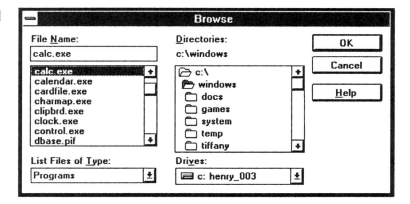

4. Look through the list of files in the box on the left. When you locate the file called SYSEDIT.EXE, double-click on it.

See Figure 7.12, below.

Figure 7.12

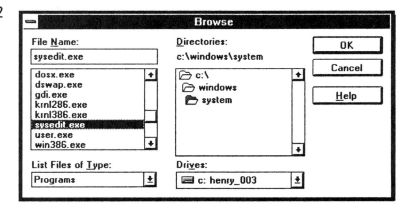

5. Look in the Command Line box. Windows will fill in the correct path.

The Item Properties box will reappear. See Figure 7.13.

Figure 7.13

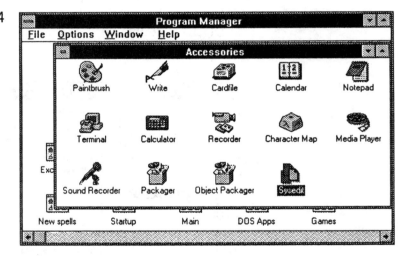

Program Item Properties

Description:	Sys Edit
Command Line:	C:\WINDOWS\SYSTEM\SYSE
Working Directory:	
Shortcut Key:	None

☐ Run Minimized

OK
Cancel
Browse...
Change Icon...
Help

6. Press the OK button to finish.

A new icon will appear in your group window. See Figure 7.14, below.

Figure 7.14

Adding an item to an existing program group

▲ **Hint** The SYSEDIT application can be used to edit your AUTOEXEC.BAT, CONFIG.SYS, WIN.INI, and SYSTEM.INI files. When SYSEDIT is launched, each file will appear in its own window. ▲

Moving or Copying Icons from One Group to Another

What to Do	**What Happens**
1. Open the group window that contains the icon that is to be moved or copied.	The selected Window will display in Program Manager.
2. Place the mouse pointer on the icon to be moved (or copied), press and hold the left mouse button, and drag the icon to its new group window. Note: The target group window does not have to be open.	The icon will be moved (or copied) to a new location.

■ **Note** If you drag an icon from one group to another, by default it is moved to the new group. If you press and hold the [Ctrl] key while you drag the icon, a copy of the original icon is placed in the new group. The selected icon will now appear in both groups.

Deleting Program Items from a Group

What to Do	**What Happens**
1. If necessary, open the group window that contains the item to be deleted.	The selected window will display in Program Manager.
2. Move the pointer to the item to be deleted, select it, and open the File menu. When the drop-down menu appears, select Delete and a dialog box will appear.	See Figure 7.15.

Figure 7.15

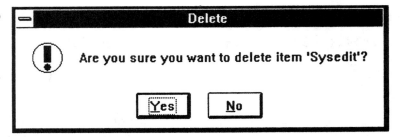

Delete

Are you sure you want to delete item 'Sysedit'?

[Yes]   [No]

3. Select OK to finish.

The selected item will be removed from the program group.

■ **Note** Effectively, when you delete a program item or program group you are just telling Windows to "forget" where the item (or group) is located. Windows does not remove the files that belong to that item from your hard disk.

Deleting a Program Group

■ **Note** Warning: If you delete a program group, all items in that program group will be lost.

What to Do   **What Happens**

1. Select the group to be   See Figure 7.16.
deleted by moving the
pointer and pressing the left
mouse button one time. If
the group's control menu
displays, just ignore it.
Note: To delete an entire
group, the group must be
minimized.

Figure 7.16

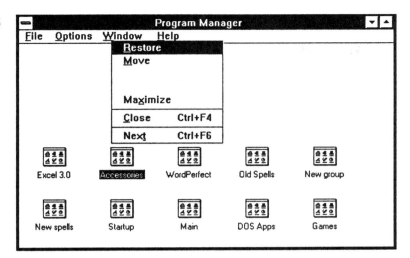

2. Open the File menu. When the drop-down menu appears, select Delete and you will see a Dialog box.

See Figure 7.17.

Figure 7.17

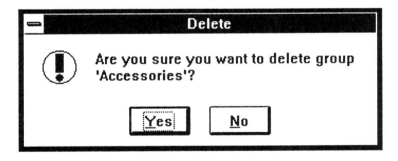

3. Select OK to finish.

The selected group will be removed from Program Manager.

How to Launch an Application Using a Data File

When a Windows application creates a data file, that data file often "remembers" which application was used to create it. In other words, the data file is said to be associated with its application. If this relationship exists (and it usually does), all you need to do is enter the name of the data file. The application will launch and the data file will load in one step. For example, if you have a data file called STOCKS.EXL that was created using the Excel spreadsheet application, you can open the File menu, choose Run, and when the dialog box appears, type the name of the data file, *not the name of the application*. Windows will automatically find the correct application, launch it, and load the STOCKS.EXL data file.

In Program Manager, it is possible to create a new program item that points to the name of a data file rather than the application. Basically, you follow the same procedure that you used to create a new group item (see Adding Items to an Existing Group). When it is time to select the application name, enter the name of the data file instead. Windows will choose an icon to represent your data file/application combination and place it in the specified group. When you are ready to use your data file/application combination, just click on its icon. Again, Windows will automatically find the correct application, launch it, and load the data file that you specified.

▲ **Hint**   Beginning with Windows version 3.1, a group called Startup is created by the Setup program. Any application placed in this group will automatically launch when Windows is started.

However, if you press and hold the ⌈⇧ Shift⌉ key as you start Windows, the applications in the Startup group will not automatically run when you boot. ▲

How to Change the Default Icon

When you add an item to a group, Windows will automatically choose an icon for you. If you want to use a different icon for any reason, change it.

Changing the Default Icon

What to Do	What Happens
1. Select the correct item by moving the pointer and pressing the left mouse button one time.	The title of the selected item will be highlighted.
2. Open the File menu and select Properties.	The Program Item Properties dialog box will appear as shown in Figure 7.18.

▲ **Hint**   You can also hold the [Alt] key and double click on a program item icon to open the Properties dialog box. ▲

Figure 7.18

3. Press the Change Icon button and a dialog box labeled Select Icon will appear.	See Figure 7.19.

Figure 7.19

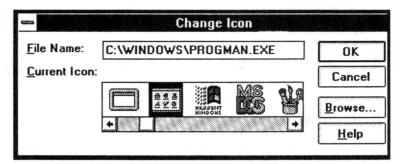

4. If necessary, enter the name of the file that contains the icon that you want to use. The scroll bar at the bottom of the icon window will let you view all of the icons in the file.

Each time you click the scroll bar, the next icon in the file will be displayed. You can also use the scroll bar to move quickly through the file.

5. To finish, click on the icon that you want and press OK in the Change Icon box and OK in the Program Item Properties box.

The new icon will display.

▲ **Hint** When you are in the Icon selection box, you can also select the new icon with a double-click. ▲

How to Change the Icon Spacing

When you use the Arrange Icons feature, Windows will place the icons on an invisible grid based on the size of the widest icon. Normally, the calculated spacing is fine, but often the icon descriptions are wider than the icons. Long icon descriptions may overlap and make everything difficult to read.

Actually, this problem has two solutions. The obvious solution is to use shorter descriptions, but sometimes this is not possible or practical.

■ **Note** Remember, the Arrange Icons feature is located in the Window drop-down menu.

How to Change the Icon Spacing

What to Do	**What Happens**
1. Open the Main Program Group and double-click the Control Panel icon.	The Control panel window will open as shown in Figure 7.20

Figure 7.20

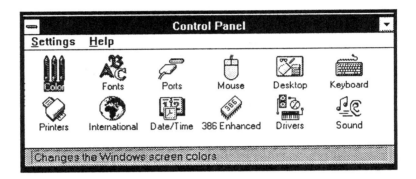

2. Double-click the Desktop icon.	The Desktop dialog box will display.
3. Find the Icon Spacing box and inside you will see a number. Type in a new value or click the Up or Down arrow to increase or decrease the value in the box. Each click will change the icon spacing by one pixel on your display screen. Increments of 10 pixels will make a noticeable difference.	If you enter a larger number, the icons will be spaced farther apart. If you enter a smaller value, they will move closer together (see Figure 7.21).

Figure 7.21

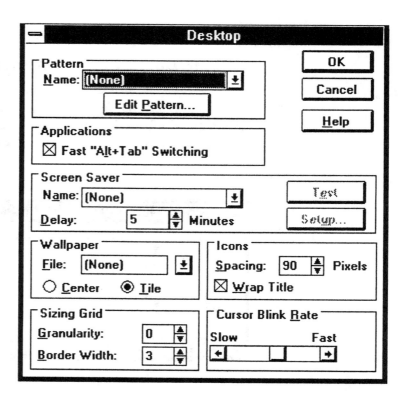

4. Click OK to finish.   The dialog box will close.

■ **Note**   The next time you use the Auto Arrange feature, the icons will move to the new grid spacing.

Summary Points

1. If you do not apply some kind of organizational structure to your data, searching for a particular file can be very difficult.

2. When the Setup program is finished, Windows is ready to use, but it is up to you to make Windows convenient to use.

3. To create a new program group, open the File menu, select New, enter a short description, and select OK to finish.

4. To add an item to an existing program group, you need to know the name of the application. Type the complete path into the Command Line box or use the Browse function.

5. To copy (or move) icons from one group to another, just place the pointer on the group and drag it to a new location.

6. To remove a program item from a group, open the group that contains the item, select it, open the File menu, and choose Delete.

7. To delete an entire group, select it, open the File menu, and choose Delete.

8. To create a program item that launches an application and loads a data file in one step, create a "normal" item, but specify the name of the data file on the command line rather than the name of the application.

9. If you want to change the icon belonging to a program item, open the File menu and choose Properties.

10. The default icon spacing can be changed if you open the Main Group and select Control Panel.

Practice Exercises

1. Create a new group called Toys. Move the calculator and the cardfile (from the Accessories Group) and the clipboard (from the Main Group) into the new group. You may need to change the size of the Program Manager window or the group windows to complete the operation.

2. Close all group windows except for Toys. Move the calculator, cardfile, and clipboard back to their original windows. Do not open the Accessories window or the Main window while performing this operation.

3. Finally, delete the Toys window from Program Manager.

Comprehension Questions

1. List the steps necessary to create a new program group.

2. What is the difference between the group filename and the group description?

3. Before you can add an item to an existing program group, what must you know about that item?

4. What must you do to copy a program item from one group to another?

5. List the steps needed to delete an item from a program group.

6. When you delete an entire program group, what happens to the program items inside it?

7. When you create a program item that uses a data file to launch an application, you do not specify the name of the application. What information is needed instead?

8. List the steps necessary to change a program item's icon.

9. What must you do to change the default icon spacing?

8

Windows Accessories

Learning Objectives

1. Identify the Windows accessories.

Performance Objectives

1. Use Windows Calculator.

2. Use Windows Calendar.

3. Use Windows Cardfile.

4. Use Windows Clock.

5. Use Windows Notepad.

Chapter Terms

Analog Clock

An Analog clock is nothing more than a clock that uses hands to display the time.

Calendar Accessory

This accessory can be used to help you keep track of your appointments. Applications of this type are sometimes called Personal Information Managers, or PIMs.

Cardfile Accessory

Cardfile is like a box of electronic filing cards. You simply fill in the cards and the computer will automatically put them in order for you.

Digital Clock

A Digital clock displays the time as numbers (or digits).

Notepad Accessory

Notepad is a simple text editor. Although it does not have all the features of a full word processor, it can be used to type notes or even to write letters.

Scientific Calculator

With this version of Calculator, you can perform base number conversions, statistical calculations, trigonometric operations, and obtain other scientific results.

Standard Calculator

This accessory can be displayed on the Windows desktop and used in exactly the same way as a standard battery-powered seven-function calculator.

Chapter Overview

It is rumored that when Merlin was imprisoned by Morgan LeFay, he managed to hide much of his magical equipment. Perhaps some of this equipment has been rediscovered in the form of the mysterious Windows accessories.

When the Setup program installs Windows, the Accessories Group is automatically created. Inside this group, you will find several small applications that can be used for many of your day-to-day operations. With the accessories, you can track your appointments, perform calculations, write yourself reminder notes, and even make phone calls.

Actually, there is nothing magical (or mysterious) about the Windows accessories, but in the hands of a knowledgeable user, they can be very powerful. You are about to become a knowledgeable accessories user. Open the Accessories Group and let's get started.

Calculator

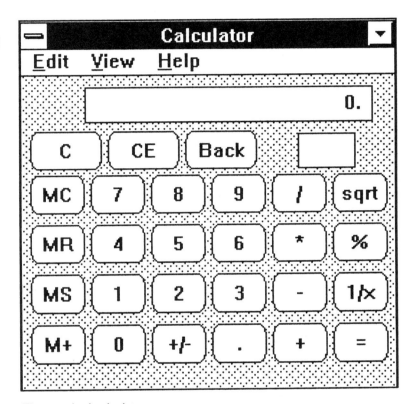

Figure 8.1

The standard calculator

Many computer users have found that it is convenient to keep a small battery-powered calculator near their computer system. Many users also find that when the calculator is needed, it is buried under a stack of papers or it has fallen behind their desk. In Windows, all you need to do to use your calculator is double-click the Calculator icon.

The first time that you open Calculator, the Standard calculator will appear (see Figure 8.1). If necessary, Calculator can be moved (or minimized), but it cannot be sized. It is a good idea to open Calculator at the beginning of a Windows session and then to leave it minimized so that is available any time you need it.

Summary of the STANDARD calculator functions

To perform this operation	Use this key	It means
+	+	Add
- (minus)	-	Subtract
*	*	Multiply
/ (slash)	/	Divide
sqrt	@	Calculate the square root of the number in the display.
%	%	Calculates percentages. If, for example, you enter 150*65%, the calculator will display 65% of 150 (which is 97.5).
1/x	r	Returns the reciprocal of the number in the display.
= (equals)	= (or [Enter◄┘])	Performs the requested calculation. If you press = (or enter) again, the last operation requested will be performed again. For example, if you enter 4+4=, the calculator will display the result 8. If you press = a second time, it will add 4 to the result and display 12 (and so on).
+/-	[F9]	Changes the sign of the number currently in the display.

. (period)	. (period) or , (comma)	Enters a decimal point.
BACK	Backspace key or ⬅	Deletes the last digit that was entered.
CE	Del	Clears the number currently in the display.
C	Esc	Clears the current calculation. Similar to the Clear All key on many calculators.
MC	Ctrl + C	Clears any value stored in the calculator's memory.
MR	Ctrl + R	Recalls any value in the calculator's memory to the display.
MS	Ctrl + M	Stores the value currently displayed in the calculator's memory.
M+	Ctrl + P	Adds the value in the display to any value stored in the calculator's memory.

In general, Windows Calculator works just like the battery-powered calculator that you can't find. To enter calculations, you can use the mouse pointer to "press" the buttons on the screen or, even better, you can use the numbered keypad on your computer's keyboard.

▲ **Hint** One real advantage of the Windows Calculator is that the results of your calculations can be transferred directly into other applications. When your answer is displayed, open the calculator's Edit menu and select Copy. Then, move to the target application, open the Edit menu there, and choose Paste.

You can also move numbers from an application into the calculator. All you need to do is reverse the operation. In the "other" application, select the number to be transferred, open the Edit menu and choose Copy. Move to Calculator, open its Edit menu, choose Paste, and the number will appear in the calculator's display just as if it had been typed in from the keyboard. ▲

The Scientific Calculator

Figure 8.2

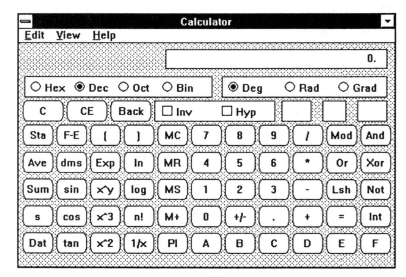

The scientific calculator

For many users, the Standard calculator is not enough. If you open Calculator's View menu and select Scientific, another more sophisticated calculator will be displayed (see Figure 8.2). With this version of Calculator, you can perform base number conversions, statistical calculations, trigonometric operations, and obtain other scientific results. A summary of the scientific calculator's functions can be found in Appendix B.

■ **Note**   Do not confuse Calculator's memory with computer memory. Calculator's memory is simply a place to temporarily store numbers needed while using Calculator. When Calculator is closed, any values stored in its memory are lost.

Using Calendar

If time didn't exist, everything would happen simultaneously. To help you keep track of time, Windows provides a calendar that you can use to store your important appointments. Double-click the Calendar icon and a window will open that displays an hour-by-hour list for the current date (see Figure 8.3). This is called the Day view and it starts, by default, at 7:00 A.M. You can use the scroll bar to view earlier or later times in the display.

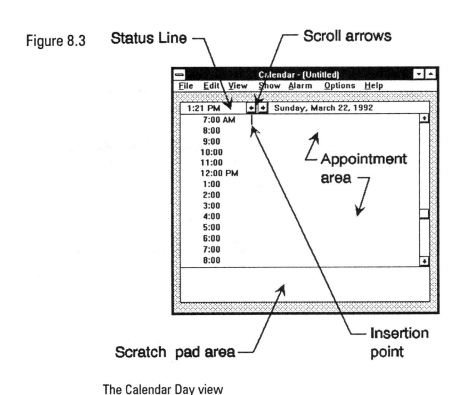

Figure 8.3

The Calendar Day view

Inside the Day view Window (in addition to the familiar title bar and menu bar) you will find several other areas of interest. Just below the menu bar, the status bar displays the date and time (as determined by the system clock) and two arrows that are used to move forward and backwards in time. If you click the left arrow, time goes backwards; if you click the right arrow, time moves forward.

■ Note If the date or the time is wrong, you can correct them from Windows Control Panel.

The area at the bottom of the window is called the scratch pad. You can use this area to attach a note (up to three lines long) to the Day view window. To enter a note, click in this area and the insertion point will move. To move quickly between the appointment area and the scratch pad just press ⌨Tab.

The main part of the Day display is called the appointment area. In this area you can enter a single line of text that describes any appointments you may have. To enter (or edit) an appointment, click on the appropriate line and type.

▲ Hint If you need to enter an appointment for a time that is not displayed, open the Options menu and select Special Time. Type the time into the text box and press INSERT as shown below. ▲

Figure 8.4

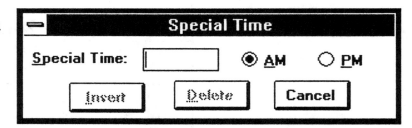

Naturally, you can use the arrows keys to move forward and backwards in time, but if you need to view appointments for next year (or even next month), pressing the arrow keys hundreds of times can get rather tiring. To move quickly to the next (or previous) month, you can press the ⌨PgUp (or ⌨PgDn) key.

Moving around in the Calendar

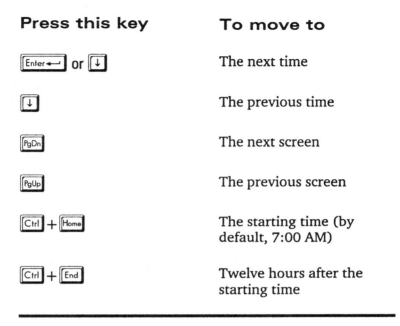

Press this key	To move to
Enter⏎ or ↓	The next time
↓	The previous time
PgDn	The next screen
PgUp	The previous screen
Ctrl + Home	The starting time (by default, 7:00 AM)
Ctrl + End	Twelve hours after the starting time

Figure 8.5

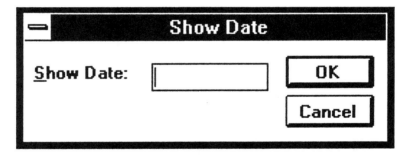

Use this dialog box to move directly to a specific date.

To move to a specific date, don't use the direction keys at all. Instead, open the Show menu and choose Date. When the dialog box shown in Figure 8.5 appears, enter the date you need and press OK (or [Enter ←]). You can enter any date between January 1, 1980, and December 31, 2099. Leading zeros are unnecessary, and the date can be entered in the forms MM/DD/YY, MM/DD/YYYY, MM-DD-YY, or MM-DD-YYYY. If you enter a two-digit year (such as 92) the Calendar program assumes that you need a date in the twentieth century. To select a date in the twenty-first century (such as 2001), you must type all four digits of the year. (You may find, however, that many people will not wait until the twenty-first century for a date).

■ **Note**   You can also move to the next (or previous) month if you open the Show menu and select Next (or Previous).

How to Set Reminder Alarms

Figure 8.6

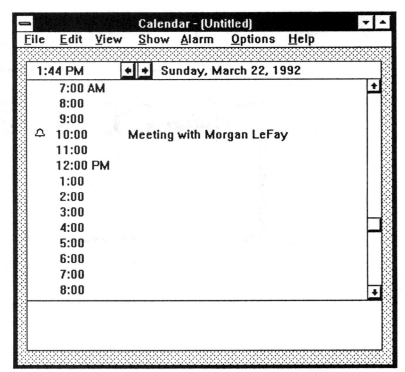

Alarm set for a meeting at 10:00 A.M.

Some people never forget appointments, but other people will forget unless they are hit on the head with a big hammer. If a little hammer will help you to remember your appointments, you can set an alarm for as many appointments as you wish.

To set an alarm, start by moving the mouse pointer to the desired time and clicking on it. Next, open the Alarm menu and choose Set. A small bell symbol will display to the left of each appointment that has an alarm (see Figure 8.6). To remove an alarm, open the Alarm menu again, select Set a second time, and the little bell symbol will disappear.

When the alarm goes off, Windows will sound an alarm. If the Calendar window is open in the foreground, a dialog box will pop up to remind you of the appointment. Press OK and the alarm will shut off. If the Calendar window is open but not in the foreground, the title bar at the top of the Calendar window will flash. If the Calendar is displayed as an icon, the icon itself will flash. (If the dialog box is not visible, you must open the Calendar window or enlarge the Calendar icon to stop the alarm.)

If necessary, you can set the alarms to go off before the appointment time. Open the Alarm menu, select Controls and type a number (between 0 and 10) into the Early Ring box. All alarms will continue to go off early until you change this setting.

■ **Note**   If you use the Calendar program frequently, you might want to launch Calendar at the beginning of your work day and leave it displayed as an icon on your desktop. If the Calendar program is not running, no alarms will sound.

How to View Your Calendar One Month at a Time   In addition to the Day view of your appointments, you can also view your calendar one month at a time (see Figure 8.7). To switch to the Month view, open the View menu and select Month. When the month is displayed, the current date will be enclosed by little arrows. If you click a different date on the month, it will highlight and when you switch back to the daily view, the appointments for the selected day will be visible. If a selected date has a note in the scratch pad area, it will display at bottom of the monthly view.

Figure 8.7

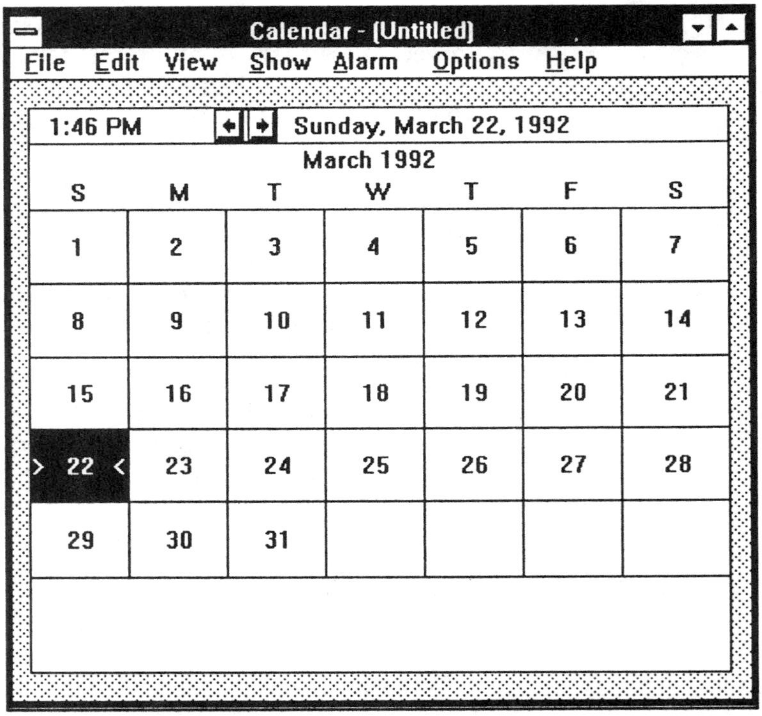

The Month view

▲ **Hint**   You can also double-click on the status bar to jump between the
Day view and the Month view. ▲

How to Print Your Calendar

Figure 8.8

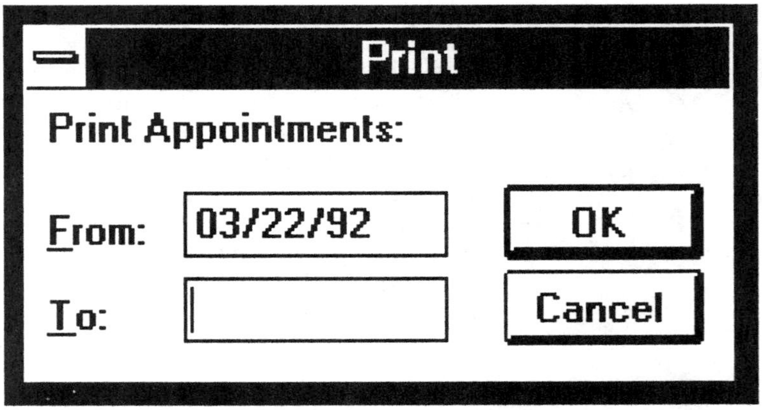

The Print dialog box for Calendar

You might find that it's not practical to carry your computer around with you just to keep track of appointments. With this is in mind, Calendar will let you print your appointments out on paper.

To print a copy of your appointments, open the File menu and select Print. When the Print dialog box appears (see Figure 8.8), enter the first and the last date to be printed and press OK. To print appointments from a single day, leave the To box blank.

Saving Your Calendar

Before you close Calendar or turn your computer off for the day, make sure that you save your Calendar file or all of your appointments will be lost. The procedure for saving a Calendar file is the same as for any other Windows application. Open the File menu and select Save (or Save As). Assign a name and press OK to finish.

Cardfile

Cardfile is like a box of electronic filing cards. You can use it for something as simple as a name and address file or as complex as a database of clip art. You can use it as a things-to-do list and store jobs in a priority order, or to keep track of magic recipes. Like all of the other parts of Windows, Cardfile is very flexible.

When you click the Cardfile icon, a window will open that displays a single blank card. To create a Cardfile database you simply fill in as many blank cards as you need. As you add cards to the file, the computer will arrange them in a neat stack that displays the entire top card (called the active card) and the index line of as many other cards as possible.

■ Note

You can change the size of the Cardfile window as necessary but you cannot change the size of the cards. If you enlarge the Cardfile window, you will be able to see more cards but they will all be the same size as the cards in a smaller window. Naturally, if you make the Cardfile window smaller, fewer cards will be visible.

Each card in the Cardfile has two parts. The main part, called the information area, is used to store anything that you want. You can place graphics or up to 11 lines of text in this part of the card. To enter (or edit) material in the information area, all you need to do is move the insertion point into the main part of the card.

Figure 8.9

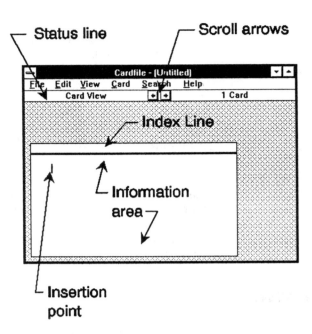

The Cardfile window

The other part of a card is called the index line. Cardfile uses the information in the index line to put your cards in order and (if you have a MODEM) dial the phone for you. To enter (or edit) information in the index line, open the Edit menu and select Index or press F6. Remember, Cardfile uses this line to sort your cards so the information you place here should be carefully selected. For example, if you are using Cardfile to store names and phone numbers, each index line should contain a person's last name, first name, and the phone number. When you are finished entering the index line, press OK and Cardfile will automatically move your card to the correct place in the stack.

▲ **Hint**   You can also edit the index of the top card if you double-click on its index line. ▲

Adding New Cards to Your File

What to Do	What Happens

1. Open the Card menu and select Add (or press F7).

The Add dialog box will open. (See Figure 8.10).

Figure 8.10

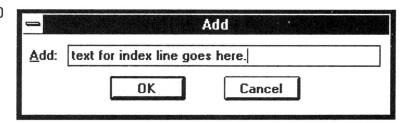

2. Type the text for the index line of the new card. Press OK when you are finished.

Cardfile will move the new card to the correct place in the card stack and the insertion point will jump to the information area (see Figure 8.11).

Figure 8.11

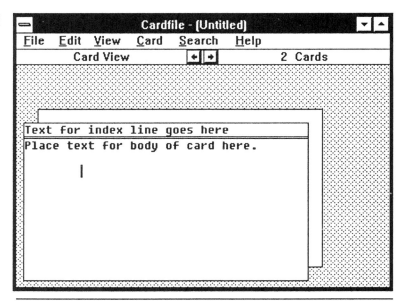

3. Place any text or other necessary information into the main part of the card.

The text will appear as you type.

▲ Hint You can even use Cardfile to store a collection of clip art. All you need to do is paste each picture on its own card, enter a descriptive name on the index line and Cardfile will automatically put your clip-art cards in alphabetical order. Now you can easily locate and transfer pictures from your collection into other Windows applications.

Figure 8.12

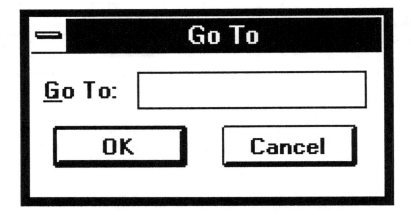

The Go To box for Cardfile

If you need to find a specific card, you can step through the cards one at a time or you can use the Go To feature and tell Cardfile to find it for you. To find a card based on information in its index line, open the Search menu and select Go To. When you see the dialog box shown in Figure 8.12, type a portion of the index line into it. Type just enough to distinguish the card you need from all the other cards, Press OK, and it will jump to the top of the stack.

If Cardfile cannot locate a card that contains the text that you specify, you will see a Not Found error message box. All you need to do is press OK to acknowledge the box, check your typing, and try again. ▲

Moving Through Your Cards

If you press the left or right arrow in the Cardfile status line, you can step through your cards one at a time. Or, if the index line of the card you need is visible, click on it and that card will jump to the front. If you want to use the keyboard to move through your cards, the following keys can be used.

Press this Key	To do this
PgDn	Move forward one card when you are in the CARD view mode. When you are in the LIST view mode, this key move the list forward one full page.
PgUp	Move backwards one card when you are in the CARD view mode. When you are in the LIST view mode, this key will move the list backwards one full page.
Ctrl + Home	Bring the first card in the file to the top of the stack.
Ctrl + End	Bring the last card in the file to the top of the stack.
↓	In the LIST view, this key will move you down to the next card.
↑	In the LIST view, this key will move you up one card.

▲ **Hint**   If you know the first letter of the index line on a card, you can quickly bring that card to the front by pressing CTRL+the letter. Cardfile will jump to the first card that begins with the letter you request and then you can scroll, card by card, to the one that you need. ▲

Figure 8.13

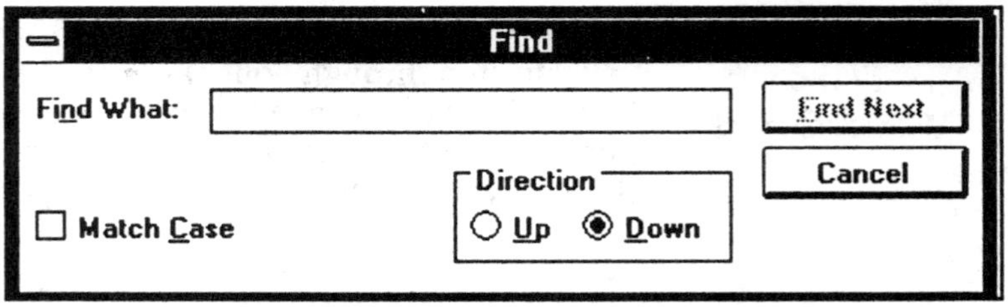

```
┌─────────────────────────────────────────────────────────┐
│ ▭                          Find                          │
│                                                          │
│ Fi_nd What:  ┌─────────────────────────┐   ┌─────────┐  │
│              │                         │   │Find Next│  │
│                                            └─────────┘  │
│                    ┌─ Direction ──────┐   ┌─────────┐  │
│              ☐ Match Case  │ ○ U_p  ◉ D_own │   │ Cancel  │  │
│                    └──────────────────┘   └─────────┘  │
└─────────────────────────────────────────────────────────┘
```

The Find box

Cardfile will also search for a card according to the contents of the information area. To do this, open the Search menu, select Find and you will see a box as shown in Figure 8.13. Type the text you want to find into the box and press OK. Cardfile will begin searching at any point in your file. If it passes the end of the file, it will jump back to the beginning, continue to search until it has come all the way around, and will stop the first time it finds the text you requested. To find the next occurrence of the same text, open the Search menu again, and choose Find Next.

If the requested text is not found, Cardfile will display a message box telling you that it could not find the text. Again, as with a Go To search, press OK to acknowledge the box, check your typing, and try again.

■ **Note**   During a Find search, Cardfile will ignore all capitalization.

Viewing the Cards in Your File as a List

There are two ways to view the cards in your file: Card view and List view. When you start Cardfile the Card view mode will be selected and your file will be displayed as a series of cards. If List view is selected, you will see only the index line of each card in alphabetical order (see Figure 8.14).

To display your cards as a list, open the View menu and choose List. To change back to Card view, open the View menu again and select Card.

Figure 8.14

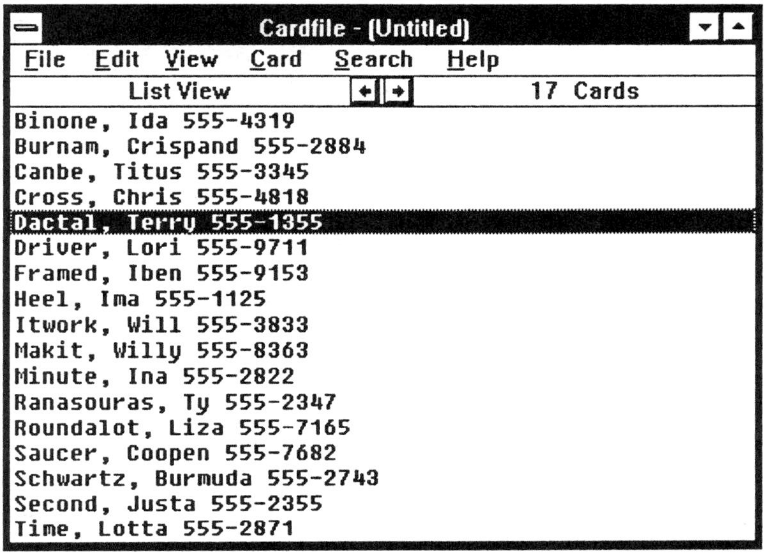

```
┌────────────────────────────────────────────────────────┐
│ ▬          Cardfile - (Untitled)              ▼ ▲       │
├────────────────────────────────────────────────────────┤
│  File   Edit   View   Card   Search   Help             │
├────────────────────────────────────────────────────────┤
│         List View          ◄ ►          17  Cards      │
├────────────────────────────────────────────────────────┤
│ Binone, Ida 555-4319                                   │
│ Burnam, Crispand 555-2884                              │
│ Canbe, Titus 555-3345                                  │
│ Cross, Chris 555-4818                                  │
│ Dactal, Terry 555-1355                                 │
│ Driver, Lori 555-9711                                  │
│ Framed, Iben 555-9153                                  │
│ Heel, Ima 555-1125                                     │
│ Itwork, Will 555-3833                                  │
│ Makit, Willy 555-8363                                  │
│ Minute, Ina 555-2822                                   │
│ Ranasouras, Ty 555-2347                                │
│ Roundalot, Liza 555-7165                               │
│ Saucer, Coopen 555-7682                                │
│ Schwartz, Burmuda 555-2743                             │
│ Second, Justa 555-2355                                 │
│ Time, Lotta 555-2871                                   │
└────────────────────────────────────────────────────────┘
```

Cardfile list view

Printing Cardfile

If necessary, you can print the contents of your Cardfile database. You can print either the active (front) card or the entire database.

To print a single card, first bring the card to be printed to the top of the stack. Then, open the File menu and select Print. The system will attempt to duplicate the top card on your printer. In fact, the printed card will even have an index line and a frame around the entire card.

To print the entire file, open the File menu and select Print All. The system will print your entire Cardfile database placing three cards on each printed page.

Automatic Dialing

If you have a MODEM connected to your computer, you can use Cardfile to dial the phone for you. Bring the card that contains the phone number you want to call to the top of the deck, open the Card menu, choose Autodial or just press F5.

If you need to set your MODEM up for dialing, press the Setup button and fill in the appropriate choices. If everything is correct, just press OK and the MODEM will take the phone off the hook and dial.

Figure 8.15

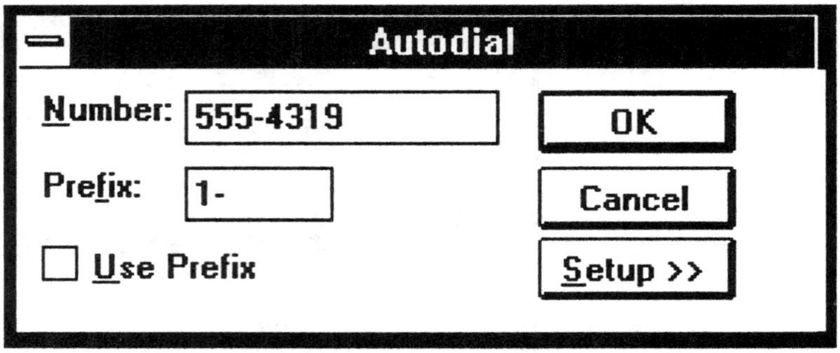

Autodial dialog box

After the MODEM has finished dialing, it will display a box as shown in Figure 8.15. Be sure to take the phone off the hook before you press the OK button on the screen. If you press the screen button before you pick the phone up, the MODEM will just hang up.

▲ **Hint**   If you are using Cardfile as a phone directory, you might want to use the information area to keep notes about your conversations. Then, anytime you call someone, you can select their card and refer to your notes. ▲

Saving   By now, you are probably getting tired of someone reminding
Cardfile   you to save your work, but Cardfile is no different than any other application. Again, if you don't save your work, it will be lost.

To save a Cardfile database, open the File menu, select Save or Save As, enter a filename, and (once again) press OK to finish.

▲ **Hint**   You may want to load your phone list at the beginning of each Windows work session. That way, all of your phone numbers are handy if you need to make a phone call or if someone calls you. ▲

Clock

Clock is a very simple but rather useful little accessory. It is simple because it only has one menu; it is useful because, on occasion, it's nice to really know what time it is.

Figure 8.16
and 8.17

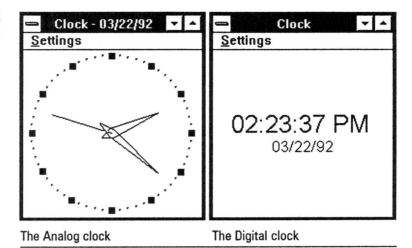

The Analog clock   The Digital clock

The first time that you launch Clock, it will display standard analog face as shown in Figure 8.16. It will be in a small square window that can be adjusted in size and moved to wherever it is needed.

■ **Note**   The clock will display the time as reported by your computer's system clock.

The clock can also be displayed in digital format (see Figure 8.17). To change to a digital display, open the Settings menu and choose Digital. The next time you start the clock, it will appear in the mode that you last used.

▲ **Hint**   Many users find it convenient to leave the clock displayed as an icon in a corner of the screen. Even as an icon, the clock will continue to display the correct time. ▲

Other Clock Options

Figure 8.18

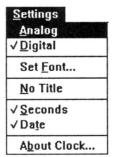

Settings menu for Clock

Beginning with Windows version 3.1 there are a couple of other options that affect the way the clock displays. When the clock is displayed in a window, (that is, if it is not minimized), it will have a menu bar with a Settings selection. When you open this menu, you can change the font and change the way the clock displays in the clock window (see Figure 8.18). For example, the Title command can be used to eliminate the title and menu bar at the top of the clock window.

■ **Note**   If you suppress the Title display, double click anywhere inside the clock window and the title will redisplay.

Notepad

Figure 8.19

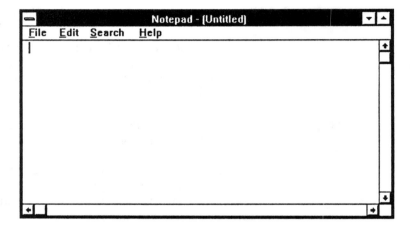

The main Notepad window

Notepad is an easy-to-use text editor. Although it does not have all the features of a full word processor, it can be used to type notes or even to write a letter. To start Notepad, locate the Notepad icon and double-click. After a few seconds, a window will appear that is similar to Figure 8.19.

Text is entered into Notepad in much the same way as any other text-processing program. The insertion point, which is moved around with the mouse (or arrow keys), marks the place that new text is going to appear. Files are saved (or retrieved) from the File menu. There are, however, a few minor differences.

Normally, if a typed line is longer than the display screen, it will "fall off the edge." If you don't want this to happen, open the Edit menu and choose Word Wrap. When Word Wrap is in effect, the text will automatically wrap around to the beginning of the next line any time it reaches the right edge of the window. The Word Wrap option remains in effect until you open the Edit menu and choose Word Wrap a second time.

▲ Hint   If you write or edit DOS batch files, Notepad can be used instead of the DOS EDLIN or EDIT program. In fact, the Word Wrap option does not affect the actual contents of your text file. Notepad retains everything, as entered, on one line. ▲

Moving Around in Notepad

In addition to normal mouse controls (and the `←` `↑` `→` `↓` arrows), the following keys can be used to move around in a notepad file.

Press this key	To move the insertion point
`Ctrl` + `→`	Right one word
`Ctrl` + `←`	Left one word
`Home`	To the beginning of the current line
`End`	To the end of the current line
`PgUp`	Up one window
`PgDn`	Down one window
`Ctrl` + `Home`	To the beginning of the document
`Ctrl` + `Home`	To the end of the document

Selecting Text

Before you can copy, move, or delete a block of text in Notepad, you must "select" or highlight the text that is to be affected. If you are using the mouse, all you need to do is move the insertion point to the beginning of the block of text, press and hold the left mouse button, and drag the pointer to the end of the block. After the text is selected, you can open the appropriate menu and continue. When using Notepad, you can also select text from the keyboard. A summary of keyboard text selection functions are described in the following table.

Press this key	To select
⇧ Shift + ← ⇧ Shift + →	text one character at a time to the left or right.
⇧ Shift + ↑ ⇧ Shift + ↓	text one line at a time up or down.
⇧ Shift + PgUp ⇧ Shift + PgDn	text one window up (or down).
⇧ Shift + Home	text from the insertion point to the beginning of the current line.
⇧ Shift + End	text from the current point to the end of the line.
Ctrl + ⇧ Shift + ←	the previous word.
Ctrl + ⇧ Shift + →	the next word.
Ctrl + ⇧ Shift + Home	text from the current point to the beginning of the document.
Ctrl + ⇧ Shift + End	text from the current insertion point to the end of the document.

**Using
Notepad
as a
Time-Log
File**

Figure 8.20

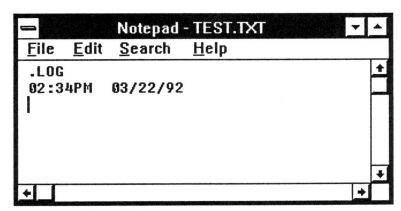

Using Notepad as a time log

If you need to keep track of your time, or if you just would like to keep an automatic diary, you can instruct Notepad to place the time and date at the end of your file every time you load your file (see Figure 8.20).

To access this feature, type .LOG, in capital letters at the beginning of your document.

▲ **Hint**   To print your Notepad document, open the File menu and choose Print. As always, when you are finished working in Notepad, don't forget to save your work. ▲

Summary Points

1. Inside the Accessories Group, you will find several small applications that can be used for many day-to-day operations.

2. Windows Calculator operates just like a real calculator.

3. Calculator can be displayed as a standard calculator or a scientific calculator.

4. Windows Calendar is a simple electronic time management system. You can display the appointments for a single day or a calendar page for an entire month.

5. Calendar will let you set alarms for as many appointments as necessary. Alarms may be set to go off up to 10 minutes before the actual time of the appointment. When an alarm goes off, the computer will sound a beep and flash the calendar window or icon.

6. Cardfile is like a box of electronic filing cards. Cardfile uses the information in the index line to sort the cards and, if the index line contains a phone number, it can even dial the phone for you.

7. Notepad is a text editor. It can be used to write (or edit) batch files, or as a small word processor.

8. To use Notepad as an automatic time-log system, place the entry .LOG (in capital letters) at the beginning of your file. If a file begins with the .LOG entry, the system will add the time and date to the end of your file each time it is launched.

Practice Exercises

Exercise One   Open the Cardfile application and create five cards that contain names and phone numbers for people that you know. Put each person's name (last name first) and phone number on the index lines, and put each person's address in the main body of each card. Remember to save your file when you are finished.

Exercise Two

1. Open the Notepad application and type the following note. When you are finished, save your work and *minimize* the notepad. *Do not close it.*

Summary of costs for training seminar

Tuition	199.95
Lunch	19.17
Travel	11.14
Parking	5.00

Total

---

2. Launch Calculator and add the figures shown in the note above. When you get the total, open Calculator's Edit menu and select Copy. Finally, close the calculator.

3. Maximize Notepad (in other words, double-click on its icon) and move the insertion point to the right of the word Total. Open Notepad's Edit menu and choose Paste. The result obtained with Calculator should appear in the correct location.

Comprehension Questions

1. Numbers can be entered into Calculator in three ways. What are they?

2. What is the difference between Calculator's memory and the computer's memory?

3. If you press the @ sign on your computer's keyboard, what will happen to the number in Calculator's display?

4. Calendar's day view begins at what time (by default)?

5. In addition to the day view, what other view is provided by Calendar?

6. If Calendar displays the wrong time and date, where do you go to correct them?

7. List the steps necessary to set an alarm that will go off five minutes before a 12:00 P.M. appointment.

8. If you set one alarm to go off early, what will happen to all other alarms?

9. A single card in Cardfile is divided into two major parts. What are each of these parts called?

10. List the steps needed to add a new card to the Cardfile accessory.

11. If you want to use Cardfile to dial the phone, where must the phone number be located on each card?

12. What is the difference between Cardfile's Search and Find features?

13. Clock can be displayed in two different formats. What are they and how are the different formats selected?

14. List at least three uses for the Notepad accessory.

15. In Notepad, what does the Word Wrap feature do (or not do)?

16. If a Notepad file begins with the entry .LOG, what will happen?

Completion Questions

1. Calculator can be displayed in a _____ or a _____ format.

2. To enter numbers into Calculator, you can use the _____ _____ or the _____ _____ on your computer's keyboard.

3. You can transfer numbers from Calculator directly into other Windows applications if you open Calculator's _____ menu and select _____.

4. You can display Calendar in the _____ or _____ view.

5. The area at the bottom of Calendar's window is called the _____ _____. You can use this area to enter a note up to three lines long.

6. To print you calendar, open the _____ menu and choose _____.

7. Cardfile is like a box of electronic _____ _____.

8. To view the cards in your file as a list, open the _____ menu and choose _____.

9. If you want to change the format of Clock, you need to open the _____ menu.

10. Notepad can be used to edit DOS _____ files.

11. Before text in Notepad can be copied or moved it must first be _____.

12. To print a Notepad file, open the _____ menu and choose _____.

Using Write: The Windows Word Processor

Learning Objectives

1. Identify the parts of the Write window.

2. Define paragraph as determined by a word processing program.

3. List several reasons to select (or highlight) text.

4. List the four ways that text can be justified in a document.

5. Define the different types of tabs available in Write.

6. Define header and footer as used by Write.

7. List the four file formats that can be used to save Write documents.

Performance Objectives

1. Enter text and format it for best appearance.

2. Perform the basic editing operations including cut, paste, and copy.

3. Use the Find feature to locate specific text in a document.

4. Use the Find and Replace feature.

5. Save and retrieve a Write document.

6. Print a Write document.

Chapter Terms

End Mark The End mark marks the end of a Write document and looks like a tiny box with four wings. When you first open a Write document, the End mark will be at the beginning of the page, and as you type, the End mark will be pushed to the right.

Font A Font is a design that is applied to all text, numbers, and other characters that is used to change their appearance on the display and the printer.

Footer A Footer is a block of text that automatically appears at the bottom of every page when it is printed.

Go-To key The Go-To key is the number 5 on the numeric keypad. To use the Go-To key, the [Num Lock] key must be off.

Header A Header is a block of text that automatically appears at the top of every page when it is printed.

I-beam Pointer The I-beam pointer is a vertical bar with wings at the top and bottom. When the mouse pointer is inside the Write work area, the mouse pointer will display as an I-beam pointer.

Insertion Point The insertion point appears on the screen as a flashing vertical bar. Any text that you enter will appear to the left of the insertion point and push it to the right as you type.

Paragraph When you are using a word processing program, a paragraph is a block of text that ends when you press [Enter←]. A word processing program will automatically put as much text as it can on every line. You only press [Enter←] when you need to start a new paragraph.

Repagination When you first type a document in Write, the computer will place all the text on one very long page. When you are ready to print, the system will divide your text into sections that will fit on 8-1/2" x 11" pieces of paper. The process of breaking the document into sections is called Repagination.

Selected Text Selected text will display in reverse (white letters on a black background) in the Write work area. If you want to move or change the appearance of any text that has already been typed, it must be selected.

Selection Area	The Selection area is at the left side of the Write work area. When the mouse pointer moves into the Selection area, it will change into a standard arrow pointer.
Work Area	The Work area is the main part of the Write screen. The Work area displays your text as you type. When the mouse pointer is in the Work area, it will appear as an I-beam pointer.

Chapter Overview

In the world of Camelot, books were rare and expensive. If a new book needed to be made, it was necessary to copy the entire text by hand. If an error was made, corrections would be difficult and time consuming. In fact, errors would often be ignored rather than corrected.

In many ways, a word processing program is nothing more than a fancy typewriter. When you are using a typewriter, you enter text and it appears, mistakes and all, on a piece of paper. Corrections and changes can still be difficult.

The Write accessory is a small, but very useful word processing program. It lacks many of the Production-typing features (such as mail merge, and columns) that are found in larger, more complex word processing programs, but many people find it to be quite adequate for personal use. When you use Write, the text still appears on a "page" but now it can be corrected or changed very easily.

Locate the Write application in the Accessories Group and double-click to launch it. A window will open that contains a blank piece of "typing paper" and you are ready to begin (see Figure 9.1).

Getting Started with Write

If you are accustomed to using a typewriter, keep in mind that when you use Write (or any word processing program), you keep typing when you get to the end of the line. Do not press Enter⮐. A word processing program will automatically put as much text as it can on every line. You only press Enter⮐ when you need to start a new paragraph.

Figure 9.1

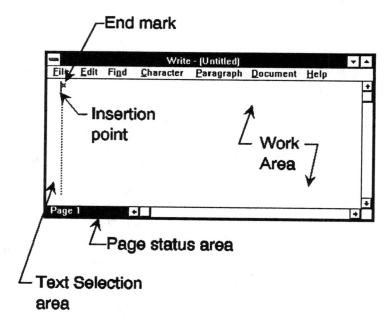

The main Write window

■ **Note** To create a blank line between paragraphs, just press Enter⮐ again. A blank line, by definition, is an "empty" paragraph.

At the top of the Write window, you will see the familiar title bar and control buttons array. If necessary, the Write window can be sized or moved. In general, the Write window is very similar to windows in other Windows applications. However, there are (as usual) a few important differences.

When the mouse pointer is in the Write work area, it changes from an arrow pointer to an I-beam pointer. You move the I-beam the same way you move the arrow, but when you click the mouse, a flashing vertical bar (called the insertion point) will jump to the location that you indicate. The insertion point marks the spot that your text will appear when you begin typing.

■ **Note** To enter text, just type. Remember, when you get to the end of the line, keep typing. Press [Enter←] only when you reach the end of a *paragraph* or if you need to insert a blank line.

When you first open a new Write document, you will see a little box with wings in the upper left corner of the work area. This little box marks the end of your document. As you type text into the work area, this end mark will move.

At the bottom left of the Write window, you will find the page status area. Here you will see an indicator that tells you which page of your text is currently on the screen but until you break your work into pages or (print it out) this indicator will always read "Page 1."

■ **Note** To automatically break your document into pages, open the File menu, select Repaginate, and Write will place two little arrows in the selection area to mark the beginning of each new page. Then, if necessary, you can insert manual page breaks to control the appearance of the finished product.

To create a manual page break, hold the [Ctrl] key, press [Enter←], and Write will place a line of dots across the work area.

Moving Around in Your Document

Note: The GOTO key is the number "5" on the numeric keypad. To use the GOTO key, the ⌨ must be off.

Press This	To move to
Ctrl + →	Next word
Ctrl + ←	Previous word
GOTO + →	Next sentence
GOTO + ←	Previous sentence
Home	Beginning of a line
End	End of a line
GOTO + ↓	Next paragraph
GOTO + ↑	Previous paragraph
Ctrl + PgDn	Bottom of the window
Ctrl + PgUp	Top of the window
GOTO + PgDn	Next page
GOTO + PgUp	Previous page
Ctrl + Home	Beginning of your document
Ctrl + End	End of your document

The easiest way to move the insertion point is to move the I-beam pointer and click. As mentioned earlier, when you click the mouse pointer, the insertion point will jump to the new location. However, many typists do not like to take their hands off the keyboard, find the mouse, move to a new spot, and resume typing. With that in mind, Write also provides several ways to move the insertion point without using the mouse. (See "Moving Around in Your Document" for a summary of these commands.)

▲ **Hint**   If you hold any of the above key combinations, the insertion point will move continuously. ▲

Selecting Text

Another of the merits of a word processing program is that you never need to type anything twice. If you decide to place your paragraphs in a different order, or to duplicate existing text in another place, all you need to do is "select" the text, copy and, move (or even delete) it from your document. Write allows you to select text in several different ways.

■ **Note**   Actually, there are many reasons to select a block of text. For example, if you need to underline a block of text, it must first be selected. In fact, before you can perform any operation that modifies the appearance of a block of text, it must first be selected.

To select a large block of text, move the insertion point to the beginning of the block, press and hold the left mouse button, and drag the pointer to the end of the block. As you drag the pointer, the selected text will display in reverse (white text on a dark background). When you reach the end of the block, just release the mouse button.

As shown in Figure 9.1, the "margin" to the left of your text (as it appears in the Write window) is called the text selection area. If you move the mouse pointer into this area it will change back into the standard arrow. Single-click, while in the text selection area, and Write will select the entire line of text immediately to the right. If you double-click, Write will select the entire paragraph.

▲ **Hint**   If you double-click and hold the mouse button on the second click, you can drag the mouse pointer and Write will select additional text a full paragraph at a time. ▲

If you need to select a block of text between two points, you can move into the text selection, select a line of text (with a single or double-click), move to the end of the block and click again *while holding the* ⟨⇧Shift⟩ *key.* Write will select all of the text between the first selection and the last click.

Figure 9.2

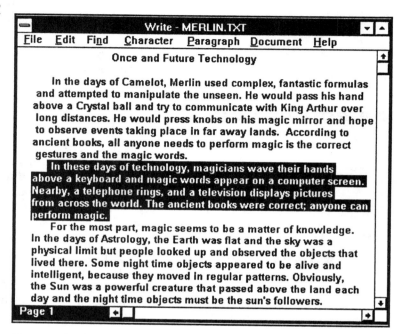

The text that is highlighted in this window is "selected."

▲ **Hint** If you move into the text selection area and click while you hold the ⟨Ctrl⟩ key, Write will select the entire document. To unselect the document (or any selection for that matter) move anywhere into the document and click again. ▲

Changing Your Text

Change can be exciting or change can be frightening, but at least when using Write, change is simple. Any time you need to add text to a Write document, move the insertion point to the correct location and type. Don't worry about erasing the text that is already there because, by default, Write will push all existing text forward to make room for the new stuff.

■ **Note**   If you do need to replace text, press the [Ins] key and Write will toggle into what is called the type-over mode. Now, when you add text, it will replace, not push, the existing text. To return to the insert mode, press the [Ins] key a second time.

Locating and Correcting Text

Figure 9.3

The Find menu

Often, it is necessary to change some specific text in a very large document. When this happens, finding the text to be changed can be time consuming and irritating.

Open the Find menu, and Write will provide some tools to help you find and correct specific occurrences of text. In fact, you can search for a string of text up to 255 characters long (see Figure 9.3).

If you need to simply locate some specific text in your document, open the Find menu and choose Find. When the dialog box appears, type the text that you are looking for into the Find What: box. Below this box are two check boxes that control the way your search will be conducted.

■ **Note**   When you perform a Find operation, Write will begin the search at the insertion point and search to the end of the document.

Figure 9.4

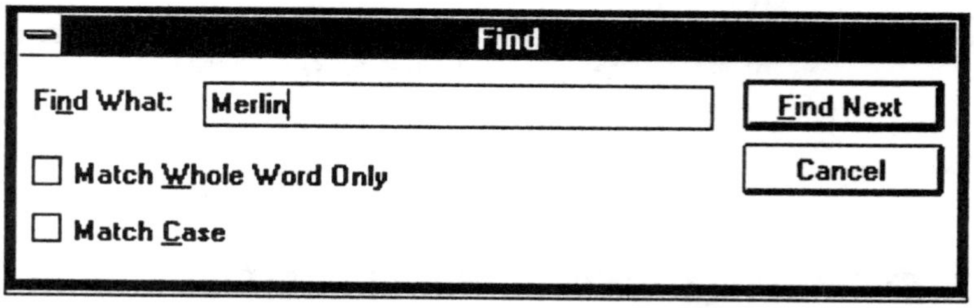

The Find dialog box.

As you can see in Figure 9.4, the first box is marked "Match Whole Word Only." When you check this box, Write will search the text for a complete word rather than a part of a word. For example, if you need to search for the word "the" and the "Match Whole Word Only" box is *not* checked, Write will find that letter combination even if it occurs inside of another word such as "*their*" or "*whether.*" Of course, if you do need to search for every occurrence of a certain letter combination, no matter where it occurs, then leave this box unchecked.

The second box tells Write to match, or not match, upper/lowercase. If upper case is important (if you are searching for a proper name, for example), make sure that this box is checked. If this box is not checked, Write will match everything.

▲ Hint   You can also use the Find function to place "bookmarks" in your text. To mark a location, type +++ or some other code you choose. Later, use the Find feature to locate your bookmarks. (Don't forget to delete all of your bookmarks before you print your finished document.) ▲

The Replace command (in the Find menu) will let you search for *and replace* specific occurrences of text with new text. You can change all occurrences, or you can tell Write which to change and which to leave alone.

To Find and Replace text, open the Find menu and choose Replace. Another dialog box will appear, but this time there will be two places to enter text. In the top box, type the text that you are looking for (in other words, put the existing text here). In the second box, enter the replacement text. Again, check the Match Whole Word Only and Match Case boxes as necessary before you press any of the buttons on the right of the dialog box.

To find the next occurrence of the search text, press the Find Next button. When Write locates the text, you can manually edit it (by clicking on the text or pressing ⌨ + ⌨), or you can continue searching.

Figure 9.5

Replace		
Find What:	Magic	**Find Next**
Replace With:	Technology	**Replace**
☐ Match Whole Word Only		**Replace All**
☐ Match Case		**Close**

The Replace dialog box

▲ **Hint**   Before you start any Find and Replace operation, you should save your work to disk. That way, if something unexpected happens, you can recall the last version and try again.

The Find and Replace function, when used incorrectly, is sometimes called Find and Destroy. ▲

When you press the Replace button, Write will replace any text that is selected (highlighted) with the specified replacement text, and then, Write will automatically search for the next occurrence of the same text.

The last button in the Replace box is marked "Replace All." When you press this button, Write will search for and replace every occurrence of the specified text automatically. Be very careful when you use this option. Remember, the computer is not intelligent. It will do exactly what you tell it to do. If you are not careful, misusing this feature could completely destroy your document.

▲ **Hint**   Anytime you find that you need to type the same long phrase (such as a name or address) again and again, type a short code such as %% or && instead. Then, when you are finished with your document, perform a Search and Replace operation and search for the code and replace it with the actual text. ▲

How to Repeat the Last Find Command

Figure 9.6

```
Find
  Find...
  Repeat Last Find  F3
  Replace...
  Go To Page...      F4
```

The selection for Repeat Last Find

When you are performing any Find or Replace operation, you do not need to leave the dialog box on the screen during the entire search. After you locate the first occurrence of the search text, simply close the dialog box until you need it again.

Then, when you need to perform your next search, open the Find menu and select Repeat Last Find (see Figure 9.6).

▲ **Hint**   You can also repeat your last Find operation if you press the [F3] key. ▲

Using Wildcards to Help in Your Search

Often, when searching for text, it is not practical (or even possible) to search for *specific* text. For example, if you are searching for the name "Merlin" and you accidently typed "Marlin," the search function would never be able to find your text. To allow for the remote possibility of human error, Write will let you use wildcards to make your search less specific.

To solve the fishy "Marlin" problem, type M?rlin (or even M?????) into the Find box. The question mark is used to represent any character.

If you type M?rlin, Write will find every word that begins with *M*, ends with *rlin* and has any character in the ? position. If you type M?????, the Find feature will locate every six-letter word that begins with M.

▲ **Hint**   To save a little time, it is not necessary to search your entire document every time you are looking for some text. Before you begin your search, you can select (highlight) the area of your document that contains the stuff to be changed. Then, when you start the search, Write will only search the selected text—not the entire document. ▲

Formatting Your Document

A uniform, continuous, monotonous block of text can be boring and difficult to read. If you want your work to be boring, you can skip this part, but if you want your finished documents to have visual appeal, then you will be interested in what is sometimes called special effects.

Figure 9.7

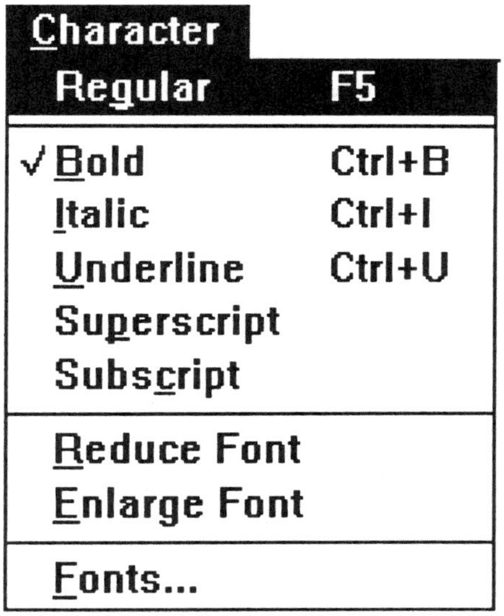

```
┌──────────────────────────────┐
│ Character                    │
│ Regular          F5          │
├──────────────────────────────┤
│ √ Bold           Ctrl+B      │
│   Italic         Ctrl+I      │
│   Underline      Ctrl+U      │
│   Superscript                │
│   Subscript                  │
├──────────────────────────────┤
│   Reduce Font                │
│   Enlarge Font               │
├──────────────────────────────┤
│   Fonts...                   │
└──────────────────────────────┘
```

The Character menu

As shown in Figure 9.7, the commands in the Character menu will let you add interest and emphasis to your document with boldface, italics, and underlining. You can also change text to superscripts or subscripts, and even change the font that is used to display (and print) your work.

Special Effects: Bold, Underline, and Italic

Write provides three options that are sometime referred to as special effects. These options change the actual appearance of your text and if used carefully can make your finished document much more appealing.

To apply any of these effects to existing text, the text must first be selected. Hold the left mouse button and drag the cursor over the text to be affected, or use any of the other text selection techniques. When everything that is to be changed is highlighted, open the Character menu and choose the tool you need. The change on your display screen will be immediately visible.

▲ **Hint**　If necessary, you can apply more than one effect to the same block of text. For example, you could have text that is underlined and boldfaced, or even boldfaced, underlined, and italicized all at the same time.To apply a special effect to text that has not been typed yet, start by opening the Character menu and selecting the effect (or effects) you need. Now, type your text and everything will appear with the effects already applied. To stop any effect, reopen the Character menu and select the effect a second time. ▲

If you would rather use the keyboard to apply special effects, press a ⌈Ctrl⌋ key combination to start (and stop) the special effects. To start boldface text, press ⌈Ctrl⌋+B, for italics press ⌈Ctrl⌋+I, and for underline press ⌈Ctrl⌋+U. To stop any of these special effects, just press the same key combination a second time.

■ **Note**　Be careful that you do not use too many special effects in a single document. These tools are easy to use and if you use them too often your document will begin to look unprofessional. Just because a tool is available does not mean that you must use it.

Changing the Font　A font is a design that is applied to all text, numbers, and other characters that is used to change their appearance on the display and the printer.

■ **Note**　The size and the type of fonts that will be available is determined by the printer that is currently selected. Not all fonts are available on all printers.

Figure 9.8

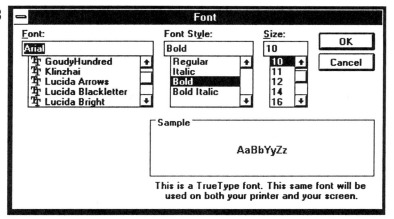

The Fonts selection box

When you open the Character menu, you display a list of additional font names by choosing the Fonts command (see Figure 9.8).

When you start a new document, Write will use the standard font for the default printer. If you want to use a different font, open the Character menu, select Fonts, and select the desired font from the dialog box.

▲ Hint If you change the font as you start a new document, the entire document will display and print using the font that you select.

If you select a different font later in the same document, the new font will be used from the selection point to the end. The text that has already been typed will not be affected.

If you need to change the font for an existing block of text, first select the text to be affected, and then select your font. Only the highlighted text will change to the new font. ▲

Changing the Font Size If you open the Character menu and choose Reduce Font or Enlarge Font, Write will change the font to the next larger or smaller size. The change will take effect at that point and continue to the end of the document (or until you change the size again).

If the text that you want to change has already been typed, you must select the text first, and only the selected text will be affected.

■ Note If you make a font size change and your printer does not support the next available size, the text on the screen will not change.

Using Superscript and Subscript Superscript and Subscript text are smaller letters and numbers that appear slightly above (or below) the other text in a line. For example, to write the chemical formula H_2O, you would want to make the 2 a subscript. If you need to indicate a number raised to a power, such as 10^6, then you would need a superscript.

Superscript and subscript are applied just like any other special effect. You can type the text first, select it, open the Character menu and choose the necessary effect; or you can open the Character menu first, then type the text, and choose the effect. (Remember, to stop the effect, you must open the Character menu a second time, and choose the effect again.)

Controlling the Appearance of a Paragraph

You will want most of the text that you type in Write to run all the way from the left margin to the right margin of your paper. To do this, just type, and Write will do the rest.

Figure 9.9

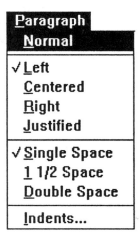

The Paragraph menu

To change the appearance of a paragraph, you need to give Write special instructions. For example, if you want the first line of a paragraph to be indented, you must press 〔Tab〕. If you need to offset a block of text to emphasize a quote or a table, you need to tell Write how far to indent, and how much text is to be affected.

None of these operations are difficult, and you already know all of the basic skills (such as selecting text and opening menus) necessary to make these changes. Open the Paragraph menu and you will find the tools that are used to make these changes (see Figure 9.9).

Changing the Paragraph Alignment

As you already know, when typing text into Write, keep typing until you reach the end of a paragraph, and like any other word processing program, your text will automatically be formatted into a preselected arrangement. Whenever you need to change this arrangement, open the Paragraph menu.

Write provides four controls that affect the arrangement of the text in a paragraph. These controls are Left justified, justified, Right justified, and Center justified.

▲ Hint

If you select Normal from the Paragraph menu, your text will be set to left justified, single-spaced text. ▲

Left justification will cause all of your text to align neatly on the left margin only. The right margin will be "rough" and will not align neatly. The number of words on each line (and the length of each word) will be used to determine where each line ends. The text in this paragraph is left justified. Look carefully at the right margin of this paragraph and compare it to the right margin of the following paragraph.

If a paragraph is justified, Write will try to fill each line of the paragraph with a full line of text. Both the left margin and the right margin should line up neatly. To perform this task, Write may adjust the spacing between each word and if necessary the spacing between letters. The text in this paragraph displays an example of justified text.

The text in this paragraph is an example of text that is right justified. It is, as you can see, the opposite of left justification. Use right justification for any application that needs text that aligns on the right rather than the left.

The last choice is text that is center justified. You may or may not find much use for this option. If you are writing a poem or typing a list of items (such as a menu for a restaurant), center justification can come in handy. The text in this paragraph is center justified.

▲ Hint You can also use center justification to automatically place a single line of text (such as a title) in the center of a page. ▲

Changing the Line Spacing Inside a Paragraph Often, to make a page of text more readable, it is necessary to change the spacing from line to line. By default, Write will advance a single space for each new line but if necessary, you can select 1-1/2 line spacing or even double spacing. Any time you need to change the line spacing, open the Paragraph menu and choose the spacing you need from the drop-down menu. The choice that has a check mark next to it is the spacing that is currently selected.

■ Note Remember, when using a word processing program, don't press ⌷Enter←⌷ at the end of each line. Only press ⌷Enter←⌷ at the end of a paragraph.

Setting Tabs Write has tabs that are preset to every half inch. You can use the tabs as they are, or change them to anything you need. You can set up to twelve tabs and these tabs can be left-aligned or decimal tabs.

■ Note Decimal tabs are often used to align a column of numbers with decimal points.

Figure 9.10

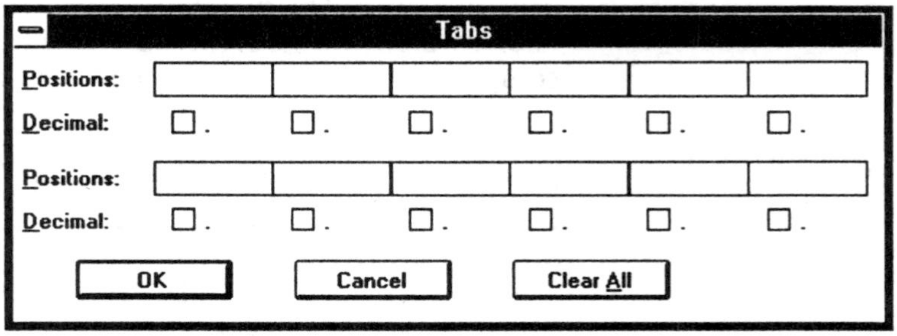

The Tabs dialog box

Choose Tabs from the Document menu and a dialog box will appear as shown in Figure 9.10. Enter a measurement in inches for each tab that you want to set. If the new tab should be a decimal tab, check the box below the entry. Use the arrow keys, the ⌷Tab⌷ key, or the mouse to move from position to position. When you are finished, press the OK button.

▲ Hint   Any time you enter text at a decimal tab stop, it will be entered to the left of the tab until you type the decimal point. ▲

You can use a decimal tab to align text on the right as long as the text does not contain a period or if it has a period only at the end.

Editing Tabs   If you need to delete or change the position of an existing tab, open the Paragraph menu, choose Tabs again, and correct (or erase) the numbers in the dialog box. To delete all the tabs (perhaps to start over), press the Clear All button.

Displaying the Ruler   If you have a mouse, you can use the ruler to change the format of your text. To display the ruler, open the Document menu and select Ruler On. The screen will change to a display similar to Figure 9.11.

Figure 9.11

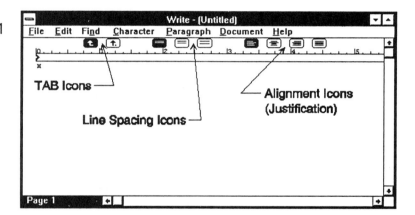

The main Write window with the Ruler displayed

The ruler will appear just below the menu bar inside the Write window. It will display three sets of icons that can be used to place tabs, control the line spacing of a paragraph, and determine the paragraph alignment.

Setting Tabs from the Ruler   The first two icons on the ruler are used to place tabs. The left icon represents a regular left tab and the other is used to place a decimal tab. Select (by clicking) the type of tab that you need, move the mouse pointer to the point (just below the line of measurements) where you want the tab to be located, and click again.

To move a tab, press and hold the left mouse button, and drag it to a new location. To delete a tab, just drag it down and "off" of the ruler.

■ **Note**   The Preset tabs do not appear in the dialog box or on the ruler.

How to Change the Line Spacing from the Ruler

What to Do	**What Happens**
1. Select (highlight) the text that is to be affected by the change.	
2. You can select an entire paragraph if you double-click in the text selection area to the left of the para-graph.	
3. To select the entire docu-ment, press and hold Ctrl and single click in the text selection area.	The selected text will display in reverse (see Figure 9.12).
4. The second group of icons on the ruler is used to select the line spacing. The first icon is used for single spacing, the second is 1-1/2 spacing, and the third is double spacing. Select the icon that represents the spacing you need.	The selected text will change to reflect the change as shown in Figure 9.13.

Figure 9.12

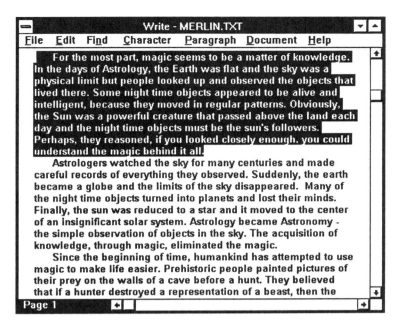

5. Click anywhere to "deselect" the block of text.

The text will revert to a normal display.

Figure 9.13

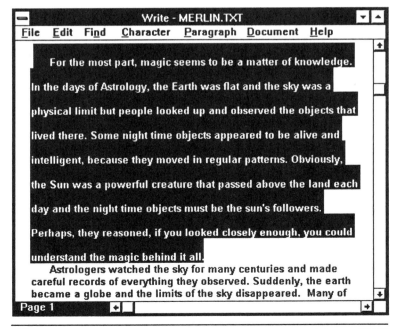

How to Change the
Paragraph Alignment from the Ruler

The last group of icons on the ruler represent the selections that affect the paragraph alignment: Left justified, Center justified, Right justified, and justified, in that order.

What to Do	What Happens
1. Select (highlight) the text that is to be affected by the change.	
2. You can select an entire paragraph if you double-click in the text selection area to the left of the para-graph.	
3. To select the entire document, press and hold [Ctrl] and single-click in the text selection area.	The selected text will display in reverse.
4. Click the icon that represents the justification that you need. The first icon is for left justification, the second is for center justification, the third is for right justification and the last one is for justification.	The selected text will change to reflect the change.
5. Click anywhere to deselect the block of text.	The text will revert to a normal display.

Hyphenation   As you proofread your finished document, you may, on occasion, find a large gap at the end of a line where a long word has been moved to the beginning of the next line. These gaps can be eliminated if you insert an "optional" hyphen in long words.

To insert an optional hyphen, first move to the point in the word where a break is allowed. Next, press (and hold) `Ctrl` and `⇧ Shift` at the same time, and then press the hyphen (dash). Optional hyphens are used only if a word appears at the end of a line.

▲ Hint   You also may want to use optional hyphens when your text is justified. If you are using narrow margins, and your text is justified, Write may change the spacing between letters to fill out the line. ▲

Placing Headers and Footers

Write makes every effort to eliminate the need to retype the same text in two different places. In the body of your text, you can use the Copy and Paste functions to duplicate text that has already been typed; however, if you need the same text at the top or bottom of every page, deciding exactly where to paste can be a problem. In fact, if you edit your text (and change its length), you may have to move everything.

Whenever you are using a computer, and feel like you are doing too much work, you are probably right. There is almost always an easier way to perform every task. For example, when you need to place text at the top (or bottom) of every page, don't type the same text again and again, put it in a header or a footer.

Creating a Header or Footer   Very simply, a header prints at the top of every page, and a footer prints at the bottom. Write will allow you to create one header and one footer per document.

What to Do   **What Happens**

1.   Open the Document menu and select Header (or Footer).   A window similar to Figure 9.14 will appear.

Figure 9.14

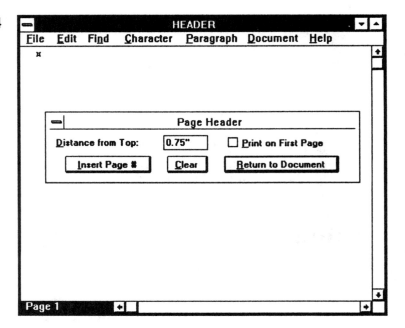

2. If necessary, change the value in the box marked Distance from Top (or Bottom). This value affects how far the header (or footer) will be from the edge of your paper.

Nothing new.

3. If your document begins with a title page, you may not want the header (or footer) to appear on the first page. If this is true, make sure the box marked Print on First Page is *not* checked.

Nothing new.

4. Enter the text for your header (or footer). It might be necessary to use the mouse to move the insertion point to the top of the header (or footer) screen. The text can be formatted just like any other text anywhere in your document.

The text will appear, as you type, in the edit screen window.

5. To place automatic page numbering in your text press the Insert Page # button.

A special code will appear. When you print your document, the correct page number will appear at that point.

6. Press the button marked Return to go back to the Document when you are finished.

The main edit screen will re-display.

■ **Note** Headers and footers will not appear until you print your document. If you need to examine (or change) a header (or footer) before you print, you must reopen the header (or footer) edit window.

Using Pictures in Your Document

Confucius was right. You need about 10,000 "words" of computer data to store some types of computer pictures. Following in the footsteps of Confucius, you can add pictures to your Write document and illuminate your text.

You can place as many graphics in your document as your computer's memory will allow, but the actual graphics must come from "outside" of Write. In fact, when a picture is loaded into Write, it cannot be edited.

■ **Note** Remember, if your image is in color it will probably print in black and white. How the finished image appears will actually depend on your printer.

By default, when you paste a picture into Write, it will appear at the left margin but once it is in, you can move and size it as necessary.

■ **Note**   When you see your graphic on the display screen, it may appear to be distorted. However, when the document is printed, it will appear correctly.

How to Paste a Picture into Your Document

What to Do	**What Happens**
1. Copy (or cut) the graphic that you wish to use from its original application. For example, start the Paintbrush program, load your picture, open the Edit menu, and select Copy or Cut.	The graphic will be loaded into Windows Clipboard.
2. Minimize (or close) the Paintbrush program so that it moves out of your way. Load (or activate) Write and move the insertion point to where the graphic is to be placed.	Nothing yet.
3. In Write, open the Edit menu and choose Paste.	The graphic will appear at the insertion point as shown in Figure 9.15.

Figure 9.15

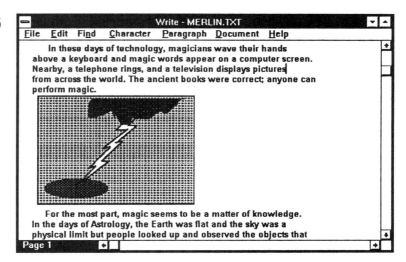

The Write main window with a graphic in place

▲ **Hint** Clipboard is a temporary storage location that is available to all Windows applications. If you want to examine the contents of the Clipboard, open the Main program group and launch the Clipboard application.

How to Move a Picture Horizontally

■ **Note** Once a graphic is placed, it can only be moved horizontally. If you need to move it vertically, you must delete it and paste it into a new location.

What to Do	What Happens
1. Click on the picture (to select it), or use the arrow keys to move the insertion point to the picture.	The graphic will display as a negative (see Figure 9.16).

Figure 9.16

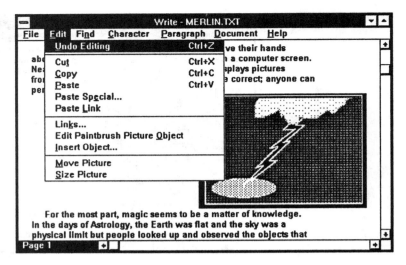

2. Open the Edit menu and choose Move.

A square cursor will appear in the middle of the graphic and it will be surrounded by a dotted frame as shown in Figure 9.17.

3. *Do not touch the mouse button.* Use the mouse to move the dotted frame to the desired location, or even better (safer), use the arrow keys to move the box.

The dotted frame will move to show the proposed new location.

4. When the frame is in the correct location, press the mouse button (or press Enter).

The graphic will move to the new location.

5. Use the arrow keys to move the insertion point or click the mouse button anywhere outside of the graphic.

The graphic will deselect.

Figure 9.17

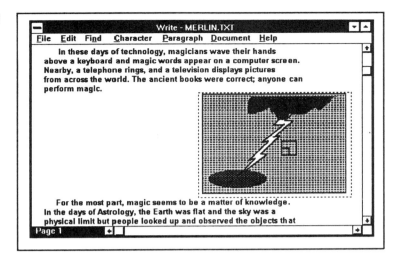

How to Change the Size of a Picture

What to Do   **What Happens**

1. Click on the picture (to   The graphic will display as
        select it), or use the arrow   a negative.
        keys to move the insertion
        point to the picture.

Figure 9.18

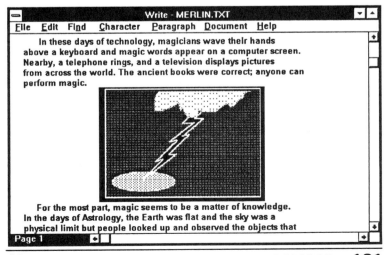

2. Open the Edit menu and choose Size.

A square cursor will appear. It will have a dotted frame attached to it.

3. *Do not touch the mouse button.* Use the mouse to move the dotted frame until it outlines the size that you want the picture to be. You can also use the arrow keys to move the box.

The dotted frame will move to show the proposed new size.

4. When the frame size is correct, press the mouse button (or press Enter←┘).

The graphic will be resized.

5. Use the arrow keys to move the insertion point or click the mouse button anywhere outside of the graphic.

The graphic will deselect.

Saving and Retrieving Write Files

When you are using Write, the rules for saving and retrieving files are pretty much the same as for any other Windows program. When you need to save a file, open the File menu, select Save or Save As, provide a filename if necessary, and press OK.

To retrieve a Write file, open the File menu and choose Open. Select the file you need from the list, and you are ready to go. The maximum size of a Write file is limited only by the amount of memory in your computer.

▲ **Hint** When you are working on a Write document (or any other project for that matter) you should save your work often. For example, make a habit of saving your work every fifteen minutes; if there is a power failure or other problem, the damage will be kept to a minimum. ▲

Saving Your Work

Four formatting choices are available when you save your work, however, unless you provide other instructions, Write will save your work in its own format.

Use this format	To save your work as
Default Format	A Write formatted document. In a file listing, a Write file will have an extension of .WRI.
Text Only Format	A Windows ANSI format. This format is often used if your document is a program or if it is to be transferred over a modem.
Microsoft Word Format	A Microsoft Word document without any additional format changes. Do not use this format if your Write document contains any graphics because they will disappear.
Text Only and Microsoft Word Format	An unformatted Microsoft Word text file.

Retrieving Your Work

If the document that you need to load was created using Write, all you need to do is retrieve it normally. Files that were created with programs other than Write may need to be converted before you can use them.

When you try to open a file that is not in Write format, a dialog box will appear. To convert the file just press the Convert button.

■ **Note** Before you convert any document into Write format, make sure you have a backup copy. Write is unable to convert some types of files created by other word processing programs and they may be corrupted.

How to Automatically Make a Backup Copy of Your Work

What to Do	**What Happens**
1. Open the File menu and choose the Save As option.	A dialog box will display as shown in Figure 9.19.

Figure 9.19

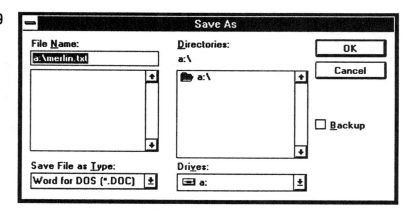

2. If necessary, type a filename into the dialog box, then check the Make Backup box.	An X will appear in the Make Backup box.
3. Click OK to finish.	The next time you load your file, Write will load a copy and save the original file with an extension of .BKP.

Printing Your Document

You are finally finished. All the hours of research and typing are about to pay off. You have saved your document, made careful backups, and are ready to submit the final version. All you need to do now is to transfer your work to paper. Make sure that the document that you want to print is displayed, open the File menu and select Print. A dialog box will display like the one in Figure 9.20. Select the print options, press OK, and you're done.

Figure 9.20

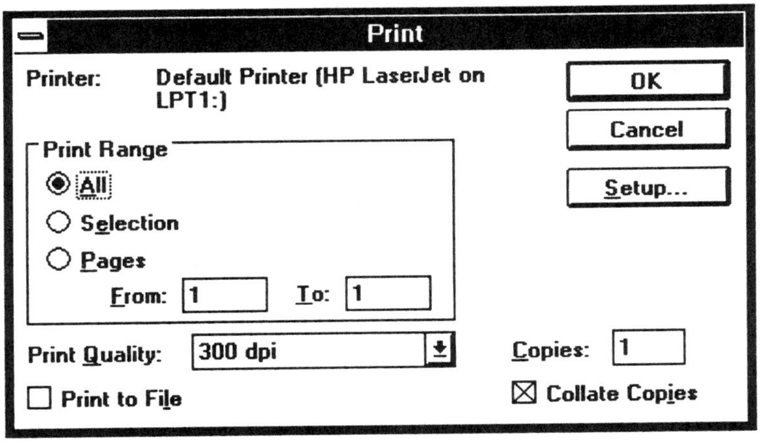

The Print dialog box

The first option will let you print more than one copy of your document. If you need more than one copy, just type a number into this box.

By default, Write will print your entire document. If you only want to print part of your document, click the radio button and put the starting page number in the From box and the ending page number in the To box.

Finally, if you have a dot-matrix printer, you can instruct Write to print a draft-quality copy of your work. A draft-quality copy will print faster and will make your printer ribbons last longer.

Summary Points

1. The Write application is normally found in the Accessories Group.

2. Write does not have all the features of a production word processing program but is more than adequate for personal use.

3. As with all word processing programs, keep typing when you get to the end of a line. Only press [Enter⏎] at the end of a paragraph.

4. To automatically break your document into pages, open the File menu and select Repaginate. Write will place two little arrows to mark the beginning of each new page.

5. To create a manual page break, hold [Ctrl] and press [Enter⏎].

6. Before you can perform any operation that modifies the appearance of a block of text, it must be selected (highlighted).

7. To automatically search for specific text in your document, open the Find menu, choose Find, and enter the search text into the dialog box.

8. If you need to search for and replace specific text with new text, open the Find menu, choose Replace, type the existing text into the first box, and the replacement text into the second box.

9. If you do not use Find and Replace carefully, you could completely destroy your document.

10. Write provides three special effects: boldface, underline, and italic.

11. A font is a design that is applied to all text, numbers, and other characters.

12. The text in a paragraph can be left justified, right justified, center justified, or justified.

13. Write has tabs that are preset to every half inch. You can use the tabs as they are, or change them to anything you need. To change the tabs, open the Document menu and select Tabs. You can set up to 12 tabs in a single document.

14. If you have a mouse, you can use the ruler to change the format of your text. To display the ruler, open the Document menu and select Ruler On.

15. To insert an optional hyphen, press and hold `Ctrl` + `⇧ Shift` +HYPHEN. An optional hyphen only displays if the word appears at the end of a line.

16. A header prints at the top of every page and a footer prints at the bottom. Write will allow you to create one header and one footer per document.

17. You can place as many graphics in your document as your computer's memory will allow, but the actual graphics must come from outside of Write.

18. To save your work, open the File menu, choose Save or Save As, and provide a filename.

19. To retrieve a Write file, open the File menu, choose Open and select the file you need from the list.

20. To print your document, open the File menu, choose Print, select the necessary options, and press the OK button.

Practice Exercises

Type the letter on the following page using Write. When finished, save and print your document. Use the following guidelines to format your work.

* Set tabs at 1.5, 3.25, 3.87, 5, and 5.5 inches to help create the table in the middle of the letter. The last tab, the one on the far right, should be a decimal tab.

  Note: This project was entered using 10 point Courier type. If you use a different font, you might need to adjust the distance between tabs.

* At the top of the letter, type today's date. Format the date so that it is right justified.

* For the main body of the letter, set the paragraph alignment to justified and use 1-1/2 line spacing.

* Change the name at the bottom of the letter to display (and print) in italic.

* When you are finished, save and print your letter.

(Place today's date here)

Digital Magic
Computer Training
St Charles, MO

To whom it may concern:

I have heard many good things about your training programs and would like to enroll myself and several of my apprentices in the following classes on the following dates. Enclosed you will find a check to cover the cost of the classes as listed in your advertising materials. We are looking forward to seeing you.

Class name	Date/time of class	Number attending	Total Cost
Windows	January 17th	4	139.95
Spreadsheets	January 26th	4	219.95
Databases	February 29th	2	99.95

Thank you,

Merlin Ambrosius
Archmage

Comprehension Questions

1. Where is the Write application icon normally stored (by default)?

2. When using Write, and your typing reaches the end of a line, what must you do?

3. When the mouse pointer is in the Write work area, how does its appearance change?

4. If you open the File menu and select Repaginate, Write will place two little arrows at various places in your text. What do these two little arrows indicate?

5. What is the fastest way to select an entire paragraph?

6. What is the easiest way to find a specific block of text in your document?

7. When using Find commands, what are Wildcards used for?

8. Before you start a Find and Replace operation, what should you do?

9. List the steps needed to apply boldface to a block of text that has already been typed.

10. List the four ways that text can be justified within a paragraph.

11. What are the two types of tabs that you can set and how are they different?

12. The Ruler can be used to change three things that affect the appearance of a paragraph. What are these three things?

13. What is an optional hyphen and when is it used?

14. To enter an optional hyphen, what must you do?

15. Define header and footer.

16. When you use graphics in a Write document, where do the graphics come from?

17. How many graphics can you use in a single Write document?

18. List and define each of the four file formats that can be used to save your work.

19. As with all Windows applications, what is the difference between the Save option and the Save As option?

Completion Questions

1. When using Write, to create a blank line, you press the _____ key.

2. The flashing vertical bar in the work area is called the _____ point.

3. To create a manual page break, press and hold the _____ while you press _____ .

4. To select the entire document, move the mouse pointer into the text selection area (to the left of your text), press and hold the _____ key and click the left mouse button.

5. A _____ is a design that is applied to all text, numbers, and other characters.

6. A _____ is a small number or letter that goes above the normal text line, and a _____ is a small number or letter that drops below the normal text line.

7. Write has tabs that are preset to each _____ inch.

8. When using Write, you can set up to _____ custom tabs.

9. To display the Ruler, open the _____ menu and choose the _____ _____ option.

10. You can place a maximum of _____ headers and _____ footers in a Write document.

11. By default, when you paste a graphic into a Write document, it will appear on the _____ margin.

10

Time for the Artist: Using Paintbrush

Learning Objectives

1. Identify the parts of the Paintbrush window.

2. Define foreground and background color.

3. List the actions that disable the Undo feature.

4. Describe the function of the various Paintbrush tools.

5. List reasons to use the cutout tools.

Performance Objectives

1. Select and use the various Paintbrush tools.

2. Create a simple drawing with Paintbrush.

3. Add text to a Paintbrush image.

4. Edit a Paintbrush image using the Erasers.

5. Print a Paintbrush picture.

6. Transfer a Paintbrush picture to Write.

Background Color   The Background color is the color that Paintbrush will use when an element is erased. The currently selected Background color will be displayed as the surrounding area of the Foreground/Background box.

Drawing Area   The main drawing area of Paintbrush is the Drawing area.

Foreground Color   The Foreground color is the color that Paintbrush will use to draw the selected elements in the drawing area. The currently selected Foreground color will be displayed as a box in the center of the Foreground/Background box.

Line Size Box   The Line size box is in the lower left corner of the Paintbrush window. A small arrow will be displayed next to the line width that is currently selected.

Palette   Along the bottom edge of the main Paintbrush window, you will find the Palette area. The Palette displays a sample of each color that is available while you are using Paintbrush.

Toolbox   the Toolbox is located on the left side of the main Paintbrush window. To select a tool, move the mouse pointer into the correct box and click. When a tool is selected, it will display in reverse.

Chapter Overview

In the days of Merlin's magic, an artist would often use pens, colored inks, and even thin sheets of gold to add ornate capital letters, tiny detailed drawings, and complicated vines to the pages of a book. These illuminations could help to clarify the text and on occasion would just be added to make the manuscript more attractive.

In these days of computer magic, you can use the Windows Paintbrush application to "illuminate" your own work. Paintbrush provides a set of tools that anyone can use to draw straight lines, circles, and square boxes to create images that can be transferred to other applications (such as Write) or even displayed as wallpaper on your Windows desktop. With a little practice, anyone can be an artist.

Using Paintbrush

Start by locating (and launching) the Paintbrush application. When the window opens, compare your screen to Figure 10.1. You will find a title bar, menu bar, Control button, and sizing controls that are similar to other Windows applications. In addition to the main part of the screen (called the drawing area), you will see the Toolbox on the left, and the Palette along the bottom of the screen.

Figure 10.1

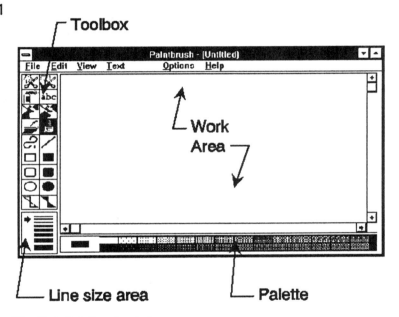

The Main Paintbrush window

■ **Note**   If you are starting a new drawing, it is usually a good idea to make sure that the Paintbrush window is maximized. If necessary, click the Maximize button in the upper right corner and you are ready to begin.

Creating a Simple Drawing

The best way to get familiar with Paintbrush is to use it. Locate the Palette area and just to the left you will find a colored box called the Foreground/Background indicator. The color in the center of the box shows the current drawing (or foreground) color, and the surrounding area displays the background color.

When you first start Paintbrush, the Brush tool will be selected. Use the mouse to move the pointer into the drawing area, and the cursor will appear as a small dot. Press and hold the left mouse button as you drag the cursor around in the drawing area and Paintbrush will draw a "freehand" line using the color in the foreground box.

To select a new foreground color, move the mouse pointer into the Palette area and press the left mouse button while positioned over one of the other colors such as red. Now when you draw, red lines will appear on the screen. You can change the foreground color as often as necessary.

▲ Hint If you make a mistake while you are drawing a line, press `←BkSp` and the cursor will turn into a small box with an "X" inside. To use this special eraser, press (and hold) the left mouse button and move the cursor over the area to be corrected. Only the last line that you placed will be erased. All other elements of your drawing will be left untouched. ▲

Changing the Background Color If you move the mouse pointer into the palette area, position it above a color and press the *right* mouse button, the *background* color will be changed. Any time you use one of the Erase tools, it will change the colors in the drawing area to the same color as the background.

For example, if you are removing some red lines from an area that is colored white, set the background to white and the lines will disappear. If you need to erase white lines from a red area, then set the background to red.

Like the foreground color, the background color can be changed as often as necessary.

Working with the Paintbrush Tools

On the left side of the Paintbrush window you will see the area called the Toolbox (see Figure 10.2). To select a tool, move the pointer into the correct box and click. When a tool is selected, it will display in reverse.

▲ **Hint** The shape of the mouse pointer will change to help you remember which tool is selected. ▲

Figure 10.2

The Paintbrush Toolbox

Using the Brush Tool

When you first start Paintbrush, the Brush tool is automatically selected and when the mouse pointer is in the drawing area, it will display as a dot. When you use the Brush to draw, a line will appear that is the same size as the dot.

If you want to draw using a thicker paintbrush, move the pointer into the line size box in the lower left corner (see Figure 10.3). Click on the line thickness you want, and the size of the pointer will change to show your selection. You can, of course, change the size of your brush any time you want to.

Figure 10.3

The line-width selection area

If you open the Options menu and select Brush Shapes, a dialog box will appear like the one in Figure 10.4. To choose a different brush shape, move the pointer to the one you want and click. The selected brush shape will be indicated by a little box.

Figure 10.4

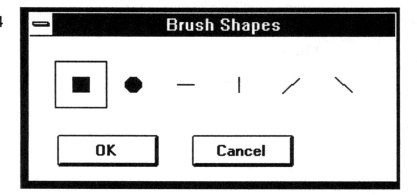

The Brush Shapes dialog box

▲ Hint   The Brush Shape box can also be opened if you double-click on the Brush in the toolbox. ▲

Using the Paint Roller Tool   The Paint Roller is used to fill an enclosed area with the selected foreground color. For example, you can use the Brush to draw a star or other irregular shape, then select the Paint Roller and quickly fill the area inside of your shape.

When you are using the Paint Roller, you need to keep a few things in mind. First, make sure that you select a color before you use the Paint Roller tool. If the wrong color is selected, you could lose parts of your drawing.

Second, the pointed tip of the Paint Roller cursor is the "hot spot." To fill an area with color, place the tip of the Paint Roller inside the outlined borders. If the area to be filled is small, be very careful.

Finally, if the area to be filled is not completely closed in, the fill color will leak out and run into other parts of your drawing. When this happens, don't panic, just select Undo from the Edit menu (or press ⌨Alt⌨ + ⌨←BkSp⌨).

▲ Hint   Any time you make a mistake, *don't do anything else.* Just open the Edit menu and select Undo or press ⌨Alt⌨ + ⌨←BkSp⌨ (or ⌨Ctrl⌨ + z).

You can use Undo as long as you have not performed one of the following actions: ▲

- Selected a new tool

- Used a scroll bar

- Opened a new application

- Resized any window

Using the Airbrush

The Airbrush tool simulates a pattern similar to the pattern produced by an actual airbrush. Often, it is used to blend colors or to produce three-dimensional shading effects. The size (diameter) of the spray produced by the Airbrush tool is controlled by the line-width selection. To change the color of the spray, simply choose a new foreground color.

To use the Airbrush, press and hold the left mouse button and drag the pointer across the drawing area. The density of the pattern produced by the Airbrush will vary depending on how fast you drag. In other words, the faster you drag, the less dense the spray. To stop spraying, release the mouse button.

Adding Text to Your Drawing

You can add text to your drawing by selecting the Text tool. To place text, move the pointer to the correct location, click the mouse button, and an insertion point will appear. Keep in mind that Paintbrush is not a word processor, so type your text carefully. To end a line of text (and start a new one) press `Enter←`.

While typing text, you can edit it "normally" if you use the `←BkSp` key and retype. However, if you select a different tool, use a scroll bar, open another application, resize the Paintbrush window, or reposition the text cursor (by pressing `Enter←` or using the mouse), then your text can no longer be edited. If you perform one of these actions, you must erase your text and reenter it. Basically, the same rules apply to `←BkSp` as apply to the Undo command.

How to Add Text to Your Drawing

What to Do	**What Happens**

1. Choose a foreground color.

When you enter text, it will appear in the color you select.

2. Select a font by opening the Text menu and selecting Font.

The Font dialog box will appear as shown in Figure 10.5.

Figure 10.5

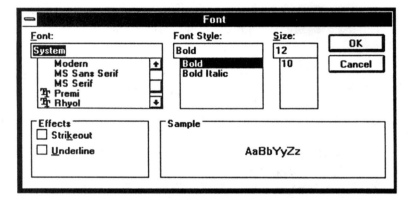

3. Select a font type by clicking on the name of the font that you want (use the scroll bar if necessary). You can also select italic, boldface, or other effects at this point. Only the fonts and styles that are available will display.

The name of the font that you select will appear in the Font Style box, and a sample of the text will appear in the Sample box.

4. Select a font size by clicking on the point size that you want. Use the scroll bar if necessary. Again, only the sizes that are available will display.

The selected size will appear in the Size box and a sample of the text will display in the Sample area.

5. Select any desired effects. You can cause your text to appear underlined or as strikeout text by checking the appropriate box in the effects area.	Again, a sample of the text will appear in the Sample box.
6. Press the OK button to return to the drawing area, move the cursor to where you want your text to appear, and click the left mouse button.	The text insertion point will appear as a thin, flashing vertical line.
7. Type your text. To start a new line, press Enter←.	Your text will appear in the drawing area.

Using the Line Tool

The Line tool is used to draw straight lines between two specified points. You can also use the Line tool to draw lines that are perfectly horizontal or perfectly vertical.

What to Do	**What Happens**
1. Select the Line tool from the Toolbox.	The Line tool icon will be highlighted.
2. Select a foreground color.	The lines that you draw will appear in the drawing area in the foreground color.
3. Select a line width. Move to the Line size box and click on the thickness of the line you need.	The lines that you draw will appear in the drawing area using the specified width.

| | **4.** | Move to the starting point of the line, press the left mouse button, *continue to hold the button,* and move to the ending point for the line. | A flexible "rubber band" line will follow the pointer. |

▲ Hint   If you press and hold the ⌈⇧Shift⌉ key while you drag the pointer it will move in a straight horizontal or straight vertical line. ▲

| | **5.** | When you are satisfied with the length (and position) of the line, release the mouse button. | The line will appear in the drawing area. |

Using the Curve Tool

The Curve tool is used to draw curved lines in the selected line width and foreground color.

What to Do	**What Happens**
1. Select the Curve tool from the Toolbox.	The Curve tool icon will be highlighted.
2. Select a foreground color.	The foreground indicator box will display the color that you select.
3. Select a line width. Move to the Line Size Box and click on the thickness of the line you need.	An arrow will appear in the Line Width Indicator Box next to the line width that you select.
4. Move to the starting point of the line, press the left mouse button, *continue to hold the button,* and move to the ending point for the line.	A flexible "rubber band" line will follow the pointer.

5.	Press and hold the mouse button again, and move the cursor. When you are satisfied with the angle and slope of the first curve, release the mouse button.	The line will curve in the direction that you move the mouse.
6.	If you want the line to curve in only one direction, move the pointer to the first end point of the line and click. If you want to curve the line in a second direction, go on to the next step.	If you are finished, the line will appear, in the foreground color, using the selected line width.
7.	To curve the line in a second direction, press and hold the mouse button again, and bend the line in the other direction. When your line is where you want it to be, release the mouse button.	The finished line will appear, in the foreground color, using the selected line width.

▲ **Hint**   Until you click the left mouse button a second time, you can click the right mouse button to Undo the curve and start over.

Using the Shape tools

■ **Note**   Once you learn to use one of the shape tools, you pretty much know how to use all of them. Using these tools you can quickly draw boxes, boxes with rounded corners, circles (or ellipses), and polygons. These shapes can be drawn as outlines (using the selected line width), or as solid (filled in) shapes.

	What to Do	**What Happens**
1.	Select the foreground color.	The foreground indicator will display your choice.

---

2. Select the line width.

The line width indicator will show your choice.

■ Note If you are drawing a filled shape, the line width will determine the thickness of the shape's border.

3. Select the background color. Remember, use the right mouse button to select the background color.

The background indicator will display your choice.

■ Note If you want to draw a filled box with no border, make the foreground and the background colors the same.

4. Select the shape tool that you need:
   Box or Filled Box
   Rounded Box or Filled
      Rounded Box
   Circle/Ellipse or Filled
      Circle/Ellipse
   Polygon or Filled Polygon

The tool that you select from the Toolbox will be highlighted.

5. Move the mouse pointer to the starting point for the shape, press and hold the left mouse button, and drag the cursor to create the shape that you need.

A "rubber band" shape will appear and follow the movement of the mouse.

■ Note If you are drawing a polygon, when you release the mouse button, the first side will appear. You can place additional sides by pressing the left mouse button again and dragging the "rubber band" line to a new location. Continue to add sides until you are ready to close your polygon. (See Step 6).

6. When you are satisfied with the size and position of the shape, release the mouse button. (To close a polygon, double-click the left mouse button.)

The shape will appear in the drawing area.

▲ **Hint** To draw straight vertical or straight horizontal lines, press and hold the [⇧ Shift] key while you drag the mouse.

If you are using the Box or the Circle tool, you can draw perfect squares (or perfect circles) if you press and hold the [⇧ Shift] key while dragging. ▲

Using the Cutout Tools

The Cutout tools are used to define an area of your drawing that is to be copied into another part of your drawing, or transferred to another application such as Write. You can also use the Cutout tools to completely erase a section of your drawing.

The Toolbox contains two Cutout tools. They are the Scissors tool and the Pick tool. If you need a cutout that closely follows the contours of an irregular shape, use Scissors. If the shape of the cutout is not critical, use Pick. The Pick tool can be used to outline any rectangular (or square) area on your drawing. In general, the Pick tool is easier to use.

■ **Note** When you use the Cutout tools to cut a part of your drawing out, it is not really erased. Actually, the specified part is copied to a special application called the Clipboard. After you place your cutout on the Clipboard, it can be pasted back into your original drawing in a new place, pasted into a completely new drawing, or even pasted into a completely different application such as the Write word processor.

Cutting and Pasting Cutouts

Use this procedure to cut a part of a drawing from one location and paste it into another location in the same drawing.

What to Do	**What Happens**
1. Move to the Toolbox and select the Scissors or the Pick tool.	The tool that you select will be highlighted.
2. Move the mouse pointer to the starting point, press and hold the left mouse button, and move the indicator until the area to be cut is completely enclosed.	A dotted line will follow the mouse pointer to indicate the selected area.
3. Release the mouse button. If you make a mistake, press the right mouse button, and start over.	The area that you define will be outlined with a dotted line.
4. Open the Edit menu and select Cut (to erase) or Copy (to duplicate) the cutout.	If you choose Cut, the area will disappear; otherwise nothing will happen at this point.
5. Open the Edit menu again, and choose Paste.	The cutout will appear in the upper right hand corner of the display screen.
6. Move the cursor to anywhere inside the cutout. Press and hold the mouse button, and drag the cutout to its new location.	The cutout will follow the mouse pointer.
7. Release the mouse button.	The cutout will be pasted into place.

▲ Hint   Remember, when you cut an area from a drawing, it actually gets copied onto the Clipboard. Once you have data on the clipboard, it can be easily pasted into new locations (including other applications) as many times as necessary. ▲

Saving and Retrieving Cutouts   Paintbrush will let you save a cutout part of your drawing as a bitmap (.BMP) file or as a Paintbrush (.PCX) file. By default, your cutout will be saved as a bitmap. To save your cutout as a Paintbrush file, open the File menu and choose Save. When the dialog box appears, press the radio button for .PCX.

Saving Cutouts

What to Do	**What Happens**
1. Use the Pick tool or the Scissors to define the cutout that is to be saved.	The cutout will be outlined.
2. Open the Edit menu and choose Copy To	See Figure 10.6.

Figure 10.6

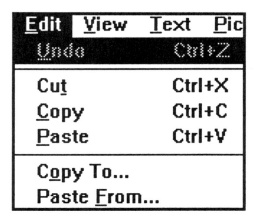

3. Type a filename into the dialog box and press the OK button.	See Figure 10.7.

Figure 10.7

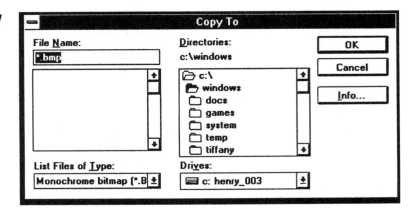

Retrieving
Cutouts

Once you have completed a drawing (or any part of a drawing) and save it to disk, it can be retrieved and used as clip art in your future work. To add cutouts to your drawing, follow this procedure.

What to Do   **What Happens**

1. Open the Edit menu and   See Figure 10.8.
       select the Paste From com-
       mand.

Figure 10.8

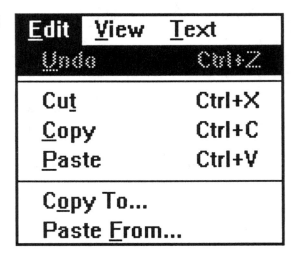

Figure 10.9

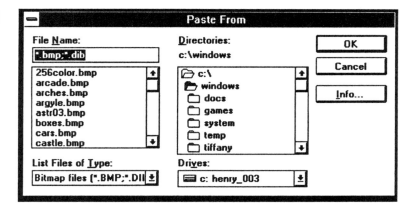

Paste From

File Name:

`*.bmp;*.dib`

256color.bmp
arcade.bmp
arches.bmp
argyle.bmp
astr03.bmp
boxes.bmp
cars.bmp
castle.bmp

List Files of Type:

Bitmap files [*.BMP;*.DII]

Directories:

c:\windows

c:\
windows
docs
games
system
temp
tiffany

Drives:

c: henry_003

OK

Cancel

Info...

2. Select the name of the drawing (or cutout) to be pasted from the list in the file box. If the name of the file that you want does not appear, you may need to select a different directory. If you know the name and location of the file to be used, you can just type it into the dialog box at the top of the window.

See Figure 10.9.

3. Press the OK button.

The cutout will appear in the upper left corner of the display screen. It will be surrounded by a dotted border.

4. Move the cursor inside the cutout and press (and hold) the mouse button.

Nothing yet.

| **5.** | Drag the cutout to its final location and release the mouse button. | The cutout will follow the cursor. |

| **6.** | Move the cursor outside of the cutout and single-click the mouse button. | The cutout will be "permanently" pasted into position. |

▲ **Hint**   It is possible to obtain collections of drawings that have been prepared by professional artists. These collections of clip art can easily be pasted into your drawings to make your finished pictures more professional and save you a lot of work. ▲

Editing Your Drawing

As you perform your drawing magic, you might change your mind along the way. Often it is difficult to visualize the finished image until you actually put the elements of your creation into place.

When you do change your mind, Paintbrush provides a series of editing tools to help you change your drawing. The Scissors and the Pick tools are two of the devices that can help you edit your work, but to make more subtle changes, use the Erasers (see Figure 10.10).

Figure 10.10

The Eraser tools

Using the Eraser   The Eraser tool is used to change all colors to the selected background color. To use the Eraser, first you must select the background color by moving the pointer to the correct box in the palette area, and pressing the *right* mouse button. (Note: The outside area of the color indicator box will change to show the color you select.)

Next, select the tool itself by moving to the Toolbox and clicking on the Eraser icon. When you move the cursor back into the drawing area, it will be shaped like a little box. If you need to erase larger (or smaller) areas, you can change the size of the box by choosing a different brush width from the Line Size box.

Finally, move the cursor to the area to be erased, press (and hold) the left mouse button, and drag the cursor around as necessary. As you move the eraser around, everything that passes under the eraser will change to the background color.

■ **Note** Remember, the eraser changes everything to the selected *background* color. For example, to erase objects in a red area, make sure that red is the selected background color before you begin. If the selected background color is white (or something else), you will end up with a white area inside of your red area.

Using the Color Eraser The Color Eraser is used to change only a single selected color to the same color as the background. It is used in basically the same manner as the standard Eraser, but the results can be much different.

Start by selecting the Color Eraser from the Toolbox, choosing the background color, and (if necessary) selecting a line width. Finally, choose a foreground color. The foreground color that you choose is the color that will be erased as you move the cursor around.

Working with Paintbrush Files

You save your Paintbrush files in the same way that you save any other Windows document. Start by opening the File menu and choose Save or Save As (see Figure 10.11). Next, enter a filename and press the OK button to finish. Windows will automatically include the correct extension.

*PCX (Paintbrush format)
*Monochrome bitmap
*16 color bitmap (default)
*256 color bitmap
*24-bit bitmap

Normally, Paintbrush will save your file as a standard Windows bitmap, that is, a .BMP file. If you need to save your work in a different form (to be exported into a different application, for example), press the Options button and choose one of the five formats listed in the box.

Figure 10.11

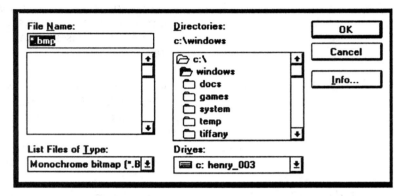

The Save dialog box

■ **Note**   For more information about graphic files and graphic file types, check the Microsoft Windows User's Guide.

Printing Your Pictures

Paintbrush will let you make a hard copy of your drawings, but remember, the output will only be as good as your printer. If you have a high quality color printer, Windows will take advantage of all the features your printer has to offer. However, if you have a black & white output device (such as a dot-matrix printer) the printout may be rather disappointing.

How to Print Your Drawings

What to Do	**What Happens**
1. Open the File menu and choose Print.	See Figure 10.12.

Figure 10.12

2. Select Draft to create a
"quick and dirty" copy or
Proof to print a high quality
printout (see Figure 10.13).

Nothing.

Figure 10.13

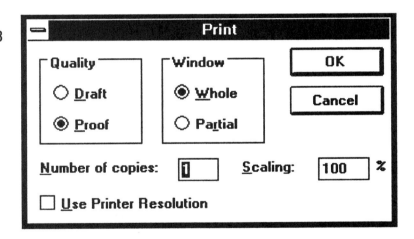

3. If you want to print more
than one copy of your drawing, enter a number into the
Number of Copies box.

Nothing yet.

4. Press OK to print.

Your drawing will appear
on the printer.

How to Print Part of Your Drawing

You can print a specified part of your drawing if you use the following procedure.

What to Do	What Happens
1. Open the File menu and choose Print.	See Figure 10.12.
2. Select Draft to create a "quick and dirty" copy or Proof to print a high quality printout.	Nothing.
3. If you want to print more than one copy of your drawing, enter a number into the Number of Copies box.	Nothing.
4. Choose Partial by selecting the proper radio button. Press OK to return to drawing area.	Paintbrush will adjust the size of your drawing so that the entire image is visible.
5. Move the pointer to the upper left corner of the area that is to be printed, press (and hold) the left mouse button, and move the pointer until the entire area to be printed is inside the border of the flexible box.	The box will surround the area to be printed.
6. Release the mouse button.	The selected area will print.

■ **Note**   The size of a dot on your printer may not be the same size as a dot on your screen. Paintbrush will try to rescale your drawing so that the printed image is as close to the screen image as possible. However, if you check the Use Printer Resolution box, the printed image may be distorted.

If You Want to Transfer a Drawing to Write

As you will remember, Windows will let you transfer graphics from Paintbrush into a Write document. Actually, when using Windows, it is possible to transfer almost any data from one application to another. In general, you simply copy the data that is to be transferred to the Windows Clipboard, open the target application and paste the data into place.

In the following procedure, we will transfer a graphic from Paintbrush into Write. Once you understand this operation it is easy to modify the procedure to transfer almost anything from one project to another.

How to Transfer a Drawing to Write

	What to Do	What Happens
1.	Open the Paintbrush application (if it is not already open) and load the drawing to be transferred into the computer.	The selected graphic will be displayed in the Paintbrush drawing area.
2.	Use the Scissors or the Pick tool to define the area of the drawing that is to be transferred.	A flexible box will appear. Use the box to outline the area that you are interested in.
3.	Open the Edit menu and choose Copy.	The area defined in Step 2 will be copied to Clipboard.

4.	Minimize (or close) Paintbrush so that it moves out of the way.	Paintbrush will no longer be displayed.
5.	Launch Write and if necessary, load the document that is to receive the graphic.	The Write word processor window will display.
6.	Move the insertion point to the place in your document where the graphic belongs.	The screen will continue to display your document.
7.	Open the Edit menu and choose Paste.	The graphic will appear at the insertion point.

▲ **Hint**   If you are making a drawing especially for use in Write, you will probably want to start it using the black and white palette. To select Paintbrush's black and white palette, open the Options menu, choose Image Attributes, and press the radio button for black and white. ▲

Summary Points

1. When starting a new drawing, it is a good idea to maximize the Paintbrush window.

2. The main part of the Paintbrush screen is called the drawing area.

3. Along the bottom of the Paintbrush drawing area, you will see the color selection area or the palette.

4. The foreground/background indicator is located just to the left of the palette. The foreground color is selected with the left mouse button and the background color is selected with the right mouse button.

5. The color of the foreground/background indicator will change to indicate what color is selected for the foreground and background. The small inside box will display the foreground color and the outside area will display the background color.

6. On the left side of the Paintbrush screen, you will find the Toolbox area.

7. When you select a tool from the Toolbox, the cursor will change shape to help you remember which tool is selected.

8. To draw freehand lines, you will need to select the Brush tool. To use the Brush tool, press and hold the left mouse button and move the cursor around on the screen.

9. The Paint Roller tool is used to fill enclosed areas of your drawing. To use the roller, place the tip of the tool inside the area to be filled, and press the left mouse button.

10. The Airbrush tool is used to simulate a spray-paint pattern. To use the Airbrush, press and hold the left mouse button, and move around the drawing area. The density of the spray is controlled by the speed at which the mouse is moved.

11. You can add text to your drawing if the Text tool is selected. The size of the text is controlled using the Size menu and the style of the text is changed with the Font menu.

12. To draw a straight line, move to the Toolbox and choose the Line tool. To create perfectly horizontal or perfectly vertical lines, press and hold the ⇧ Shift key while using the mouse to define the line.

13. The Curve tool is used to draw lines that curve smoothly. The line will appear in the foreground color using the line width as selected from the line size box.

14. The Shape tools can be used to draw boxes, boxes with rounded corners, circles, ellipses, and polygons. The shapes can be drawn as outlines or as filled shapes.

15. Whenever you need to define a part of your drawing that is to be copied, moved, or erased, the Cutout tools are used. The Cutout tools can also be used to transfer all or part of your drawing to other applications (such as the Write word processor).

16. The Scissors tool is used to cut an irregular object and the Pick tool is used to cut a rectangular shape.

17. The Erase tools are used to change parts of your drawing from one color to the background color. The Eraser changes all colors and the Color Eraser changes only the foreground color.

18. By default, when you save your drawings to disk, they will be saved as Bitmaps (or .BMP) files. When you assign a filename, Paintbrush will automatically assign the correct extension.

19. If necessary, Paintbrush files can also be saved as monochrome bitmaps, 16-color bitmaps (by default), 256-color bitmaps, 24-bit bitmaps, and as PCX (Paintbrush) files.

20. To print your drawings, open the File menu and choose Print. You can print all of your drawing or any part of it.

21. To create a drawing especially for use in Write, start by opening the Paintbrush Options menu, selecting Image Attributes, and pressing the radio button for the black and white palette.

22. To move a drawing to another application, copy the drawing to the Clipboard, open the target application, and paste the drawing into position.

Practice Exercises

1. Open the Paintbrush application and experiment with the various tools. You might want to try signing your name inside a brightly colored box or just use the Shape tools to draw areas of overlapping color.

2. Draw a picture of a simple stained glass window. Use the Line tools to outline some geometric shapes and then use the Paint Roller to add some color.

3. In the Windows subdirectory, you will find a file named PAPER.BMP. Load this file into Paintbrush, place it on the Clipboard, and transfer it to a Write document.

Comprehension Questions

1. List the five main parts of the Paintbrush screen.

2. What must you do to select a new foreground color?

3. What must you do to select a new background color?

4. How can you tell which color is selected for the foreground color and which is selected for the background color?

5. If you want to draw using a thicker paintbrush, what must you do?

6. List two ways to open the Brush Shapes selection box. Write a short description of each of the shapes found there.

7. What is the Paint Roller tool used for?

8. Explain how to use the Airbrush tool.

9. You can use the Undo feature to "take back" your last operation as long as you do not perform certain actions. List these actions.

10. What tool is used to add text to your drawing?

11. What is the difference between the Line or Curve tools and the regular Drawing tool?

12. List and define the eight Shape tools.

13. List three reasons to use the Cutout tools.

14. The two Cutout tools available are Scissors and Pick. When do you use the Pick tool and when do you use the Scissors?

15. What is the difference between the Eraser and the Color Eraser?

16. Describe the procedure used to save only a cutout portion of your drawing.

17. List the steps needed to retrieve a cutout or a piece of clip art from a disk into an existing drawing.

18. What is the difference between a "Draft" printout and a "Proof" printout?

19. What will happen if you transfer a color drawing into a Write document?

Completion Questions

1. The main area of Paintbrush is called the _____ area.

2. Along the bottom edge of the main Paintbrush window, you will find the _____ area which displays a sample of each color available.

3. The _____ color is the color that Paintbrush will use to draw the selected elements in the main Paintbrush area.

4. The _____ color is the color that Paintbrush will use when an element is erased.

5. If you are starting a new drawing, it is a good idea to make sure that the Paintbrush window is _____.

6. You can select a different font if you open the _____ menu and choose _____.

7. To draw a line that is perfectly vertical or perfectly horizontal, press and hold the _____ key while you drag the mouse pointer.

8. If you are drawing a shape, the _____ _____ will determine the thickness of the shape's border.

9. By default, your drawing will be saved as a _____ file.

10. To print your picture, open the _____ menu and choose _____.

11

Starting
File Manager

Learning Objectives

1. Identify the parts of the File Manager window.

2. List the four icons used to help identify files in File Manager.

3. Describe the four types of disk-drive icons.

Performance Objectives

1. Start File Manager.

2. Select a disk drive.

3. View the directory window of the selected drive.

Directory Tree Area	The Directory Tree area is located on the left side of a directory window. The Directory Tree area displays a diagram of the structure of the directories and subdirectories on the active disk.
Directory Window	Each directory window is found in the main working area of File Manager. A directory window will display a drive bar, a Directory Tree, and a file list. You can open as many directory windows as your system resources will allow.
Disk-drive Icons	Each of the disk drives attached to your system are represented by a Disk-drive Icon. The Disk-drive Icons are located on the Drive Bar.
Drive Bar	The File Manager window contains an area that displays an icon to represent each of the disk drives attached to your system. This area is called the drive bar.
File Manager	In general, you will use File Manager to copy, move, organize, and delete files and subdirectories. Unlike DOS, File Manager displays the tree structure of your hard disk (and floppy diskettes) in a graphic format.
File List Area	The File List area is on the right side of the directory window. It displays a list of the files for the directory that is currently highlighted in the Directory Tree area.
Status Bar	The Status bar is found at the bottom of the File Manager window. The Status bar displays the name of the drive that is currently active, the free space on that drive, and the total number of files displayed in the active window.

Chapter Overview

When you type the command DIR at the DOS prompt (and press [Enter←], of course), you will see a meaningless list of files. If you are lucky (or are a fast reader), you might see something that looks familiar or interesting, but how do you get to it?

Once again, it's Windows to the rescue.

Windows contains a second major tool called File Manager that helps you organize, display, find, and use your valuable files. To start File Manager, open the Main Group and click the icon for the File Manager. Your screen will display a window similar to Figure 11.1.

Figure 11.1

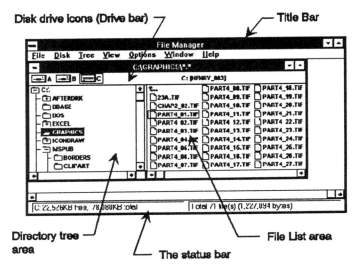

When you first launch File Manager, your screen will look something like this.

Across the top of the main File Manager window will be the familiar title bar with its Control Menu button and the Maximize/Minimize buttons, but at the bottom, you will see something new called the status bar. The left side of the status bar displays three items: the name of the drive that is currently active, how much of that drive is *not* being used (free space), and the total space available on that drive. The right side of the status bar displays two items: how many files are shown in the File List area, and how much disk space those files use.

The Directory Window

The main window inside File Manager is called the directory window. The directory window has its own title bar and control buttons, and will display the current drive, the current path, and the types of files that are displayed. By default, the directory window will show all files as indicated by the wildcards (*.*) in the title bar.

▲ Hint   If you want to work with only one type of file, open the View menu and select By File Type from the drop-down menu. When the dialog box appears, make any necessary selections and a new file list will display. ▲

As you can see, the main work area of the directory window is divided into two parts: the Directory Tree area (on the left) and a File List area (on the right). Between these areas you will see a vertical dividing line and a scroll bar. You will also find scroll bars at the bottom of each area.

■ Note   If only one directory window is displayed, it cannot be closed — it can only be moved or minimized.

It is convenient (and logical) to compare a disk drive to a little filing cabinet. Inside each of these cabinets you can put a number of files, and if necessary, these files can be placed in expanding folders (subdirectories) to keep all the related information together.

Each drive icon at the top of the window represents one of your filing cabinets. To "open" a filing cabinet, you simply select it from the drive bar by clicking its icon. The contents of the directory window will change to show the structure and the file list for the new drive.

▲ Hint   If you double click on the Drive bar in the File Manager, a list of available drives will appear.

If you double click directly on a Disk Drive Icon, a new window will open that displays a list of files on that drive. ▲

The Directory Tree Area   The left side of the directory windows is called the Directory Tree area. Inside the Directory Tree area, you will see a diagram that shows the arrangement of the directories (and subdirectories) of the disk that is currently highlighted on the drive bar. If you need to see the Directory Tree structure for a different disk drive, click the icon (on the drive bar) that represents the drive that you need to examine.

■ Note   The drive bar is located near the top of the directory window. It will display the volume name of the current disk and a set of icons that represent each of the drives attached to your system. Think of the drive bar as a kind of menu bar for the directory window.

If you are attached to a network, the name of the network will display rather than the volume name of the current disk.

Figure 11.2

 This icon looks like the front of a little floppy disk drive. It even has a little indicator light.

 This one looks like the front of a little hard disk drive. On your system, the indicator for Drive C: will probably be highlighted.

 The Icon for a RAM disk looks like it has a tiny integrated circuit on the top.

 Any Network drives will look as if they contain a tiny network connector.

These icons represent each of the different types of disk drives

The File List Area

On the right side of the directory window, you will find the File List area. In this part of the window, you will see a list of files and sub-subdirectories on the current drive. Every time you select a new disk drive or subdirectory, the list of files in this area will change. By default, the files in this list will be in alphabetical order with any sub-subdirectories at the beginning. If you want to display your file list in a different order, open the View menu and choose one of the Sort By options.

▲ Hint

Any time a list of files from a subdirectory is displayed, the list will begin with a special symbol that looks like a tiny arrow followed by two dots. If you double-click on this tiny arrow, the system will move back one level in your subdirectory structure. ▲

Windows File Management

Windows makes it easy to impose some order on your file collection. You start by placing related files in subdirectories (expanding folders), and if necessary, you can divide these subdirectories into sub-subdirectories.

Any time you need to see a list of files in a subdirectory, just single-click on its folder in the Directory Tree area. The selected File Folder icon will change to an "open" file folder and the list of files in that subdirectory will display in the File List area on the right.

How to Identify a File by Its Icon

As you examine a list of files in the File List area, you will notice that each file is preceded by an icon (see Figure 11.3). These icons help you identify the file type. Subdirectories will be listed first and will be preceded by an icon that resembles a file folder. Program files, that is, files that have an .EXE, .COM, .BAT, or .PIF extension, will be preceded by an icon that resembles a tiny window. All data files (called documents in Windows) are attached to an icon that looks like a piece of paper with the corner turned down.

Figure 11.3

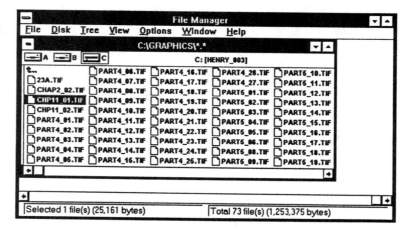

A typical directory listing

A document file associated with an executable file will resemble a little piece of paper filled with lines of text. If a file is associated, it can automatically launch the application that was used to create it (see Figure 11.4).

■ **Note**

When using Windows, all data files are referred to as documents and all programs are referred to as applications.

Figure 11.4

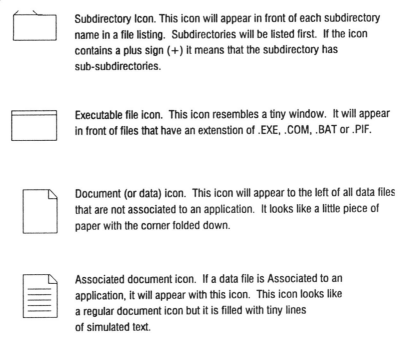

Subdirectory Icon. This icon will appear in front of each subdirectory name in a file listing. Subdirectories will be listed first. If the icon contains a plus sign (+) it means that the subdirectory has sub-subdirectories.

Executable file icon. This icon resembles a tiny window. It will appear in front of files that have an extenstion of .EXE, .COM, .BAT or .PIF.

Document (or data) icon. This icon will appear to the left of all data files that are not associated to an application. It looks like a little piece of paper with the corner folded down.

Associated document icon. If a data file is Associated to an application, it will appear with this icon. This icon looks like a regular document icon but it is filled with tiny lines of simulated text.

Hidden file icon. If you have File Manager set to display hidden files, they will display using this icon.

Icons used to identify the different types of Windows files

If you double-click on one of the file-folder icons in the File List area, you will see a new list that displays the files in that directory. If the new list contains any sub-subdirectories, additional file folders will be displayed at the top of the new list. If you single-click on one of these new folders, a new list will display. You can continue to click on file folders in the File List area or in the Directory Tree area until you find the file list you are searching for.

▲ **Hint**   If you open the Tree menu and select Indicate Expandable Branches, folders in the Directory Tree window that have sub-subdirectories will display a plus sign (+) when they are closed, and a minus sign (-) when they are open. As always, subdirectories in the Directory Tree area can be expanded (or collapsed) with a double-click. ▲

1. To launch File Manager, open the Main window and double-click the File Manager icon.

2. All of the standard features of a window (such as the control buttons and the title bar) are displayed as part of the File Manager window.

3. Each disk drive in your system will be represented by a disk drive icon.

4. The main File Manager window is divided into two areas: the Directory Tree area and the File List area.

5. The Directory Tree area displays a diagram of the tree structure for the selected disk drive.

6. The File List area displays the list of files in the currently selected subdirectory of the currently selected disk drive.

7. If you wish to view a list of files from a different disk drive, simply select the icon for the desired drive from the drive bar.

8. To view a list of files in a different subdirectory, single-click on the file folder that represents the desired subdirectory.

Identify each of the following parts of the File Manager window.

Figure 11.5

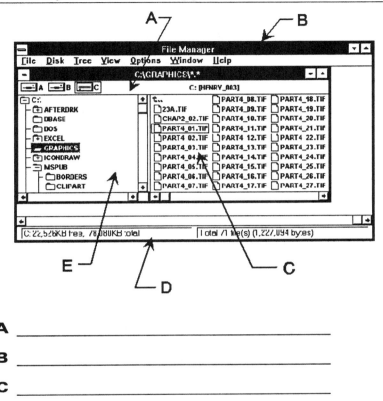

A _____

B _____

C _____

D _____

E _____

Comprehension Questions

1. What is File Manager used for?

2. Name the four types of disk drive icons.

3. What will happen if you double click on an icon in the Drive Bar?

4. What happens if you select a different disk-drive icon drive from the drive bar in the main directory window?

5. How many directory windows can be open at the same time?

6. The contents of drive C: are currently displayed in a directory window. If you click on the icon for drive A:, what will happen?

7. What will happen if you double click on the drive bar in the File Manager?

8. What do you have to do to start File Manager from Program Manager?

9. What does the status bar tell you?

10. By default, the files in a file list appear in what order?

11. There are, as far as Windows is concerned, only two types of files. What are they?

12. What does it mean if a file-folder icon in a file list displays a plus sign?

13. What is a subdirectory?

14. What are subdirectories used for?

Completion Questions

1. When you are at the DOS prompt, you can display a list of files by typing _____ and pressing ⌴Enter◄─⌴.

2. To start the File Manager, open the _____ Group and double-click the File Manager icon.

3. The icon that precedes a subdirectory name looks like a little _____.

4. The icon that displays along with the name of an executable file resembles a tiny _____.

5. In Windows, all data files are referred to as _____.

12

General File Manager Operations

Learning Objectives

1. Identify the Directory Tree area.

2. Identify the File List area.

3. Identify the directory window divider bar.

Performance Objectives

1. Open a window that displays only a Directory Tree.

2. Open a window that display only a File List.

3. Display the Directory Tree and the File List in one window.

4. Open more than one directory window.

5. Arrange the open directory windows in File Manager.

Directory Window Divider — The Directory Window divider is a vertical bar that divides the Directory Tree area from the File List area in a directory window. If a Directory Window displays only a File List or a Directory Tree (rather than both), the Directory Window divider will be located at the extreme left side of the window, next to the window border.

Expandable Branch — If a subdirectory branch has additional lower levels, then it is an Expandable branch.

Subdirectory Branch — A Subdirectory branch is an entire substructure in a tree structure. In other words, a Subdirectory branch is a subdirectory and all of the sub-subdirectories below it (see Figure 12.1).

Subdirectory Level — A Subdirectory level is a single subdirectory. A Subdirectory level may have other levels below it, but a single subdirectory level consists of only a single subdirectory name (see Figure 12.1).

Tree Structure — The Tree structure is a graphic representation of the arrangement of the directories and subdirectories on a hard disk (or diskette). Subdirectories are used to divide a disk into convenient divisions for simplified data storage (see Figure 12.1).

Figure 12.1

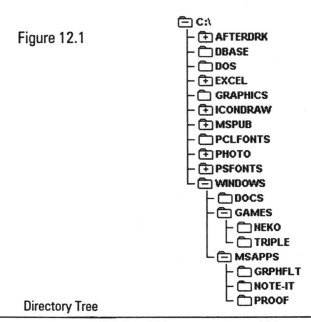

Directory Tree

Chapter Overview

As you already know, when you first start File Manager, a single directory window will be displayed. That window will be divided into the Directory Tree area and the File List area. For most people this arrangement will work very well, but Windows tries to be as flexible as possible. The View menu, as shown in Figure 12.2, will let you control the way Windows displays information in File Manager. You have three choices: display the Directory Tree and the File List in a single window, display the Directory Tree alone, or display only the File List. As always, Windows will work the way you want it to work.

Figure 12.2

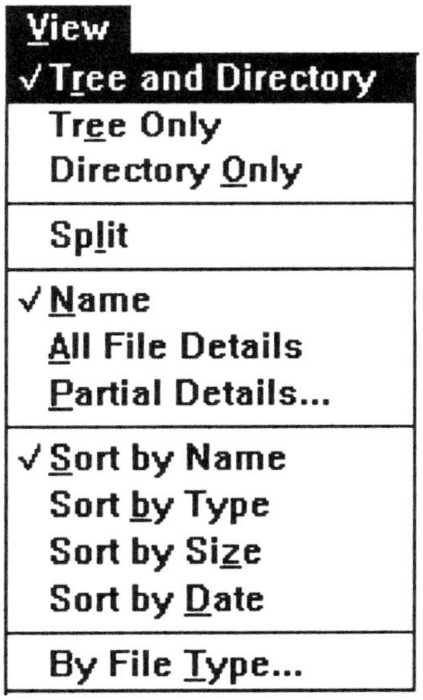

View

√ Tree and Directory
  Tree Only
  Directory Only

  Split

√ Name
  All File Details
  Partial Details...

√ Sort by Name
  Sort by Type
  Sort by Size
  Sort by Date

  By File Type...

The View menu in File Manager

How to Control the Directory Window Division

Whenever a Directory Tree window displays both a Directory Tree and a File List, you will see a vertical dividing line through the middle of the screen. As you know, on the left side of the divider, you will see the Directory Tree area, and on the right you will see the File List. By default, this "split" divides the window into two equal areas. If you have a large File List, or a complicated Directory Tree, most of the information that you need may not be visible. However, you can easily fix this problem by moving the dividing line anywhere you need it to be.

The easiest way to move this dividing line is to place your mouse pointer directly over it. When you are in the correct place, the pointer will change into a short vertical bar with arrows that point to the left and right. Now, press (and hold) the left mouse button, and a dark vertical line will appear. Drag this line to a new location, release the button, and the change is made.

▲ **Hint** You can also move the dividing line between the two areas if you open the View menu and choose Split. A dark line will appear, but this time *do not press the mouse button*. Use the arrow keys or the mouse to move the line to the left or right. When you are finished, press the mouse button or the ⌷Enter◄┘⌷ key. ▲

The Directory Tree Area

The left side of the directory window is called the Directory Tree area. Inside this area you will see a tree structure that describes the arrangement of the directories and subdirectories of the disk that is currently selected (highlighted) on the drive bar. By default, you will only see the directories that are visible from the root directory. If you double-click on one of these directories, the File Folder icon will open, and all of the sub-subdirectories will display (if there are any sub-subdirectories). If the file folder that you choose does not have any sub-subdirectories, you can double-click on it all day, but nothing will happen.

You can also open the Tree menu and use the selections in the drop-down menu to control the display in the Directory Tree area (see Figure 12.3). If you choose Expand One Level, or press the plus sign (+), the current file folder will open up one level. The Expand One Level choice is the same as a double-click with the mouse. However, if you choose Expand All, the entire tree structure will display.

Figure 12.3

Tree	**View**	**Options**	**Window**	**Help**
Expand One Level				+
Expand Branch				*
Expand All				Ctrl+*
Collapse Branch				-
√ Indicate Expandable Branches				

The Tree menu

▲ **Hint** If you open the Tree menu and select Indicate Expandable Branches, a tiny plus sign (+) will appear inside the File Folder icon of any subdirectory that has sub-subdirectories. ▲

How to Display Only the Directory Tree

If your tree structure is very large or very complex, you may wish to open a window that displays only the tree structure. All you need to do is open the View menu and select Tree Only (see Figure 12.4).

Figure 12.4

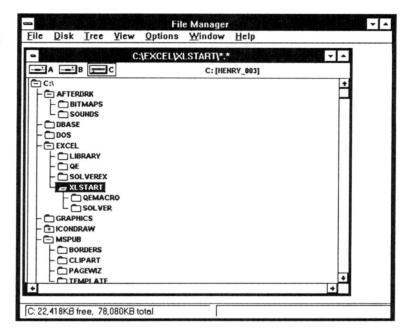

A window showing only a Directory Tree

The File List Area

The right side of the directory window normally displays a list of the files on the currently selected drive. You can move the divider between the Directory Tree area and the File List area to make the File List area larger (or smaller) as necessary.

How to Display Only the File Listing

To create a window that displays only a File List, open the View menu and choose Directory Only. A window will open similar to the window shown in Figure 12.5.

Figure 12.5

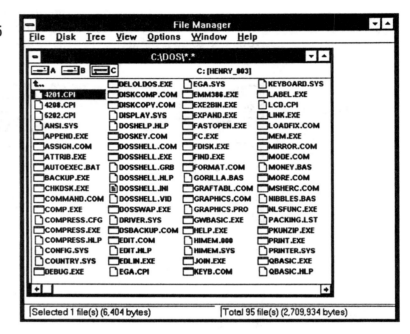

A window showing only a File List

Displaying More Than One File List

If your Directory Tree is very large or very complex, you can change the window so that only the Directory Tree area displays. If your File List is very long or very complex, you can change the window so that only the File List area displays. If your Directory Tree and your File List are both very large and complex, you might want to place each display in a window of its own.

How to Open More Than One Directory Window

What to Do	**What Happens**
1. Open File Manager and select the file-folder icon that represents the directory containing the file list that you need to examine.	The folder that you select will be highlighted and the file list will display on the right side of the directory window.
2. Open the View menu and select Tree Only or Directory Only.	The directory window will change to show your choice.
3. Open the Window menu and choose New Window.	See Figure 12.6.

Figure 12.6

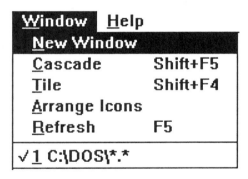

| **4.** A new window will open but it will be in the same format as the old window. Open the View menu again, and choose the opposite setting. For example, if you selected Tree Only for the first window, choose Directory Only for the new window. | See Figure 12.7. |

Figure 12.7

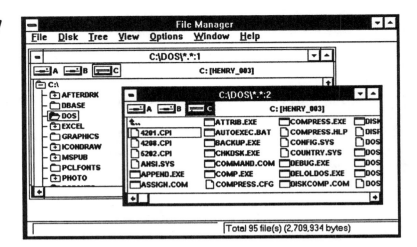

5. Move or resize the windows   See Figure 12.8.
so that the information that
you need is visible.

Figure 12.8

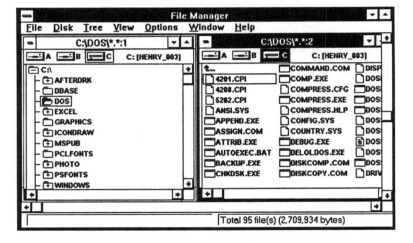

The rearranged windows

**Arranging
Your Open
Windows**

Now that you know how to open more than one directory window, occasionally you may end up with a rather cluttered desktop. You can move or size your windows normally, or arrange them automatically. To automatically arrange open windows in File Manager, open the Window menu and choose Tile or Cascade.

Figure 12.9 shows four windows in a tile pattern. The two windows in the top of the File Manager area show only Directory Trees and the two windows in the bottom half show "split" windows that display both the Directory Tree and the File List. You can (of course) arrange your windows in any pattern that meets your needs.

Figure 12.9

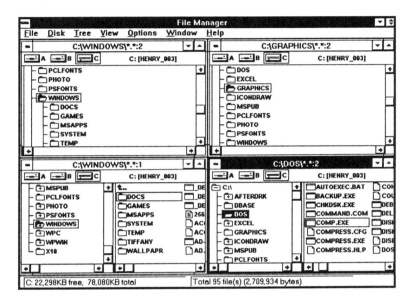

Four windows arranged in tile pattern

How to Leave File Manager

When you exit Program Manager, you end your Windows session, but when you exit File Manager, you simply return to Program Manager. Remember, File Manager is really nothing more than another Windows application.

▲ Hint   You may want to minimize File Manager rather than close it. If you minimize File Manager, it is always ready to be used. You don't have to wait for it to load each time you need it. ▲

How to End
a File
Manager
Session

If you want to preserve any changes that you made while using File Manager, open the Options menu and select Save Settings on Exit (see Figure 12.10). When you are finished, open the File menu, choose Exit, and Windows will return to Program Manager.

Figure 12.10

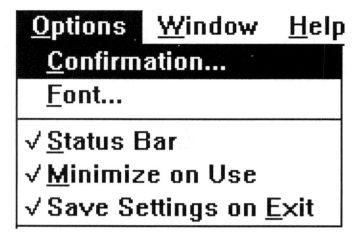

▲ **Hint**   If you open the File menu in the File Manager, press and hold the ⟨⇧Shift⟩ key while you choose Exit, Windows will save the File Manager's settings, but will not close. ▲

Summary Points

1. By default, a directory window will display a Directory Tree structure and a File List for the drive and subdirectory that is currently active.

2. The View menu will let you choose from a display that shows both the Directory Tree area and the File List area, or the Directory Tree or File List only.

3. The Directory Tree area is divided from the File List area by the directory area divider.

4. You can move the directory area divider with the mouse or with the Split command from the View menu.

5. The Tree menu will let you expand an entire branch of the Directory Tree structure, expand it by one level only, or expand the entire structure. You can also use the Tree menu to collapse a single branch of the Directory Tree structure.

6. The Window menu is used to open more than one directory window.

7. Any Directory Tree windows that are open in the File Manager work area can be sized, moved, or even minimized, just like any other window.

8. You can (as always) use the Tile and Cascade commands to arrange all of your open windows in the File Manager work area. To use these features, open the Window menu and choose Tile or Cascade.

Practice Exercises

1. Open File Manager and select the root directory of your hard disk. A Window will open that displays the Directory Tree on the left and the File List on the right.

2. Locate the Windows subdirectory and select it. Now, open a new window (from the Window menu) and use the Tree Only feature (from the View menu) so that the new window displays only the Directory Tree display. Move the borders of the new window so that it only covers the left half of your screen.

3. Move the mouse pointer into the new window and double click on the Windows file folder. It will expand and display another file folder labeled System. Select the System folder with a single-click.

4. Open a third window from the Window menu. When the new window appears, it should contain a directory listing. Open the View menu again and select Directory Only. The new window will change to display a file listing.

5. Move the border of the new window so that it covers only the right half of your screen. When you are finished, your screen should resemble Figure 12.11.

Figure 12.11

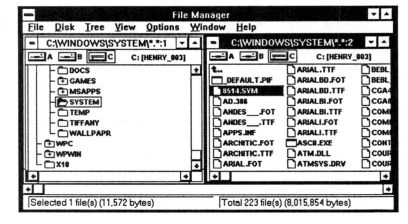

Illustration of finished project

■ **Note** Your finished project will not look exactly like this. Yourt system will almost certainly display a slightly different list of files and subdirectories.

Comprehension Questions

1. What is the vertical dividing line called that separates the Directory Tree area from the File List area in a directory window?

2. How many directory windows can be open at the same time?

3. There are two ways to move the split between the Directory Tree area and the File List area. What are they?

4. If you choose Expand One Level from the Tree menu, what will happen to the display of the current subdirectory level?

5. If you choose Expand All from the Tree menu, what will happen to the Directory Tree area display?

6. What is the difference between Expand One Level and Expand Branch (in the Tree menu)?

7. What happens if you try to close the last Directory Tree window in File manager?

Completion Questions

1. By default, the left side of a directory window displays a
_____ _____ and
the right side shows a _____
_____.

2. A directory window can contain a
_____ and a _____
_____ or a _____ or
_____ _____ by itself.

3. If you open the Tree menu and choose
_____ _____
_____, a tiny plus sign (+) will appear inside the file folder of a directory that has subdirectories or sub-subdirectories.

4. You can arrange your windows automatically if you open the
_____ menu and choose Tile or Cascade.

5. To exit File Manager, open the _____
menu and choose _____.

13

Using the File Manager for Basic Disk Operations

Learning Objectives

1. Describe the difference between a data disk and a system disk.

2. List reasons to make backup disks.

Performance Objectives

1. Format a DOS data disk.

2. Create a bootable system disk.

3. Add or change a disk label.

4. Make a backup copy of a diskette.

Chapter Terms

Backup Disk A Backup disk is an extra copy of your important data or program files. When your primary disk fails, you can always use your Backup disk and continue working.

Bootable Disk A Bootable disk is another name for a system disk.

Data Disk A Data disk is a formatted disk or diskette that is used to store programs or data files.

Destination Disk When you are making a backup disk, the Destination disk is the disk that will contain a copy of your original files when you are finished. After the backup operation is complete, the Destination disk is usually called the backup disk.

Disk Label A Disk label is a name that is given to an entire disk or diskette. When using Windows, a disk's label appears on the drive bar in File Manager.

Format Before a disk can be used to store data or programs, it must be formatted. In other words, when you format a disk, you prepare it so that it can be used by your computer.

Quick Format If a disk has been formatted once and you want to reuse it (as a blank disk) you can always reformat it and it will be completely erased. Beginning with Windows 3.1 (and DOS 5.0) you can choose to quick format a disk. A quick format is much faster than a standard (or unconditional) format.

Source Disk When you are making a backup disk, the Source disk is the original disk that contains your original files. The source disk is sometimes called the primary or original disk.

System Disk A System disk is a data disk that contains a copy of the critical DOS files. A System disk can be used to boot your computer system. The primary hard disk in your computer should be a system disk.

Chapter Overview

Windows does not eliminate DOS, it just hides it. That means that all of the basic disk operations that DOS requires are also needed when you use Windows. You must still format data diskettes, make proper backups, and perform all the proper housekeeping chores.

How to Format a Data Disk

Open the Disk menu and select Format Diskette from the drop-down menu. A dialog box similar to the one shown in Figure 13.1 will be displayed. Select the disk to be formatted and press the OK button. *Choose carefully!* If the disk you want to format is not displayed, click the arrow next to the Drive Selection box. Make certain that Windows is going to format the disk that you intend to format. Formatting a disk erases all the data on that disk—it cannot be recovered.

Figure 13.1

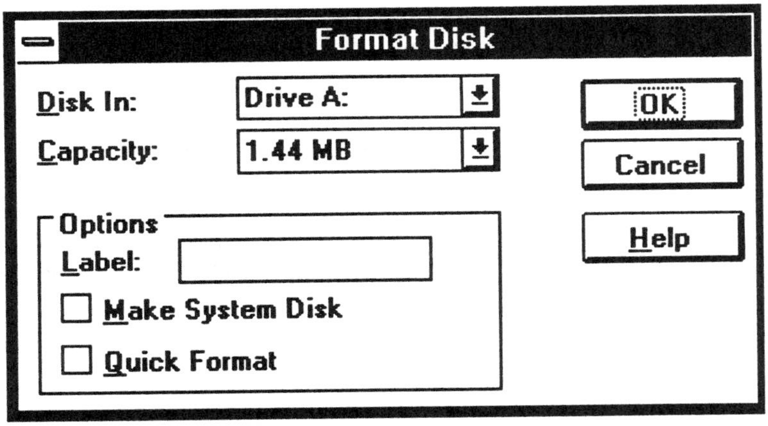

The Format Disk dialog box

DOS will allow you to format disks in several different ways. From the DOS command line you would have to include one or more switches to select the format options you need. When using Windows, just check the box for any desired options, and then press OK.

If you select System Disk, then Windows will create a bootable disk. If the disk to be formatted is a high-capacity disk, then the High Capacity option should be selected.

How to Format a Data Disk with File Manager

		What to Do	**What Happens**
1.		Obtain a blank floppy disk. Place it in the correct disk drive. Remember to close the drive door.	Nothing yet.
2.		Open the disk menu and select Format Diskette.	The Disk menu will display.
3.		Select the disk to be formatted. If the correct disk is not displayed, click on the Down arrow and the list of available floppy disk drives will be displayed. Choose the correct disk and click OK.	The selected disk will become active (see Figure 13.2).

Figure 13.2

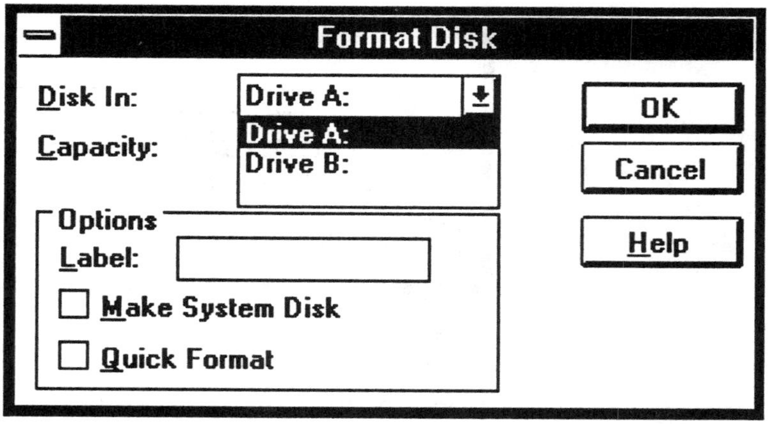

4. Make sure that the correct capacity value is displayed in the text box. If the incorrect capacity is displayed, click on the Down arrow next to the box. Choose the correct capacity with a single-click.

See Figure 13.3.

Figure 13.3

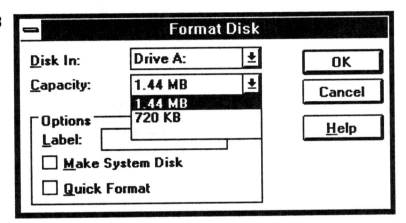

5. At this point, select any options that you need. Supply a disk label, and check the System Disk box and the Quick Format box. When everything is ready, click OK.

The Confirm Format box will appear (see Figure 13.4).

Figure 13.4

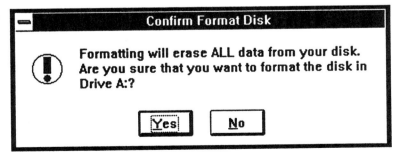

The Confirm Format Box

▲ **Hint** If you are reformatting a diskette that has been used before, you may want to select the Quick Format option. This option formats a disk much faster than the regular command.

If you select Quick Format for a disk that has never been formatted before, the system will simply format your disk normally. Nothing bad will happen, but you may receive an additional warning. Just press OK to continue. ▲

6. Press the OK button in the Confirmation box. A dialog box will keep you informed of the operation's progress (see Figure 13.5).

The disk will be formatted.

Figure 13.5

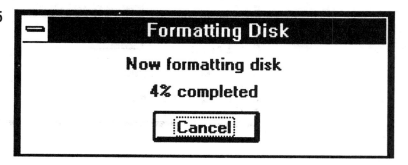

7. When the operation is finished, a final dialog box will appear. The box will display the capacity of the disk that just finished formatting and it will ask, "Do you want to format another disk?" If you are finished, press NO. If you have more disks to format, press YES and the process will repeat.

See Figure 13.6.

Figure 13.6

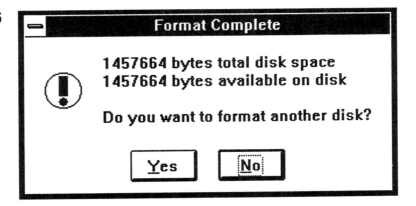

Format Complete

1457664 bytes total disk space
1457664 bytes available on disk

Do you want to format another disk?

Yes   No

Creating a System Disk

A system disk can be placed in your boot drive and used to start up your system. If your computer is equipped with a hard disk (and if you are using Windows, it almost has to be) you almost never need to create system disks. Putting the system files on a floppy disk is pretty much a waste of disk space.

There are, however, several reasons to create system disks. For example, most people have one or more memory-resident programs (such as device drivers) that automatically load into your system when it is started up. If it becomes necessary to start your system without these resident programs, a special start up disk is required.

If the DOS files on your hard disk are accidently erased, you can use a floppy system disk to start your computer. Once started, you can often access your hard disk normally.

There are two ways to create a system disk. You can format a data disk as described previously and be sure that the Make System Disk box is checked. If the disk has already been formatted, you can copy the system files onto it if you open the Disk menu and select the Make System Disk feature (see Figure 13.7).

Figure 13.7

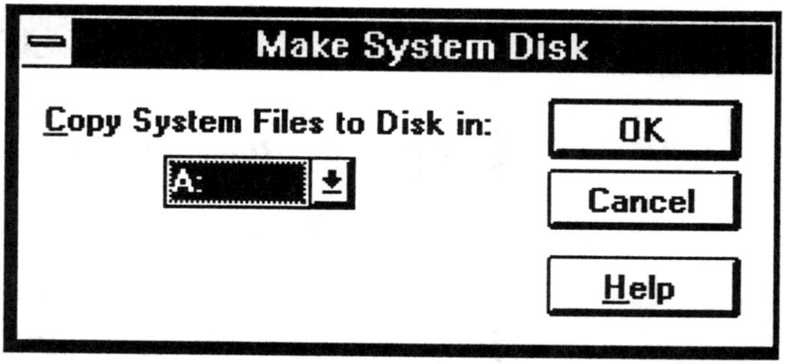

```
┌─────────────────────────────────────────────────┐
│ [▬]            Make System Disk                  │
├─────────────────────────────────────────────────┤
│  Copy System Files to Disk in:    ┌──────────┐   │
│                                   │    OK    │   │
│   ┌─────────────┬───┐             └──────────┘   │
│   │ A:          │ ± │             ┌──────────┐   │
│   └─────────────┴───┘             │  Cancel  │   │
│                                   └──────────┘   │
│                                   ┌──────────┐   │
│                                   │   Help   │   │
│                                   └──────────┘   │
└─────────────────────────────────────────────────┘
```

The Make System Disk dialog box

Making a Backup of a Diskette

Disks fail. It's a simple fact of computer life. The only way to protect yourself from disk failure is to make backup copies of your valuable data. Fortunately, Windows makes this job quick and easy.

The disks that you copy must be the same size and format. For example, you can use this process to copy a 360K 5-1/4" disk to another 360K 5-1/4" disk, but you cannot use it to copy a 5-1/4" disk to a 3-1/2" disk.

Place the disk to be copied in the correct drive and select it. Next, open the Disk menu and choose Copy Diskette. When the dialog box appears, select the location of the destination disk and click OK. Windows does the rest. Note: If the source drive and the destination drive are the same, you will need to swap disks one or more times during the operation. Windows will tell you when to switch.

How to Make a Backup Disk

What to Do	**What Happens**
1. Write protect the disk that is to be copied. If you are copying a 5-1/4" disk, place a piece of write-protect tape over the notch on the side of the disk. For a 3-1/2" disk, just move the write-protect switch.	The source (original) disk will be write protected.
2. Place the disk to be copied into drive A:, open the Disk menu and select Copy Diskette.	See Figure 13.8.

Figure 13.8

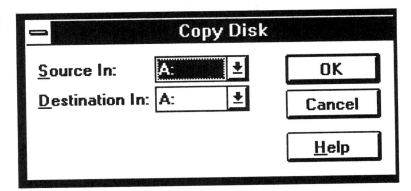

What to Do	**What Happens**
3. If necessary, select the correct source and destination from the list boxes that are displayed. When everything is ready, press OK.	A confirmation box will appear (see Figure 13.9). Press YES to begin.

Figure 13.9

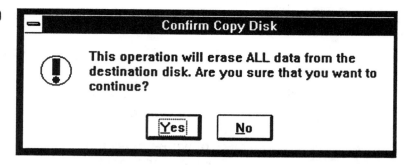

4. A dialog box will appear that reads, "Please insert the source diskette into drive A:." Press OK (see Figure 13.10).

The computer will begin to read data from the disk into the memory.

Figure 13.10

5. After a short delay you will see another dialog box. It will say, "Insert destination disk." Remove the original disk from the drive, insert a new disk and press the OK button.

The destination disk will be in the drive.

6. While the copy is being made, a message box will keep you informed about the status of the process. It may be necessary to swap the disks a second, or even a third time. Read the dialog boxes and change disks as necessary. When the copy is completed, the directory window will return.

Data will be read from memory and placed on the destination disk.

Adding (or Editing) a Disk Label

DOS lets you name each of your diskettes to help you identify them. The name of the selected diskette will appear in the Directory Tree window below the disk drive bar. If you want to change the name of a disk, begin by selecting Label Disk from the Disk menu. If the disk has no name, simply enter the desired name into the box. If the disk already has a volume label, it will be displayed for editing.

A disk label may be up to eleven characters long. Some versions of DOS will even allow spaces in a disk label. When finished, select OK.

Figure 13.11

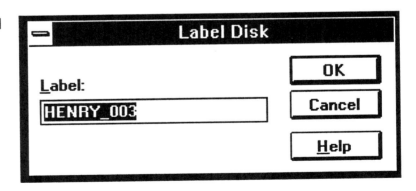

The Label dialog box

How to Add (or Edit) a Disk Label

	What to Do	**What Happens**
1.	Place the disk to be named into a floppy disk drive. Close the drive door.	Nothing.
2.	Select the drive icon that represents the drive that contains your disk.	Selected drive will be high-lighted.
3.	Open the Disk menu and select Label Disk.	A dialog box will appear.

Figure 13.12

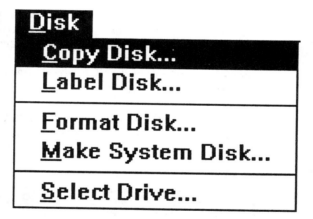

4.	Type the disk label into the box. Call this disk WIN-DOW-DATA. Press [Enter◄─┘] or click OK when you are finished.	The computer will place the label on the disk.

Summary Points

1. To format a data disk, open the Disk menu and select Format Diskette.

2. To create a system disk, check the Make System Disk box in the Format Disk dialog box.

3. If your disk has already been formatted, you can create a system disk if you choose the Make System Disk feature from the Disk menu.

4. When you format a disk, the correct disk capacity must be displayed in the list box before you begin.

5. Open the Disk menu and select Copy Diskette to backup your floppy disks.

6. A disk label may be added or changed by opening the Disk menu and choosing the Label Disk option.

Practice Exercises

At your computer, perform the following practice exercises:

1. Obtain two blank floppy diskettes. Format one of the disks as a data disk and the other as a system disk.

2. Use File Manager to label the data disk as WINDOW-DATA and the system disk as WINDOW-BOOT.

3. Obtain a DOS or other prepared diskette from your instructor and use File Manager to make a backup copy of it.

Comprehension Questions

1. What is the difference between a data disk and a system disk?

2. What are two reasons to create a system disk?

3. Why should you *not* put a copy of the system files on every disk that you format?

4. If a disk has a label, where will File Manager display the name?

5. Why is it necessary to make copies of your diskettes?

6. If you format a disk a second time, what happens to the data on that disk?

7. If you try to quick format a disk that has never been used before, what will happen?

8. What will happen if you try to copy a 3-1/2" disk to a 5-1/4" disk using the Copy Diskette feature?

9. Once a disk has been named (labeled), is it possible to change that name? If so, how is it done?

Completion Questions

1. The only way to protect yourself from disk failure is to make _____.

2. To make a backup of a floppy disk, open the _____ menu and select Copy Diskette.

3. The original disk, that is, the diskette that is being copied, is called the _____ disk.

4. A disk label can be up to _____ characters in length.

5. If you want to add or edit a disk label, open the _____ menu and choose the _____ option.

14

Basic File Operations

Learning Objectives

1. Define directory window.

2. Describe the difference between the ⌂Shift key and the Ctrl key when used to select files.

3. Describe the difference between the Ctrl key and the Alt key when copying and moving files.

4. List ways to recover from a Disk Full error.

5. Describe the file deletion process.

Performance Objectives

1. Select a file in a file list.

2. Select groups of files in a file list.

3. De-select files in a file list.

4. Copy a file (or a group of files) from one location to another.

5. Move one or more files from one location to another.

6. Change the name of an existing file or group of files.

7. Remove (delete) a file or a group of files from a disk.

8. Search for (and find) files that have been misplaced in your storage system.

Copy   The Copy function is used to make a duplicate file. When the Copy function is finished, you will have two files with exactly the same contents. You can force Windows to copy a file if you press and hold the ⎇Ctrl key.

Delete   When a file is deleted, it is removed from disk storage. The disk space that it used is released and is reused by the system to store other files.

Deselect   If a file that has been highlighted is selected a second time, the highlight will go off. In this case, a file is said to be deselected.

Move   When you move a file, an existing file is actually located in a new place. After a Move operation, you still only have one file. It is the same file as before the Move operation, it is just in a new location. You can force Windows to move a file if you press and hold the ⎇Alt key.

Rename   The Rename operation only changes the name of a file. After Rename, you still only have one file and it is still in the same place as it was before the operation. Often the Rename feature is used to correct a typing error that was made when the file was first created.

Search   This feature is found in the File menu. In general, this feature is used to find groups of files on your hard disk.

Select   When a file is highlighted in a File Manager window, it is said to be selected.

Chapter Overview

As the name suggests, Windows File Manager is designed to perform file-based operations. If you are using DOS, you can copy, move, delete, and rename files, but you had better have your DOS manuals handy.

Windows makes these basic tasks simple. You select the files and choose the operation. Windows does the rest.

When File Manager opens, the directory tree window will be displayed. If you double-click a folder on the left side, a new list of filenames will appear on the right. You can now begin to select files.

How to Select Files

In File Manager it is possible to work with a group of files, or just one file at a time. In general, you just highlight the files you want to modify. To select a single file, you must move the mouse pointer to that file and click. If you want to select a different file, move the pointer again and click again. The first file will automatically deselect.

If you want to select multiple files, hold the ⌜Ctrl⌟ key, move to the next file and click again. If the ⌜Ctrl⌟ key is down, the files that have already been selected will *not* de-select (See Figure 14.1).

Figure 14.1

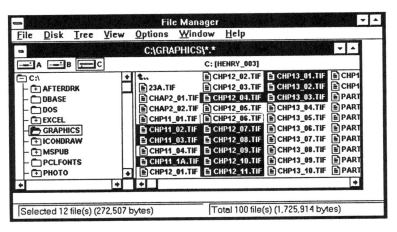

Selecting multiple files

Shortcuts for Selecting Files

Selecting a large number of files one at a time is both time consuming and error prone. To simplify this process Windows provides several shortcuts.

To select a successive group of files, start by highlighting the first file of the group you are interested in. Move to the last file in the group, hold the ⌜⇧Shift⌟ key, and click again. In addition to the first file and the last file, all of the in-between files will be selected.

If you want to select more groups of files, move to the first file of the next group, hold the [Ctrl] key, and select. Finally, move to the last file of the next group, and hold both the [⇧ Shift] key and the [Ctrl] key before you click. Repeat this process until all files or groups of files have been highlighted.

To select all of the files in a window, press the [Ctrl] key and the slash (/) at the same time.

▲ **Hint**   You can also select all of the files in a window if you open the File menu, choose Select Files, and press the Select button. ▲

How to Deselect Files

Even if you never make mistakes, sooner or later you will need to deselect one or more files. Fortunately, Windows provides tools to make this easy.

To deselect all of the files in a window, hold the [Ctrl] key and press the backslash (\), or simply close the window. To deselect a single file, hold the [Ctrl] key down and click the file again.

▲ **Hint**   You can also use the Select Files feature (in the File menu) to select (or deselect) certain types of files. For example, to select all files, except files that end with the extension .EXE, open the File menu, choose Select Files and press the Select button. Next, type *.EXE into the dialog box and press Deselect. Finally, press the Close button and all of the files in the window *except* the .EXE files will be highlighted. ▲

Copying and Moving Files

There is not much difference between the steps for copying a file and moving a file. The results however, are very different. When you finish copying files, you will have two copies of every file that was selected. One file will be in the original location, and a second, identical file will be in another place. To copy files, press and hold the [Ctrl] key (See Figure 14.2).

Figure 14.2

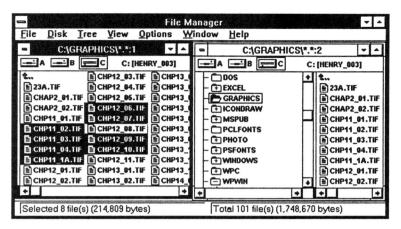

Windows arranged as tiles prior to a Copy or Move operation

When you complete a move, you still only have one file, but that file will be in a different location. To move files, press and hold the [Alt] key.

The general procedure for copying and moving files can be used in many different situations. If you need to move files from one disk to another, from one subdirectory to another, or from a hard disk to a floppy disk, just open the necessary directory windows and go. If you try to perform an operation that is not allowed, Windows will let you know.

During the operation, Windows might display one or more warning boxes. Read the text in the boxes and respond as necessary. In later lessons, you will learn how to get rid of these boxes if you want to.

▲ Hint   This might help you to remember when to use the [Ctrl] key and when to use the [Alt] key. ▲

- To copy files, hold the [Ctrl] key. Remember, C for copy and C for [Ctrl].

- To move files, hold the [Alt] key. Remember, hold [Alt] for an alternate location.

Method One: Select and Drag Between Windows

This method is probably the easiest to understand. Everything that happens is very visual. You just pick the files up and drag them. You don't have to type in any filenames or remember any complicated pathnames. Windows will display a slashed circle (similar to the international NO symbol shown in Figure 14.3) if you try to move or copy the files to an illegal location.

Figure 14.3

The International NO symbol

Start by opening a window that displays the original file or files. Next, open another window to receive the files. The second window could be on another disk drive or just a different subdirectory on the same disk. At this point, you might want to open the Window menu and choose Tile. This makes everything easier to see.

Figure 14.4

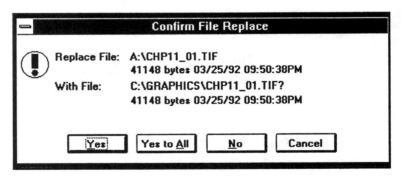

The Replace File warning box

If you want to copy the files, press and hold the [Ctrl] key and drag the files to their destination. If you want to move them, hold the [Alt] key. If the destination contains a file with the same name as the incoming file, a dialog box will appear, similar to the box shown in Figure 14.4. If you wish to replace the existing file with the new file, press the Yes or Yes To All button. To leave the existing file unchanged, select No. If you want to completely stop the operation, use CANCEL.

▲ Hint If you try to copy or move files to a diskette that is not for-matted, you will receive an warning as shown in Figure 14.5. You can then format the target disk or cancel the operation if necessary. After the disk is formatted, Windows will automatically complete the Copy or Move operation. ▲

Figure 14.5

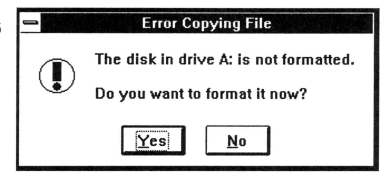

The Disk Not Formatted warning

How to Copy Files Between Windows

	What to Do	**What Happens**
1.	Open a window (if necessary) and display the files that are to be copied or moved.	The source window will display.
2.	Open a new window to receive the files that are going to be copied or moved.	The destination window will be displayed.
3.	Open the Window menu and select Tile. Now, all of the windows that are open will be visible.	Windows will arrange the open windows into tiles.

4. Select (highlight) the files that are to be copied or moved. If necessary, use the shortcuts as described earlier.

The selected files will be highlighted.

5. Drag the files to their new location. Remember, to copy the files, hold the ⌨Ctrl key; to move the files, hold the ⌨Alt key. If copies of the files already exist in the destination location, a dialog box will appear as shown in Figure 14.6.

The files will be copied or moved to their new location.

Figure 14.6

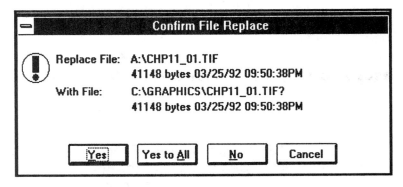

Method Two: Sending Files to a Specified Location

If you know where you want your files to end up, it is not necessary to open a second window. Just open a directory window that contains the original files and select the files to be copied or moved. Now open the File menu and choose Copy. When the dialog box appears (see Figure 14.7), enter the full pathname of the destination and press the Copy button to transfer the files.

Figure 14.7

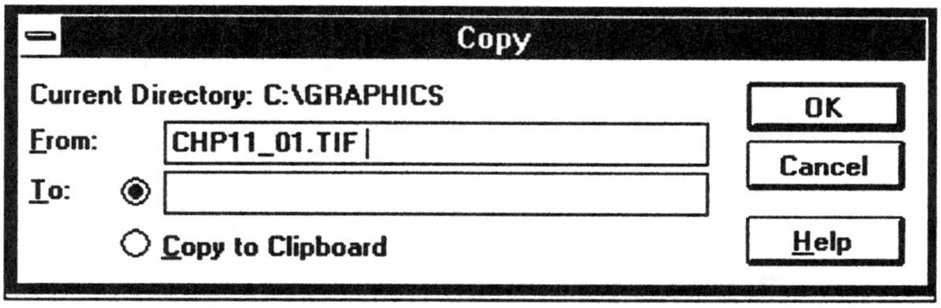

The Copy dialog box

It is even possible to perform the entire copy process without opening any windows at all. If you know the full pathname of both the source and the target, simply open the File menu, select Copy, and fill in the blanks. However, if you are going to do it this way, you may as well do it from the DOS prompt.

How to Send Files to a Specific Location

	What to Do	**What Happens**
1.	Open a window that displays a list of the files that are to be copied or moved.	The source window will be displayed.
2.	Select (highlight) the files that are to be copied or moved. If necessary, use the shortcuts as described earlier.	The selected files will be highlighted.
3.	Open the File menu and select Copy (or just press the F8 key).	The Copy dialog box will appear (see Figure 14.7).
4.	Type the full pathname (and filename) into the box and click Copy (or just press Enter⏎).	The selected files will be copied or moved.

▲ **Hint**   The source filename does not have to be the same as the destination filename. Specifying a destination name that is different from the source is the same as copying (or moving) a file and then renaming it. If you do this, a two-step procedure is combined into a single step. ▲

Method Three: Sending Files to the Drive Bar

Almost everything on the Windows display is active. For example, the title bars can be dragged to move a window, the borders can be moved to size a window, and almost any icon that is displayed can be selected. Occasionally, a feature will have another, almost hidden function. The disk-drive icons on the drive bar fall into this category.

Open a directory window and select a group of files to be copied or moved. Now drag that group of files to a disk-drive icon on the drive bar. Remember, to copy the files, press and hold the Ctrl key; to move them, hold the Alt key. When you get to the right place, a box will appear around the disk-drive icon. Release the mouse button, and the files will be placed in the default directory of the selected drive.

How to Send Files to the Drive Bar

	What to Do	**What Happens**
1.	Open a window that displays the list of files that are to be copied or moved.	The source window will display.
2.	Select (highlight) the files that are to be copied or moved. If necessary, use the shortcuts as described earlier.	The selected files will be highlighted.
3.	Drag the files to the correct disk-drive icon on the drive bar. Remember, to Copy the files, hold the Ctrl key; to move the files, hold the Alt key.	The files will be copied or moved to the default directory of the selected drive.

How to Fix Disk Full Errors

Figure 14.8

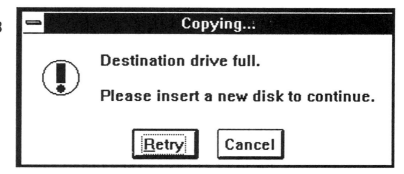

The Disk Full dialog box

If the target disk runs out of space during a Copy or Move operation, a warning box will appear (see Figure 14.8). This box will tell you to place a new disk into the drive, and press OK to continue.

▲ **Hint**   The best way to deal with this problem is to never let it happen. Always make sure that there is plenty of room on your target disk before you begin. ▲

How to Rename Files

To rename a file, first select it from within a directory window. Open the File menu and choose Rename. A dialog box will appear that contains the current name of the file as shown in Figure 14.9. Type a new name in the To box and press the Rename button. Renaming a file does not move or alter the contents of the file in any way.

Figure 14.9

Rename		
Current Directory: C:\GRAPHICS		OK
From: PART4_01.TIF		Cancel
To:		Help

How to Rename files

■ Note   If you try to rename a file to a name that already exists, an error box will appear. Just press OK to continue.

There are some dangers to renaming files. The rule of thumb is: Don't rename any files that don't belong to you. Remember, computers are very stupid. If you are not sure where the file came from, leave it alone.

▲ Hint   You can also use the Rename feature to change the name of a subdirectory. All you need to do is to select the subdirectory from the File List, and choose Rename. ▲

How to Delete Files

If you delete a file, it is removed from your storage system permanently. All you have to do is open a directory window and select the files to be deleted. Press the [Del] key on your keyboard and a dialog box will appear that displays a list of the files you selected (See Figure 14.10). If necessary, this list may be edited. You can remove files that got in there accidently or add any files that were missed. Click OK and they are gone.

Figure 14.10

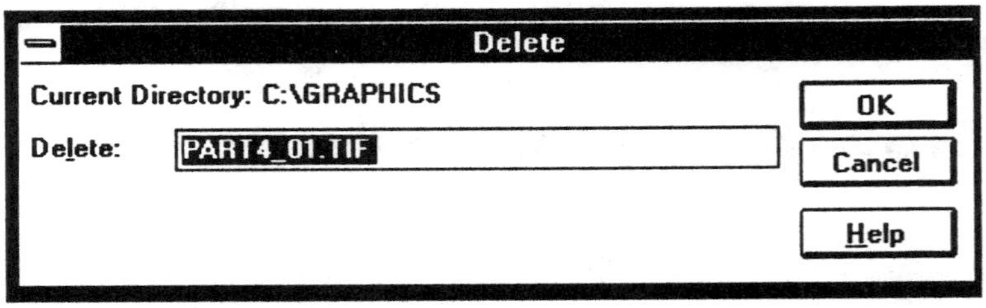

The dialog box for deleting files

If any of the selected files are marked Read-Only or are Hidden, an additional warning box will appear. If you want to go ahead and delete the file, select Yes. To skip the file and continue deleting the other selected files, select No. To completely cancel the delete operation, select Cancel.

You may also delete files from the File menu. Again, open a window and select the files to be deleted, but this time open the File menu and choose Delete. You will again see the dialog box that contains the list of files. You can edit this list if necessary. Deleting files is like running a document through a paper shredder. You might be able to put things back together again, but don't count on it. There are several utility programs (including the UNDELETE command in DOS version 5.0) that can be used to undelete files. They usually work—but not always. The best solution to this problem is prevention. *Delete files carefully.* If you don't know for sure, don't delete it.

The Disk Detective: Finding Missing Files

Your computer system provides several places to store files. If you can't remember where a file is stored, Windows will help you find it. Type in a filename, or even part of a filename and let the "disk detective" go to work (See Figure 14.11).

Figure 14.11

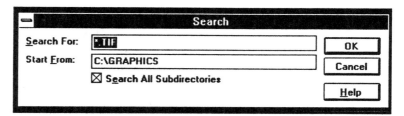

Finding misplaced files with the Search feature

Start by selecting the disk drive that is to be searched. Next, open the File menu, choose Search, and a dialog box will open displaying the current directory. Enter the name of the file into the Search For box and click OK. If you can't remember the exact name of the file, or if you want to search for a group of related files, you can include wildcards as part of the filename.

Windows will search for your file in the current directory. If you want to search the entire disk, make sure the Search Entire Disk box is checked.

If the search is successful, a Search Results window will open. This window will display the path and the names of the files that were found. You can use the Search Results window just like any other window. You can copy, move, delete, rename, or even launch any of the files that are found.

If the search is not successful, you have several choices. You might want to select another drive and repeat the search. Also, make sure that you typed the filename correctly. If you were using wildcards, try a different combination. Above all, don't give up. It has to be there somewhere; just keep digging.

Summary Points

1. Windows File Manager is primarily intended for file-based operations.

2. To work with a file or a group of files, they must first be selected.

3. To select an individual file, simply move to the file and click the mouse button.

4. To select additional files, move to the next file, hold the [Ctrl] key, and click the next file.

5. To select a successive group of files, move to the first file in the group, and select it. Next, move to the last file, hold the [⇧ Shift] key, and click the mouse.

6. To copy a file, first select it, then press (and hold) the mouse button and drag it to a new location. In general, the steps for moving a file are the same as the steps for copying a file.

7. When you are copying files, press and hold the [Ctrl] key, and the file will be copied to a second location. To move a file, press and hold the [Alt] key.

8. To change the name of a file, select the file, open the File menu and choose Rename. Type the new name into the dialog box and click OK.

9. To delete a file, select the file, and press the [Del] key. Alternate method: Open the File menu and choose Delete.

10. To find missing files, open the File menu and choose Search for. Enter the name of the missing file into the dialog box and click OK.

Practice Exercises

At your computer, perform the following practice exercises:

1. Place the WINDOW-DATA disk (created in the previous lesson) into drive A: and open a directory window to display its contents. Select the disk-drive icon for your hard disk, and open a new window to display its root directory. Select the AUTOEXEC.BAT, CONFIG.SYS, and COMMAND.COM files and *copy* them to your floppy disk.

2. On your floppy disk, copy the file AUTOEXEC.BAT to a new file on the same disk and name the new file AUTOEXEC.XXX. Hint: Use Method Two.

3. On your floppy disk, rename the file called AUTOEXEC.XXX to AUTOEXEC.BAK.

4. A file called SYSEDIT.EXE is located somewhere on your hard disk. Use the Search feature to find it. Finally, *copy* SYSEDIT.EXE from the Search Results window to your floppy disk.

5. Delete the file called AUTOEXEC.BAK from your floppy disk. Please be careful. Make sure that the file is being deleted from your floppy disk — not from the hard disk.

Comprehension Questions

1. You need to select a series of files in a directory window. You move to the first file and select it. Which key do you hold to select additional files, one at a time?

2. Describe, step by step, the procedure for selecting a single group of successive files.

3. If you hold the ⟦Alt⟧ key down and drag a group of files to a new location, what happens?

4. What happens if you try to rename a file to a name that already exists?

5. If you press and hold the ⟦Ctrl⟧ key and drag a group of files to a new location, what happens?

6. Under what circumstances would you use both the ⟦⇧ Shift⟧ key and the ⟦Ctrl⟧ key *at the same time*?

7. If you have selected three files, and then select another file but do not hold any other keys, how many files (total) will be selected at the end of this operation?

8. You have selected six files and you are attempting to move them to another disk. In the middle of the third file, you get a Disk Full error message. How many files were moved successfully and how many were left behind?

9. How do you deselect a single file?

10. Describe two ways to select all of the files displayed in a window.

11. If you hold the `Ctrl` key and drag a group of files to the disk-drive icon for drive C:, what happens?

12. If you try to delete a file that is marked as Read-Only or Hidden, what will happen?

13. If you have a group of files selected and you press the `Ctrl` key and the `\` (backslash) key at the same time, what will happen?

14. What additional key do you hold to *move* a group of files from one location to another?

Completion Questions

1. In addition to the mouse button, the _____ key is used to copy files, and the _____ key is used to move files.

2. To select a successive group of files, select the first file in the group, press and hold the _____ key, move to the last file and click the mouse button.

3. To select all of the files in a window, hold the _____ key and press the _____.

4. To De-select all of the files in a window, hold the _____ key and press the _____.

5. To deselect a single file in a group, move to the file, press and hold the _____ key and click the mouse button.

6. If a file is copied or moved to the drive bar, the new file will be located in the _____ directory of the destination drive.

7. To find lost files, open the _____ menu and select the _____ feature.

15

Advanced File Operations

Learning Objectives

1. Define file attributes.

2. List each of the four file attributes.

Performance Objectives

1. Change the system attributes of a file.

2. Control the appearance of the information displayed in a directory window.

3. Change the order of the files that display in a directory window.

4. Display the font used by File Manager.

5. Allow or suppress confirmation messages as desired.

Archive Attribute When a file is first created or modified, the Archive attribute is set. The Archive attribute tells the system that the file is a brand new file.

File Attribute A File attribute is like a flag that is up or down. When the flag is up, then the attribute is active. If the flag is down, then the attribute is inactive.

File Details The File details includes the size of the file, the time and date the file was last modified, and the files attributes.

Hidden Attribute If the Hidden attribute is set on a file, then that file or subdirectory will not display in normal directory listings.

Read-Only Attribute When the Read-Only attribute is active, a file can only be read, it cannot be changed or erased.

System Attribute If the System attribute is set, the file will be hidden and it cannot be run from the command line — it must be run by another program.

Chapter Overview

There is more to file maintenance than just copying and moving files. For example, when DOS creates a file, four file attributes are assigned. The attributes are like little flags that are either up or down. If a flag is up, the attribute is active or set. If the flag is down, the attribute is said to be inactive or unset. DOS provides commands to change some of these attributes, but Windows provides tools to change all four of the attributes as needed. Changing these attributes can help control the way files are utilized and displayed.

Another way to control the file display is through the View menu. You can instruct Windows to only display certain types of files, or to display files in a different order. You can even choose to display files in all uppercase or lowercase letters. These changes can be temporary or set as the system default.

Finally, if you are getting tired of clicking the OK box to confirm multiple operations, you can choose to suppress any (or even all) of the dialog warning boxes. Windows makes every effort to be flexible. If Windows is not compatible with your work habits, don't change your work habits, change Windows.

How to Change the Attributes of a File

When a file is created, four attribute flags are automatically assigned. These flags can be set (or unset) to help you with file management.

■ Note   Actually there are six file attributes, but only four of them apply to files. The other two are for disk labels and subdirectories and cannot be changed by Windows.

To change any (or all) of a file's attributes, first select the files to be changed. Then open the File menu and choose Properties. (The Properties dialog box is shown in Figure 15.1.) If a box is checked, the attribute is set. Make your selections and press OK.

▲ Hint   Hide all of the files in the root directory. This protects them from accidental change or deletion. If key files such as COMMAND.COM or AUTOEXEC.BAT are damaged or changed, your system may be not be able to boot. ▲

Figure 15.1

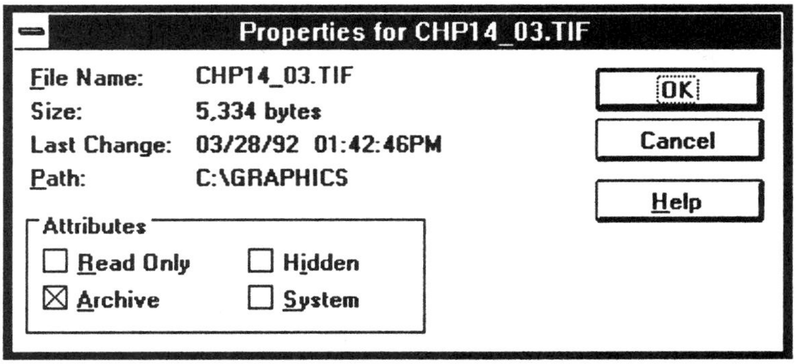

The Windows Properties dialog box

The System Attribute   If the System attribute is set, the file will be hidden and cannot be run from the command line — it must be run by another program. Normally this flag is used to mark the files that are actually part of the DOS operating system, but it is possible to mark any file as System. Although Windows will let you change this attribute, its use should primarily be restricted to DOS.

The Hidden Attribute

If the Hidden flag is set on a file, then that file or subdirectory will not display in normal directory windows. The system files are usually hidden to protect them, but you can manually set the Hidden flag on any file or subdirectory, and it will still work normally. This flag is often used to protect confidential files. For example, an employee may want to set the Hidden attribute on important files such as CHESS.EXE or POKER.COM. Obviously, you would not want an unauthorized supervisor tampering with these files.

▲ Hint

Beginning with Windows 3.1, you can set the Hidden attribute for subdirectories as well as files. If a subdirectory is hidden, everything works normally, it just doesn't display in file listings. ▲

The Read-Only Attribute

The Read-Only attribute helps protect a file or subdirectory from accidental change or deletion. For example, an office may have a master memo form. An employee would load the form into a computer, change it as necessary, and print it. If the employee tried to save the modified memo form using the same filename, an Access Denied message would be displayed. To save the memo after changing it, a new filename would have to be used.

The Archive Attribute

When a file is first created or modified, the Archive attribute is set. Several DOS commands (such as BACKUP and XCOPY) can access this attribute. If it is unset, the file will be ignored. For example, if you are making a full backup of your hard disk, the DOS BACKUP command will unset the Archive bit of every file that it copies. Next time you make a backup, you can tell the BACKUP command to ignore all the files that have the Archive bit set.

▲ Hint

You can examine the attributes (properties) of a file if you press (and hold) the ⌥Alt key while you double click. ▲

How to Change the Way Windows Displays Your Files

When you first use Windows, it will display all files and all subdirectories in several columns across the screen. The View menu allows you to display (or not display) all of the file details in the order that is most useful.

Figure 15.2

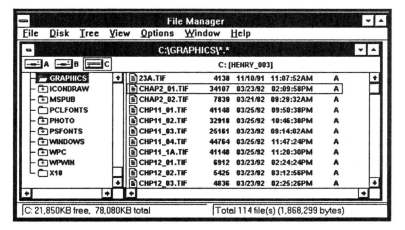

```
View
√ Tree and Directory
  Tree Only
  Directory Only

  Split

√ Name
  All File Details
  Partial Details...

√ Sort by Name
  Sort by Type
  Sort by Size
  Sort by Date

  By File Type...
```

The View menu

Start by opening the View menu from the menu bar (see Figure 15.2). The items that are checked are the current settings. To change the settings, simply select one of the options. For example, to list the files with all the file details displayed, you must first choose All File Details. The file details include the size of the file, the time and date the file was last modified, and the file's attributes (see Figure 15.3).

Figure 15.3

File Manager						
File	Disk	Tree	View	Options	Window	Help

C:\GRAPHICS*.*

A B C   C: [HENRY_003]

GRAPHICS	23A.TIF	4138	11/10/91	11:07:52AM	A
ICONDRAW	CHAP2_01.TIF	34107	03/23/92	02:09:58PM	A
MSPUB	CHAP2_02.TIF	7839	03/21/92	09:29:32AM	A
PCLFONTS	CHP11_01.TIF	41148	03/25/92	09:50:38PM	A
PHOTO	CHP11_02.TIF	32918	03/25/92	10:46:38PM	A
PSFONTS	CHP11_03.TIF	25161	03/23/92	09:14:02AM	A
WINDOWS	CHP11_04.TIF	44764	03/25/92	11:47:24PM	A
WPC	CHP11_1A.TIF	41148	03/25/92	11:20:30PM	A
WPWIN	CHP12_01.TIF	6912	03/23/92	02:24:24PM	A
X10	CHP12_02.TIF	6426	03/23/92	03:12:56PM	A
	CHP12_03.TIF	4836	03/23/92	02:25:26PM	A

C: 21,850KB free, 78,080KB total   Total 114 file(s) (1,868,299 bytes)

A typical file display showing all of the file details

You can choose to display all of this information, part of this information, or only the filenames and their icons. By default, only the filenames display. To override the defaults, open the View menu, select Partial Details, and make your choices.

If All File Details is selected, the information will display in columns similar to a standard DOS display. The first column displays an identifying icon followed by the filename and its extension. In the next column, you will see the size of the file in bytes. Columns Three and Four display the time and date stamp. These columns tell you when the file was created, or the last time it was updated.

The last column indicates the status of the four file attributes. A letter R means Read-Only, A means Archive, H is for Hidden, and a letter S indicates a System file. If no letter is displayed, then the attribute is not set.

Figure 15.4

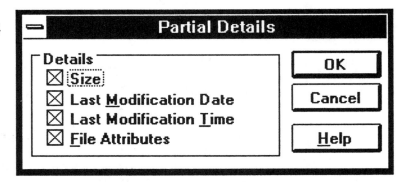

The Partial Details dialog box

If you select Partial Details, the display can be customized. Check (or clear) any or all of the boxes as desired. You can choose to display (or not display) the file size, modification date, modification time, and attribute flags, as shown in Figure 15.4. The only thing that cannot be turned off is the filename and extension.

Changing the Order of Your Files

The second group of choices under the View menu allows you to modify the display order of your files. The first choice, Sort By Name, displays the files in alphabetical order by filename. Sort By Name is the default. If you choose Sort By Type, the second choice on the View menu, the files will be alphabetized by extension. The third choice is Sort By Size. If you select this option, the largest files will be displayed first. The last choice, Sort By Date, will list the newest files first.

How to Display Specific Files

If you want to display only a certain groups of files, open the View menu and choose By File Type. This dialog box will contain a text box and several check boxes (see Figure 15.5). The text box is used to select files with very specific names or extensions. When the dialog box first opens, the text box displays *.* which means that by default, File Manager will display all files. You could, for example, display only files with the extension .EXE by entering *.exe into the box.

Figure 15.5

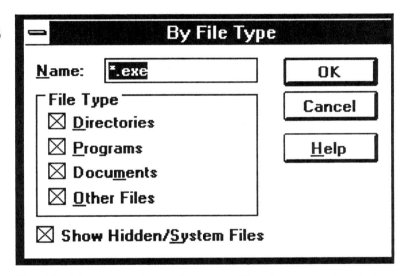

Use this dialog box to choose the types of files that you want to display.

The Directory check box (in the File Type area), causes File Manager to display the names of all subdirectories within the current directory.

The Programs option will display only files that end with .EXE, .COM, .BAT, or .PIF extensions.

The check box for Documents will cause all files associated with an application to display.

If Other Files is checked, any file that is not covered by one of the options listed previously is covered here.

The last check box in this window toggles the display of hidden and system files. Normally, these files are invisible. If you want to be able to see them, then check this box.

■ **Note** If you change the Hidden attribute on a file or subdirectory, it may not disappear right away. To make the file (or subdirectory) disappear, it might be necessary to refresh your screen. To refresh the screen, press [f5] or select the highlighted disk-drive icon a second time. If the file still does not disappear, then you probably have the Show Hidden/System Files option checked.

Other Display Options

The Options menu provides several more controls that you can use to control the way that your file lists displays. The Font choice allows you to display the information in File Manager using any font that is supported by your system. When you select Font, a dialog box will display the choices that are available (see Figure 15.6). Select a base font from the Font box, a style (such as Bold or Italic) from the Font Style box, and a size from the Size box. As you make your selection, you can preview your choice in the Sample box at the bottom of the window. If you want the information in the file list to display in all lowercase, click the check box at the bottom. When you have everything set the way you want, press OK to finish.

Figure 15.6

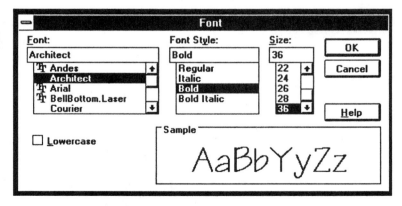

The File Manager Font dialog box

The Options menu will also let you control three other items (see Figure 15.7). If an item in this menu has a check mark next to it, then it is active.

The first choice, Status Bar, will enable (or suppress) the display of the status bar located at the bottom of the File Manager main window. When the status bar is not displayed, you have a little extra room in the File Manager work area. However, most people find that the information in the status bar is useful.

 Figure 15.7

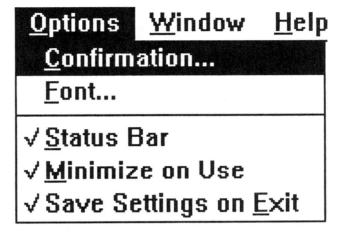

The Options menu

If the second choice, Minimize On Use, is selected, File Manager will automatically minimize any time an application is launched from it. If your desktop tends to get cluttered, this selection can be useful.

The last selection, Save Settings On Exit, can be important. If you exit File Manager and this selection is not checked, then all of your careful choices will be lost.

How to Suppress the Display of Confirmation Boxes

One of the major advantages of using Windows is its ability to work with a group of files. For example, you can select a large group of files and delete all of them with a single command. If you want to delete a large group of files, you save a lot of time. If you selected Delete accidently, Windows can also create work for you.

Figure 15.8

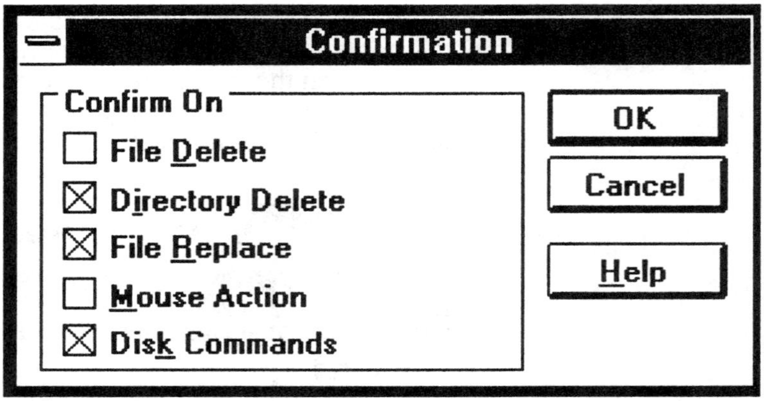

```
┌─────────────────────────────────────────────────────┐
│ ▬        │        Confirmation                       │
├─────────────────────────────────────────────────────┤
│ ┌─ Confirm On ──────────────┐    ┌──────────────┐    │
│ │  ☐ File Delete            │    │     OK       │    │
│ │  ☒ Directory Delete       │    └──────────────┘    │
│ │  ☒ File Replace           │    ┌──────────────┐    │
│ │  ☐ Mouse Action           │    │   Cancel     │    │
│ │  ☒ Disk Commands          │    └──────────────┘    │
│ │                           │    ┌──────────────┐    │
│ └───────────────────────────┘    │    Help      │    │
│                                  └──────────────┘    │
└─────────────────────────────────────────────────────┘
```

The Confirmation dialog box

Every time a "dangerous" operation is requested, Windows will display a confirmation box. To complete the requested operation, you must give Windows additional permission. If seventy-five files are involved, you have to give Windows permission to continue seventy-five times. As you gain confidence with Windows, these confirmation boxes will become a nuisance. The Confirmation option allows you to control the appearance of these messages.

To make these choices, open the Options menu and choose Confirmation. The dialog box displayed in Figure 15.8 will appear. All selections made here become the system defaults, and like other dialogue boxes, if an option is checked it is active.

The File Delete option will display a warning box every time a file-delete operation is requested. It will display once for every file selected.

Directory Delete will display if you attempt to delete a subdirectory. When Windows deletes a subdirectory, all files and sub-subdirectories are also removed from the disk.

The third selection is File Replace. This dialog box will appear if an operation is requested that will overwrite an existing file. If you intended to replace the file involved (such as replacing an old copy of a file with a new one), just give Windows permission to continue. It is probably a good idea to leave this option enabled. Nobody can easily remember the name of every file on every disk. If you unintentionally assign a name to a file and that name is already being used, you could destroy important data.

The fourth choice is Mouse Action. If this option is selected, Windows will ask for additional permission before completing any mouse action such as copying, dragging, or moving.

The Fifth choice is Disk Commands. If this option is selected, a confirmation box will display each time you try to format or copy a disk.

When all selections are made, choose OK to close the box.

Summary Points

1. Windows allows you to control the state of the System, Hidden, Archive, and Read-Only attributes. The attributes can be set or unset.

2. The System attribute is normally used to mark files that are part of the DOS operating system. If the System attribute is set, it cannot be run from the DOS command line.

3. If the Hidden attribute is set on a file, then that file will not display in a normal directory listing. Hidden files can be used normally even though they are invisible.

4. If a file is set to Read-Only, it is protected from accidental change or deletion.

5. The Archive attribute is set when a file is created or modified. Many backup or copy procedures will unset this attribute indicating that the file is not new.

6. The View menu contains options for changing the way your files display. The actual order of the files on the disk is not affected.

7. The By File Type dialog box (in the View menu) allows the user to control the display of directories, programs, documents, and files with a specific filename.

8. The Options menu allows you to change the font used by File Manager, controls upper/lower case display of files, the display of the status bar, and the display of the various confirmation boxes.

9. The Confirmation options include File Delete, Directory Delete, File Replace, Mouse Action, and Disk Commands. These options can be enabled or disabled from the Options menu.

Practice Exercises

At your computer, perform the following practice exercises:

1. Open the View menu and select the All File Details option.

2. Open the View menu again, choose the By File Type option and check the box to make system and hidden files display. Now open a directory window and display the files in the root directory of your hard disk. Write a list of the filenames, extensions, size, date/time stamps and file attributes for the files you find there.

3. Change the attributes of your AUTOEXEC.BAT and COMMAND.COM to Read-Only.

4. Open the Options menu and set all confirmation choices on.

Comprehension Questions

1. How many file attributes are there in all?

2. How many of the file attributes will Windows let you change?

3. What are the four choices in the Partial Details dialog box, and what does each of these selections control?

4. What is the difference between "radio buttons" and "check boxes?"

5. What are the five options in the Confirmation dialog box?

6. If All File Details is selected, what information will display in a directory window?

7. What are the only items that *cannot* be turned off in a file listing?

8. There is a text box in the By File Type dialog box. What is this text box used for?

9. If you choose to arrange files by size, which is listed first, the largest files or the smallest?

10. How do you change the font that File Manager uses to display file listings?

11. What are the four ways that your files can be sorted?

12. The Confirmation dialog box will allow you to disable all warning boxes. Decide which of these choices *you* would enable (or disable) and explain your choices in all five situations.

Completion Questions

1. The _____ attribute can be changed, but its use should be restricted to DOS.

2. If the Read-Only attribute is set an _____ message will be received if you attempt to delete that file.

3. The Partial Details dialog box allows you to display (or not display) the _____

4. Screen clutter can be minimized if the _____ _____ _____ option is selected from the Options menu.

5. Any time a "dangerous" operation is requested a _____ box may appear.

6. If the _____ attribute is set, the file will not appear in a normal directory listing.

7. The Archive attribute is set when a file is _____ or _____

8. If a file has the _____ attribute set, then that file cannot be run from the DOS command line.

16

Directory Tree Operations

Learning Objectives

1. Define subdirectory.

2. Identify a folder with subdirectories.

3. Describe three ways to expand or collapse a subdirectory display.

Performance Objectives

1. Create a subdirectory.

2. View the subdirectory tree structure on a disk or diskette.

3. Expand or condense the subdirectory display.

4. Copy or move a subdirectory and its contents.

5. Delete a subdirectory and its contents.

Chapter Terms

Root
Directory

When you format a hard or floppy disk, DOS creates a directory that will be used to store all other files and subdirectories. This "base" directory is called the root directory.

Subdirectory

A subdirectory is a division of the root directory (or of another subdirectory) and is used to help keep related files organized.

Chapter Overview

Subdirectories are used to organize your files. If you put all of your tax information in one shoe box, your insurance forms in another shoe box, all of your bank statements in a third shoe box, and then put all of your shoe boxes in a big storage box, you already understand subdirectories. Subdirectories on a disk (or diskette) are nothing more than subdivisions that you can create and then use to organize your information.

Subdirectories (electronic shoe boxes) on a disk have at least two advantages compared to a shoe box under your bed. First, the electronic shoe boxes take up a lot less space and are easier to maintain. Second, an electronic shoe box can be further subdivided into sub-subdirectories to make things even easier (shoe boxes inside of shoe boxes). You can create as many levels of subdirectories as you need. There are almost no limits to the depths you can reach.

Directory Tree Basics

The filing system that DOS provides is very flexible. You begin with a large, empty "filing cabinet." To keep related files together, you create "expanding folders" or subdirectories. If necessary, these subdirectories can be divided into sub-subdirectories. DOS keeps track of everything for you, but as your structure gets more complex, it can get confusing. If you examine a list of files, it is easy to tell the subdirectories from the files, but everything is all jumbled together and it is impossible to tell if there are any sub-subdirectories hiding anywhere.

In a Windows Directory Tree window, you will see a graphic (see Figure 16.1). This graphic represents the arrangement of the subdirectories. Next to each subdirectory name you will see a little file folder and a directory name. Subdirectories can be copied, moved, deleted, and renamed as if they were files, but remember, a subdirectory usually represents a number of files. Deleting a subdirectory can do an incredible amount of damage if you are not careful.

Figure 16.1

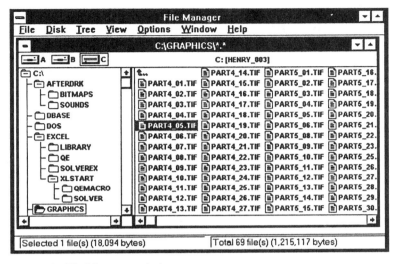

The main File Manager window

Viewing the Subdirectory Structure

When you start File Manager, you will see a directory window. It will contain a graphic that represents the arrangement of the directories and subdirectories on your disk, and a list of files in the directory that is currently selected (see Figure 16.2). If a directory has subdirectories that are not visible, the directory icon will display a plus sign. By default, only the first level of subdirectories will be visible.

Figure 16.2

Tree	View	Options	Window	Help
Expand One Level				+
Expand Branch				*
Expand All				Ctrl+*
Collapse Branch				-
√ Indicate Expandable Branches				

The Tree menu

There are several ways to expand or condense a subdirectory tree. The easiest way is to just position the mouse pointer on a folder and double-click. If the folder has subdirectories, it will expand and display the next level of subdirectories. Double-click a second time and the folder will "collapse."

▲ **Hint**　If you open the Tree menu and check the Indicate Expandable Branches feature, then subdirectories that have sub-subdirectories will display a tiny plus sign (+) when they are collapsed and a minus sign (-) when they are open. ▲

There are also several hot keys that can be used to control the display. Once a folder is highlighted, you can press the plus sign (+) key on the keyboard to expand the structure by one level. If you press the asterisk, all levels below the current level (in other words, the entire branch) will be displayed. You can also press and hold the [Ctrl] key and then press the asterisk. This causes *all* levels in *all* subdirectories to become visible. (Note: If the asterisk is not on a key by itself, you may need to press and hold both the [⇧ Shift] key and the [Ctrl] key to perform this operation.) These functions can also be performed from the Tree menu. The keyboard hot keys are listed next to the functions.

To collapse a directory display, just select the correct folder and press the minus key. To collapse all subdirectories, close the folder for the root directory and then reopen it.

How to Create a New Subdirectory

To create a new subdirectory, first select the directory that is to contain the new subdirectory. This could be the root directory or any other file folder in the display. Open the File menu and select the Create Directory option. When the dialog box appears (see Figure 16.3), type a name for the new directory and press OK or [Enter←]. You can create subdirectories and sub-subdirectories as needed.

In general, the same rules that apply to filenames also apply to subdirectory names. The name cannot be longer than eight characters, and spaces are not allowed. You can even assign an extension to a subdirectory name, but in practice this in rarely done.

Figure 16.3

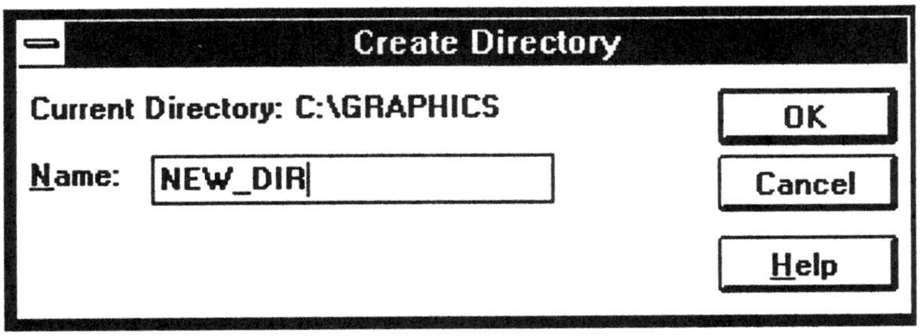

```
┌──────────────────────────────────────────────────┐
│ ▬               Create Directory                  │
├──────────────────────────────────────────────────┤
│  Current Directory: C:\GRAPHICS      ┌──────────┐ │
│                                      │    OK    │ │
│  Name:   ┌─────────────────────┐     └──────────┘ │
│          │NEW_DIR|             │     ┌──────────┐ │
│          └─────────────────────┘     │  Cancel  │ │
│                                      └──────────┘ │
│                                      ┌──────────┐ │
│                                      │   Help   │ │
│                                      └──────────┘ │
└──────────────────────────────────────────────────┘
```

The Create Directory dialog box

How to Create a New Subdirectory with File Manager

What to Do	What Happens
1. Select the directory that is to contain the new directory. This could be the root directory or any of your subdirectories.	The selected directory will be highlighted.
2. Open the File menu and select Create Directory from the list.	A dialog box will appear.
3. Type the name of the new subdirectory into the dialog box. When finished, click OK or press [Enter←].	The new subdirectory will be created.

How to Copy, Move, Delete, or Rename a Subdirectory

Actually, Windows doesn't care about the real differences between a file and a subdirectory. Almost anything that can be done to a file can also be done to a subdirectory. Subdirectories can be copied, moved, renamed, and erased using the same techniques that are used on files.

For example, to move a subdirectory (and all of its files) to a new disk, you can just select it, hold the [Alt] key, and drag it to the new disk. If you want to copy rather than move it, hold the [Ctrl] key. If you want to rearrange the subdirectory structure within a disk, select the directory to be changed, hold the appropriate key ([Ctrl] or [Alt]), and make the change.

It is important to remember, however, that a subdirectory can contain a great deal of information. Whatever happens to a subdirectory also affects its files. If you delete a subdirectory, you also delete all the files in the subdirectory. If you change the name of a subdirectory, the program that uses that directory will not be able to find any of its files.

■ **Note**   It is also very easy to confuse Windows if you change the tree structure. Windows must know the name of the program, its subdirectory, and in some cases, sub-subdirectories before an application can be launched. If you are not careful, your icons can become nothing more than pretty pictures on your desktop.

Summary Points

1. Subdirectories are subdivisions on a disk that are used to help keep related information or files together.

2. Like files, a subdirectory name can be a maximum of eight characters long.

3. To create a new subdirectory, open the File menu and choose Create Directory.

4. Subdirectories can be placed in the root directory of a disk, in any subdirectory, or any sub-subdirectory as needed.

5. You may use the same techniques for copying, moving, renaming, and deleting files to copy, move, rename, or delete subdirectories.

6. Deleting a subdirectory also deletes all of the files in that subdirectory.

Practice Exercises

Project One

1. Place a formatted floppy disk in your disk drive and select (highlight) its icon on the drive bar. Open the File menu and create three subdirectories. Call the first one TAXES90, the second TAXES91, and the third TAXES92.

2. Select the TAXES90 subdirectory, and create two sub-subdirectories called INCOME and EXPENSES.

3. Expand the subdirectory structure so that all of its elements are visible.

4. Copy the INCOME and EXPENSES subdirectories into the TAXES91 and the TAXES92 subdirectories.

5. Delete the TAXES90 subdirectory and its contents.

6. Collapse all subdirectories on your diskette.

Project Two

Devise (on paper) a subdirectory structure that would organize the following programs and files:

*a spreadsheet program

*spreadsheet data for taxes

*spreadsheet data for stocks

*a word processing program

*a set of standard memos for the word processing program

*a set of letters used for producing a mail merge

*a desktop publishing program

*a set of files for the publishing program that are used to create a monthly newsletter including text files and scanned graphics

*also provide a place for each program to store its day-to-day data files

Comprehension Questions

1. What is the primary use for subdirectories?

2. What does a minus sign on a subdirectory file folder indicate?

3. What are the two ways to completely expand the picture of a subdirectory structure?

4. If a subdirectory name is deleted, what happens to the files in that subdirectory?

5. If the name of a subdirectory is changed, what happens to the files in that subdirectory?

6. What are the rules for naming a subdirectory? Can a subdirectory name have an extension?

7. If you wish to create a new subdirectory, what menu must be used and where will the new subdirectory appear in the tree structure?

8. What key do you hold if you wish to copy a subdirectory? Which key do you hold to move a subdirectory?

9. What are some of the problems that can be created by changing the name of a subdirectory?

10. What is the maximum number of levels allowed in a subdirectory structure?

Completion Questions

1. By default, only _____ level of subdirectories will be visible in a Directory Tree window.

2. If a folder icon contains a _____
_____ it means that there are additional levels of subdirectories that are not currently displayed.

3. One way to display all levels of all subdirectories is to press and hold the _____ key and then press the _____ key.

4. To create a new subdirectory you must first open the _____ menu.

5. The same general rules that apply to _____ also apply to subdirectory names.

17

Starting Applications from File Manager

Learning Objectives

1. Identify a program by its icon.

2. Identify all files that are associated with an application.

3. List three ways to launch applications from File Manager.

Performance Objectives

1. Launch an application from File Manager.

2. Use a document to launch an application.

3. Copy executable files from File Manager to Program Manager.

4. Associate a document to the application that created it.

5. Activate the Minimize On Use feature as desired.

Associated File
If a file is associated, it knows which application was used to create it. An Associated file will have an icon that looks like a little piece of paper with the corner folded down. This icon looks similar to a regular document icon filled with tiny lines of text.

Minimize On Use
If the Minimize On Use feature is selected, File Manager will automatically minimize any time an application is launched from it. The Minimize On Use feature can be used to help eliminate screen clutter.

Chapter Overview

File Manager is such a flexible tool that many Windows users don't use Program Manager at all. Program Manager is easier to use (once it is set up correctly) but many die-hard DOS users refuse to give up control of their keyboard. You can start both Windows applications and non-Windows applications from File Manager. All you need to know is the name of the file and where the file is stored. If you don't know where the file is stored, you can use Search to help you find it.

Figure 17.1

File	
Open	**Enter**
Move...	F7
Copy...	F8
Delete...	Del
Rename...	
Properties...	Alt+Enter
Run...	
Print...	
Associate...	
Create Directory...	
Search...	
Select Files...	
Exit	

The File menu

File Manager will let you launch any file that has a program icon with a double-click. However, some programs (especially DOS utility programs) that work directly on disks can undermine the way Windows operates. Even some DOS commands can do unpredictable things when run from Windows. At best, Windows may crash and force you to reboot your machine. At worst, your favorite utility—the one that always worked so well before—could completely trash your hard disk.

Launching an Application from File Manager

There are several ways to launch an application from File Manager. The easiest is to find the filename and double-click on it; the application will run just as if it were launched from Program Manager. You may also select (highlight) the file, open the File menu, and choose Open. When you close the application, File Manager will return, ready for further commands.

Applications can be launched from any window inside File Manager. If you don't remember where a file is, use the Search feature. When Windows locates the file, it can be launched directly from the Search Results window.

Launching a File from the File Menu

There is another option in the File menu called Run. If you know the complete pathname and the name of the application to be launched, type that information into the text box and your application will start. If you are launching a standard DOS application, this is the same as typing the command at the normal DOS prompt. However, if the application will only run under Windows, there may be no other way to get it started (See Figure 17.2).

Figure 17.2

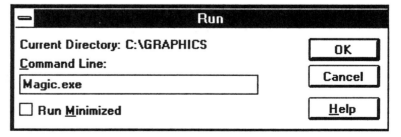

The Run dialog box

A good example would be a new program that needs to be to installed from floppy disks. If you place the startup disk in the floppy drive and type INSTALL at the DOS prompt, you might get a message that says "This program requires Microsoft Windows."

Grab your trusty mouse and follow this procedure.

Get Windows running and launch File Manager. Open the File menu and type the complete pathname and filename into the dialog box. For example, to run an Install program from drive A: you would type A:INSTALL. Press OK (or [Enter◄─┘]) and it will launch.

Using a Document to Launch an Application

File Manager makes it easy to tell which files are programs and which contain data. As a general rule, the difference between a data file and a program file is that program files create data files.

If you know which data file was created by which program file, File Manager provides another tool for launching your programs. Find the data file you need to work on, and drag it to the application that created it. File Manager will launch your application *and load your data file automatically.*

For example, if you need to update information from a July stockholders' meeting in a word processing program, find the file that contains the information and drag it to the program file for your word processor. Windows will launch your word processor and load the requested data file. In one step you are ready to begin work. If your data files and application are in different locations (or even on different disks), open the necessary windows, and move or size them so that you can see everything.

There are, however, two things to watch for when using this technique. First, make sure that you match the data file to the program that created it. If the file format is not what the application is expecting, it will not launch.

Second, for this technique to work, your application must be able to accept a filename as a command-line argument. If you can start an application from the DOS prompt and specify a filename at the same time, then no problem. For example, if you are using a word processor called Editor, enter the command EDITOR letter.txt at the DOS prompt. The word processor will run and load the file named letter.txt. In Windows, simply drag the file letter.txt to the file EDITOR and Windows does the rest.

How to Use a Document to Launch an Application

What to Do	**What Happens**
1. In File Manager, open a window that contains the application to be launched.	The window that contains the application will be displayed.
2. Open a second window (if necessary) that contains the data file to be used.	The window that contains the data file will be displayed.

■ **Note** Actually, step One and step Two can be performed in any order. It really doesn't matter which window is opened first.

3. Tile (or arrange) the open windows so that everything can be viewed easily. To arrange the windows as tiles, open the Window menu and choose Tile.	The windows will arrange as tiles.

▲ **Hint** You can also arrange the windows as tiles by pressing `Ctrl` + `Esc` (to activate Task List) and selecting Tile from the buttons at the bottom. ▲

4. Use your mouse to drag the data file on top of the application file. Release the mouse button and the application will launch.	The application will launch and the selected data file will be loaded into memory.

Launching the Correct Application Automatically

DOS will allow you to enter a filename up to eight characters long with an optional extension of up to three more characters. Traditionally, the extension is used to help identify the file. For example, if a file ends with .EXE, .COM, .BAT, or .PIF, Windows assumes that the file is an application. As far as Windows is concerned, everything else is data.

Figure 17.3

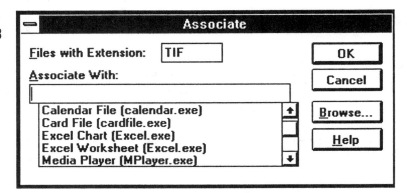

How to associate a data file with its application

File Manager will allow you to associate a file with a certain extension to a specific application. For example, if all of your database files have the extension .DBF, simply tell Windows to launch your database program if a .DBF file is selected.

To make this connection, start by selecting a file with the .DBF extension. Now, open File menu and choose Associate. A dialog box will open and display the current association if there is one (see Figure 17.3). You can now enter or edit this information as desired.

After the association is made, the icon in front of all files with a .DBF extension will change to an associated icon. To load and run a file with an association, double-click on its name. Windows will automatically locate the correct application, launch it, and load the data file you requested.

How to Associate a Data File with the Correct Application

	What to Do	**What Happens**
1.	In File Manager, open a window that contains the file to be associated, and select that file.	The file will be highlighted.
2.	Open the File menu and select Associate.	The Associate dialog box will appear.
3.	If the application that you need appears in the list that is displayed, choose that application and click OK.	The document icon will change to an Associated document icon.
4.	If the required application is not displayed, press the Browse button.	The Browse dialog box will appear (see Figure 17.4).

Figure 17.4

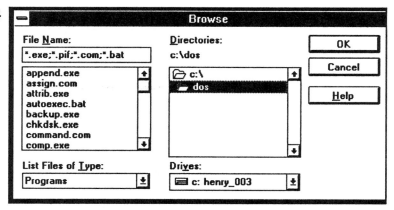

	What to Do	**What Happens**
5.	Search the disks and subdirectories until you find the name of the application that is to be associated. When you find it, double-click on it.	The pathname and filename will appear in the text box.

6. Press OK to finish.

The document's icon will change into an Associated icon.

Moving Executable Files to Program Manager

Running applications from File Manager is easy, but running them from Program Manager is even easier. If you find that you are running an application from File Manager over and over, why not move it into Program Manager?

Figure 17.5

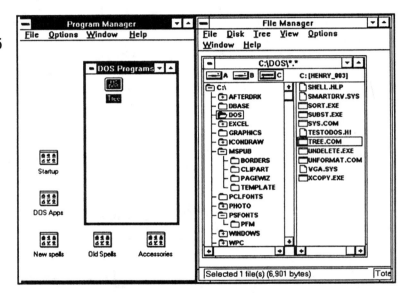

Moving an Application from File Manager to Program Manager

Start by opening Program Manager and sizing the window to only fill half of the screen (as shown in Figure 17.5). Next, open or create a group to receive the new applications. Open File Manager and size its window to fit the other half of the screen. Find the name of the file to be moved, and drag it to the open group in Program Manager. Windows will automatically create an appropriate icon for the new application.

How to Move Executable Files to Program Manager

	What to Do	**What Happens**
1.	Start Program Manager (if it isn't already running) and size the window to fit on half of the screen.	Program Manager will display.
2.	Start File Manager and size its window to fit on the other half of the screen.	Both Program Manager and File Manager should be visible.
3.	In Program Manager, open (or create) a group to receive the new applications.	A new window will open ready to receive the new items.
4.	In File Manager, find the file to be moved and drag it to the open window in Program Manager.	Windows will create an icon to represent the application.

■ **Note** When an application file is moved using this method, it doesn't really go anywhere. Actually this procedure is just another easy way to add application icons to Program Manager.

File Manager Housekeeping

Windows is a multitasking system; it is designed to let you do more than one job at a time. If you launch applications from File Manager, you could have a word processor, a spreadsheet, and a few games all running at the same time. Needless to say, your desktop will get pretty cluttered. One solution to this problem is to activate the Minimize On Use feature. Open the Options menu (see Figure 17.6) and select Minimize On Use. When this feature is active, File Manager will automatically shrink to an icon any time an application is launched.

Figure 17.6

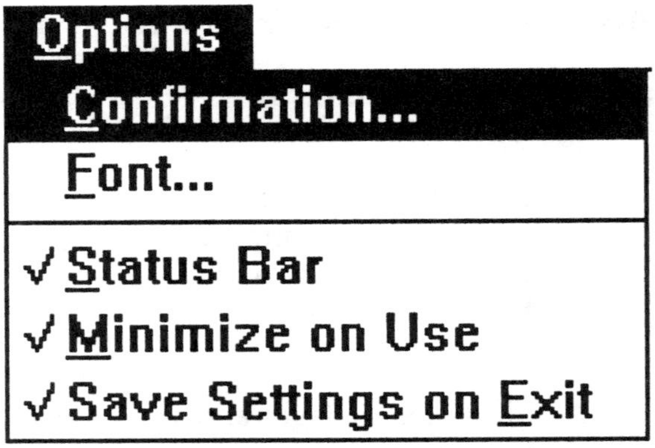

```
Options
    Confirmation...
    Font...
  √ Status Bar
  √ Minimize on Use
  √ Save Settings on Exit
```

The Options menu

When you close the application, File Manager will stay mini-mized. All you have to do is double-click the File Manager icon, and it will restore itself to the original size.

▲ **Hint**   By the way, this same feature is available in Program Manager.
▲

Summary Points

1. File Manager will let you launch any file that has a program icon displayed with it.

2. If you know the filename and the path of an application, that application can be launched from the File menu. Select Run from the File menu and enter the name and the path of the application into the text box.

3. Applications can be launched from any window in File Manager.

4. You can launch an application and load a data file automat-ically if you drag the name of the data file to the name of the application.

5. To load an associated data file, double-click the filename. Windows will automatically launch the application and load the requested data file.

6. Executable files can be moved from File Manager directly into Program Manager.

7. To minimize desktop clutter select the Minimize On Use feature. When this feature is active, File Manager will shrink to an icon whenever an application is launched.

Practice Exercises

At your computer, perform the following practice exercises:

1. Set the File Manager options so that it will Minimize On Use.

2. Locate (in File Manager) the program file named NOTEPAD.EXE. Next, on your hard disk, find a file that ends with the extension .TXT. (Hint: use the SEARCH feature.) When an appropriate file is located, drag this file on top of the NOTEPAD.EXE file. The Notepad program should launch and the data file you selected will be loaded.

3. Create a new program group in Program Manager called DOS COMMANDS. Move the following commands from the DOS subdirectory in File Manager to the new group in Program Manager.

    TREE   ATTRIB   DOS KEY   HELP

Comprehension Questions

1. Certain types of programs should not be run from Windows. What are they?

2. If you double-click a filename that has a program icon next to it, what will happen?

3. If you double-click a file that has a regular document icon next to it, what will happen?

4. How do you use a regular document file to launch an application?

5. What selection under the Files menu will allow you to launch an application from File Manager?

6. What is the difference between an associated document and one that is not associated?

7. Why would you want to move an executable program to Program Manager?

8. If the Minimize On Use feature is active, what happens when an application is launched from File Manager?

9. How do you create an association between a data file and the application that created it?

10. It is possible to launch an application by dragging a data file on to the top of it. Under some conditions this will not work. What two things do you need to watch for?

18

Other File Manager Functions

Learning Objectives

1. List reasons to use the Refresh command.

2. Identify printable files.

Performance Objectives

1. Refresh the information in a window.

2. Print text files from File Manager.

Refresh   On occasion, when a change is made to a file list in File
Manager, the screen will not change to display that change. If
this happens, it may be necessary to refresh the screen, When
a screen is refreshed, it simply means that Windows will reread
the disk and display an updated tree structure and/or file list.

Text File   A Text File is a special type of file that contains text and a min-
imal number of formatting codes. Several specialized programs
can be used to create text files including the Windows Notepad
accessory, the DOS EDIT command, and the DOS EDLIN command. Text Files usually end with a .BAT or a .TXT extension.

Chapter Overview

There are a few File Manager functions that just don't fit neatly
into any category. They are, however, important features and
cannot be left out of a discussion of File Manager. These features
have to do with the way Windows displays information in File
Manager, and the printing of certain types of files.

How to Refresh a Window

On occasion, Windows get confused about what should be displayed in a window. When files are deleted or moved, Windows
does not always inform the display about what happened. This
is usually not a problem and seems to occur mostly when a
network drive is involved.

Figure 18.1

Window	Help	
New Window		
Cascade	Shift+F5	
Tile	Shift+F4	
Arrange Icons		
Refresh	F5	
√1 C:\DOS*.*		

The Window menu

To make certain that your display is up to date, open the Window menu, and select Refresh. Windows will reread the disk drives and update your display.

Shortcut: Press the ⌨[F5] key.

▲ **Hint**　You can also refresh a window by choosing a new disk icon or by choosing the same disk icon a second time. ▲

Using File Manager to Print Text Files

Several DOS (such as EDLIN) and Windows utilities (like the Notepad) save their files in a form known as ASCII. The technical details are not important right now, but these files are often called text files. File Manager can take these text files and print them for you.

Figure 18.2

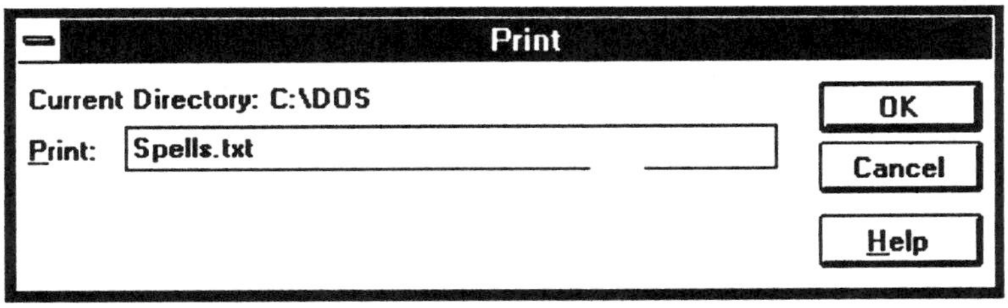

The Print dialog box

To send the contents of these files to the printer, select the files to be printed and open the File menu. Choose Print from the menu and press OK (see Figure 18.2).

To print a single file, you can just press [Alt]+F. Type the name and path of the file into the dialog box and press OK.

How to Print Text Files from File Manager

	What to Do	**What Happens**
1.	Open File Manager and locate the file (or files) to be printed.	File Manager will be displayed.
2.	Use the mouse to select the files.	The selected files will highlight.
3.	Open the File menu (use the mouse or just press [Alt]+F) and select the Print feature.	File menu will display.
4.	The Print dialog box will appear. The text box will contain a list of the files to be printed. This text can be edited if necessary.	Print dialog box will display.
5.	Press OK (or [Enter◄─]) and the selected files will be printed.	Windows will print the files you have selected.

Summary Points

1. If the display does not update after a file operation, select the Refresh function from the Window menu or just press [F5].

2. To print a text file, open the File menu and select Print.

3. You may also print a text file by pressing [Alt]+F and selecting Print.

Practice Exercises

At your computer, perform the following practice exercises:

1. Locate the text file (in the Windows\System sub-subdirectory) called TESTPS.TXT. Print this file from File Manager by pressing ⌨+F.

2. Select the file named SETUP.TXT and print it from File Manager. Incidentally, this file is additional Windows documentation. You may want to keep it for future reference.

■ Note The SETUP.TXT file is rather long. You may need to check with your instructor before you print it.

Comprehension Questions

1. How do you refresh a display window?

2. Why do windows need to be refreshed on occasion?

3. What type of files can be printed from File Manager?

4. What is the name of one of the DOS utilities that creates printable files?

5. What is the name of one of the Windows utilities that creates printable files?

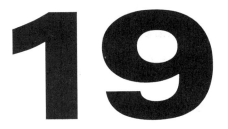

Print Manager

Learning Objectives

1. Describe the main function of Print Manager.

2. Define print queue.

3. List the different types of print queues.

Performance Objectives

1. Access Print Manager.

2. Change the order of the files in the print queue.

3. Cancel jobs in the print queue.

4. Modify the printing speed.

5. Control the display of Print Manager messages.

6. Troubleshoot many common printing problems.

7. Close Print Manager.

Print Queue   A Print Queue is a list that indicates which file is currently printing and which files are waiting to be printed.

Local Queue   A Local Queue is the Print Queue that is directly under the control of the computer that you are using.

Network Queue   A Network Queue is a print queue that is managed by the network file server. Any printers attached to a Network Queue are shared by all users on the network.

Chapter Overview

Your computer displays data as mysterious little dots of light on your monitor. These dots are manipulated into meaningful relationships that can represent letters of the alphabet, numbers, or even the shapes and colors that make up a graphic design. It can be difficult to put these little dots of light into an envelope and mail it, but once again, using computer magic, Windows can change the lights on the screen into characters and designs on paper.

Data from Windows applications are printed through an application called Print Manager. Print Manager icon is stored (by default) in the Main Group, but any time a print operation is requested, Windows will create a print file and launch Print Manager. From that point until the job is completed, Print Manager takes care of printing your data.

■ **Note**   Printers are different. That is, different printers have different abilities and the final appearance of your output may not be exactly what you expect. It may be necessary to do a little experimenting to get the results that you need.

Printing with Print Manager

You don't have to do anything special to use Print Manager. Any time you open the File menu (from any Windows application) and select Print, Print Manager goes to work. It launches itself automatically and when it is finished, it closes automatically. Usually, a Print dialog box will open that is similar to the box shown in Figure 19.1. If you need more than one copy of the printout, or if you only want to print a part of the document, make the necessary selections and press the OK button. Print Manager does everything else.

Figure 19.1

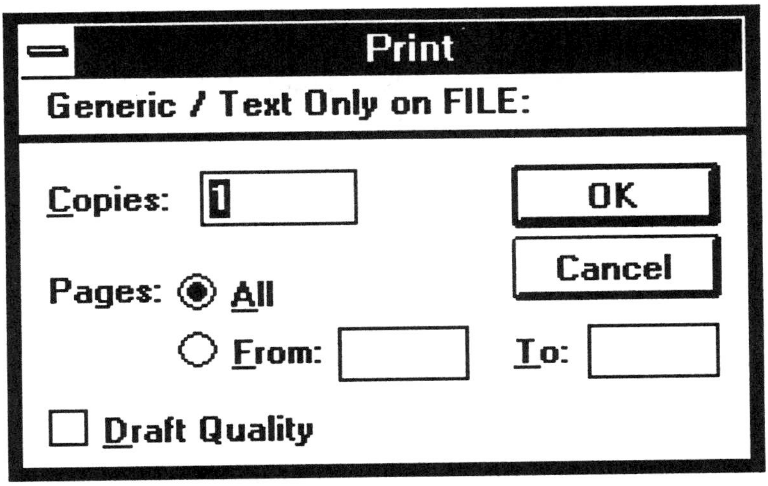

A typical Print dialog box

Printing from a DOS Application

When you are printing from a DOS based application that is running under Windows, the DOS application will print just as if it were running under DOS. *DOS applications do not use Print Manager.*

If you want to print the output from a DOS application through Print Manager, you must first transfer the information to be printed into a Windows application.

▲ Hint

If you are running in Enhanced mode, and you have a DOS application running in a window, you can cut the information to be printed to the Clipboard, and paste it into a Windows application to be printed. ▲

Printing to a File

One of the ways to transfer information from a DOS application to a Windows application is to "print" the output from the DOS application to a file, and then load it into a Windows application to be printed. Unfortunately, different DOS applications will use different procedures for printing to a file. To learn the specific procedure for a specific DOS application, you will need to consult that application's documentation.

If necessary, you can also "print" the output of a Windows application to a file. Once this file is created, it has many uses. For example, if you need to merge two documents—one from a spreadsheet and one from your word processor—you could print the spreadsheet to a file and then easily load it into your word processor. You could also create a document on one computer and print it from a different computer.

■ **Note**   Actually, to transfer information between your spreadsheet and word processor as described here, you should have the Generic/Text Only printer driver installed and selected.

To print the output from a Windows application to a file, use the following procedure.

What to Do   **What Happens**

1.   Open the Control Panel and   See Figure 19.2.
         double-click the Printers
         icon. Remember, by default,
         the Control Panel is in the
         Main Group.

Figure 19.2

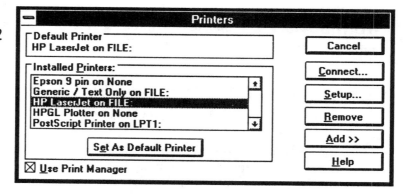

2.   Select the name of the   The name of the printer
         printer to be used. To cre-   that you choose will be
         ate a file that is to be trans- highlighted.
         ferred to another
         application, choose the
         Generic/Text Only printer.

3. Press the Connect button and another dialog box will appear.

See Figure 19.3.

Figure 19.3

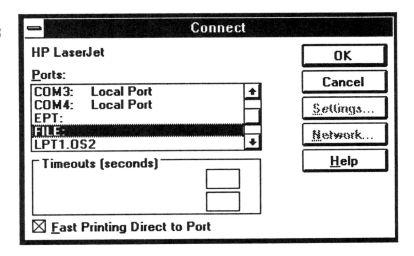

4. Look through the list of choices in the Ports box and choose File:. When you are finished, press OK.

Your choice will be highlighted.

5. Make sure that the correct printer is highlighted and press the Active radio button. Now, double-click on the printer's name (or press the Default Printer button) and the selected printer will become the default printer. When you are finished, press OK.

The name of the default printer will be displayed in the Default Printer box.

6. Return to your application (close Control Panel and the Main Group if necessary) and print normally. When the dialog box appears, type a filename and press Enter⏎.

See Figure 19.4. When you press Enter⏎, Windows will create a file that contains the output data.

Figure 19.4

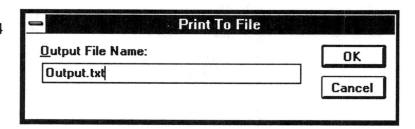

The Print Queue

As you already know, when you print a document from Windows, it is sent to Print Manager. Print Manager works in the background printing your documents, in the order that they are received, while you go and do other things. When Print Manager receives a file, it is placed in a Print Queue.

■ **Note**   A Print queue is a list that indicates which file is currently printing and which files are waiting to be printed.

Looking at the Print Queue   When Print Manager starts a print job, the Print Manager icon will appear on the desktop near the bottom of your screen. If you double-click this icon the Print Manager window will open and you can check on the status of all your print jobs (see Figure 19.5).

When the Print Manager window is open, you can interrupt, cancel, or change the order of your print jobs.

■ **Note**   Actually there are two types of print queues—a local queue and a network queue. If you are printing to a network printer, the Print Manager will use the network queue. The Print Manager icon will *not* appear on your desktop. If you need to check on the status of your Network print jobs, you must launch Print Manager by

---

double-clicking on it's icon. By default, the Print Manager icon will be located in the Main group.

Figure 19.5

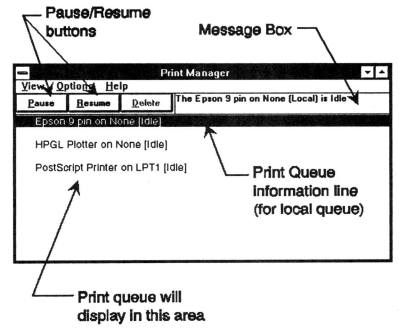

Pause/Resume buttons

Message Box

Print Queue information line (for local queue)

Print queue will display in this area

The Print Manager window

Changing the Order of the Jobs in the Print Queue

If a local file has not started printing, you can change it's position in the print queue. All you have to do is select the file that you want to move, and drag it to a new position in line. From the keyboard, you can select the file, press and hold [Ctrl] and press [↑] or [↓] to move the file to a new place. When the file is where you want it to be, release the [Ctrl] key.

■ Note   You cannot change the position of a file in a network queue.

Pausing and Resuming Printing

Below the menu bar in the Print Manager window, you will find three buttons. These buttons are marked Pause, Resume, and Delete, and they do exactly what you expect them to do.

If you need to stop the printer for any reason, press the Pause button, or from the keyboard, press Alt+P. When you look at the information line, you will see a message that indicates that the printer is paused.

To resume printing, press the Resume button, or from the keyboard, press Alt+R.

■ **Note** You may (or may not) be able to interrupt a network queue. Some networks will let you pause an individual print file but it will depend on the specific features that your network supports. Check with your network administrator for more information.

Deleting a Job from the Print Queue

If a job has not started printing, you can select it and press the Delete button (or press Alt+D on the keyboard). A dialog box will appear. Press OK (to confirm) and the selected job will be removed from the print queue.

On occasion, you will need to delete a job that has already starting printing. Before an active print job can be deleted, you must press the Pause button to stop the printer. After you press Pause, press the Delete button, and the job will terminate.

■ **Note** If you cancel a print job that includes graphics or special fonts, it might be necessary to reset your printer before starting the next print job.

Changing the Print Speed Print Manager performs its job as a background operation. In other words, additional operations can take place at the same time in the foreground. You can control how much time Windows spends on the foreground task and how much time is spent on Print Manager by changing the *priority*. In general, if Print Manager has higher priority, the foreground jobs will run slower.

To increase the printing speed (and slow the foreground tasks) open the Options menu (as shown in Figure 19.6) and select High Priority. This setting will give more of your processor's time to Print Manager and less to the foreground tasks.

If you choose Medium Priority from the Options menu, then Windows will split the time as equally as possible between Print

Manager and the other active tasks. Medium Priority is Print Manager's default setting.

Figure 19.6

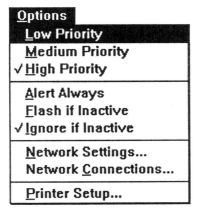

The Print Manager Options menu

Finally, if you need your computer to give most of its attention to the foreground tasks, then open the Options menu and select Low Priority.

Displaying Print Manager Messages

The Options menu also contains three options for controlling the way that Print Manager communicates with you any time it needs to display a message.

The first option, Alert Always, will cause Print Manager to immediately display a message box anytime anything happens that needs your attention. You can then open (or activate) the Print Manager window and take any necessary action.

If you choose Flash If Inactive, Print Manager will beep once and flash the Print Manager icon anytime it needs your attention. If the Print Manager window is open but not active, its title bar will flash. Flash If Inactive is the default setting.

The third choice, Ignore If Inactive, will not pay any attention to the problem condition if Print Manager window is not active or if it is displayed as an icon.

■ **Note**   The message control options *do not* affect the display of system messages such as "printer off-line" or "out of paper."

In any case, the display option that you choose will remain in effect unless you open the Options menu and change it.

Displaying Time, Date, and File Size

When Print Manager receives a file for processing, by default it will display the time and date that the file was received and the file's size. If you do not need to see this information, open the View menu and turn off one (or both) of the options.

If a check mark appears next to the command (as it is listed on the menu) then the option is active. To deactivate either option, open the View menu and choose the option again (see Figure 19.7).

Figure 19.7

<u>V</u>iew   <u>O</u>ptions   <u>H</u>elp
√ <u>T</u>ime/Date Sent
√ <u>P</u>rint File Size
<u>R</u>efresh
<u>S</u>elected Net Queue...
<u>O</u>ther Net Queue...
E<u>x</u>it

The Print Manager View Menu

Printing Without Print Manager

Most of the time you will want to let Print Manager take care of printing tasks in the background, out of your way. However, on occasion, you may want to print directly to a local printer or to a network. If you print without Print Manager, your computer will be completely tied up by the printing task. You will not be able to use your computer until after the print job is finished.

To print without Print Manager, open Control Panel and double-click on Printers icon. When the Printers dialog box appears, clear the Use Print Manager box as shown in Figure 19.8.

Figure 19.8

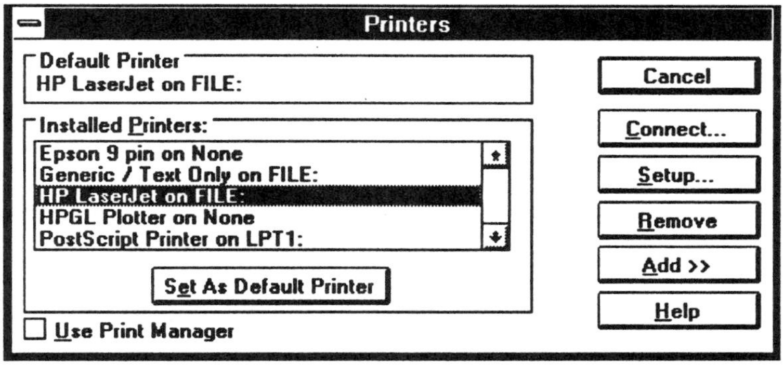

```
┌─────────────────────────────────────────────────────────┐
│ ▄                         Printers                        │
│ ┌─Default Printer──────────────────────┐  ┌───────────┐  │
│ │ HP LaserJet on FILE:                 │  │  Cancel   │  │
│ │                                      │  └───────────┘  │
│ ┌─Installed Printers:──────────────────┐  ┌───────────┐  │
│ │ Epson 9 pin on None              [▲] │  │ Connect...│  │
│ │ Generic / Text Only on FILE:         │  └───────────┘  │
│ │ HP LaserJet on FILE:                 │  ┌───────────┐  │
│ │ HPGL Plotter on None                 │  │  Setup... │  │
│ │ PostScript Printer on LPT1:      [▼] │  └───────────┘  │
│ │                                      │  ┌───────────┐  │
│ │       ┌──────────────────────┐       │  │  Remove   │  │
│ │       │ Set As Default Printer│       │  └───────────┘  │
│ │       └──────────────────────┘       │  ┌───────────┐  │
│ │  □ Use Print Manager                 │  │  Add >>   │  │
│ └──────────────────────────────────────┘  └───────────┘  │
│                                            ┌───────────┐  │
│                                            │   Help    │  │
│                                            └───────────┘  │
└─────────────────────────────────────────────────────────┘
```

Printing without Print Manager

▲ **Hint**   In general, your print jobs will run faster without Print Manager. If you are using a network printer, your print jobs may or may not speed up. Check with your network administrator for more information. ▲

Trouble in Paradise

Print Manager is very easy to use and, as you have seen, its operation is almost completely automatic. However, there is always a dark side. It doesn't matter how much you wave your magic wand, minor problems can (and will) occur.

If a problem does occur, before you do anything else, open Print Manager window and see if there are any messages there that could help. If the printer was working and suddenly stops, the difficulty is probably a loose cable, or other bad connection. If you are trying to print using a new system for the first time, start by checking the documentation that came with your printer, or (if possible) contact the technical support people where you bought your equipment. Most important, don't give up.

No Printing at All   If your printer will not print at all, use the following checklists to help locate the problem:

_____   Is the Printer plugged in and the power switch turned on?

_____   Check the indicator switches on the printer's front panel. Is the printer on-line?

_____ Check the printer's connection cable. Is it snug on both ends?

_____ Check the printer physically. Is it loaded with paper? Is the ribbon seated properly? If you have a laser printer, does it have enough toner?

If your printer still will not print, open the Main Group and double-click on the Printers icon and continue.

_____ Is the correct printer selected, and is it selected as the default printer?

_____ Check the radio buttons in the status box. Is the selected printer set to ACTIVE?

_____ Press the Configure button in the printer dialog box. Is the correct port selected?

_____ Press the Setup button. Is the correct paper size and paper feed selected?

If you still can't print, save your work, and exit the current application.

_____ Open the File Manager and try to print a text file such as WIN.INI or SYSTEM.INI. Does the printer respond?

Finally, leave Windows and return to the DOS prompt.

_____ At the DOS C: prompt, type the following command: DIR>PRN
[Enter ←]

Does the printer print now? If yes, run through the above checklist again.

_____ If it still does not work, check all the connections one more time and try the DIR>PRN command again. Does it print now?

If your printer still does not work, contact the printer manufacturer or your dealer.

Printer Advances Paper but Does Not Print

If your printer feeds one (or more) pieces of paper through your printer but does not print, open Control Panel and double-click on the Printers icon, then use the following checklist:

_____ Check the Installed Printers box. Is the correct printer driver installed and selected as the default printer? (You may need to contact Microsoft or your printer manufacturer to obtain the correct driver for your printer).

_____ Press the Setup button in the printer dialog box. Are the correct paper size and type selected?

_____ Does the printer have a good ribbon and is it installed correctly?

_____ If you are using a laser printer, check the front panel. Is the printer set up to match the selections in the Installed Printers box? (You may need to consult the laser printer's documentation to find out.)

_____ If you are printing to a network printer, contact the network administrator. Ask if anything has been changed or if something is wrong with the network.

Incorrect Format

If your data prints but the document contains extra lines, is paginated wrong, has incorrect margins, or any other formatting problem, use this checklist:

_____ Check the Installed Printers box. Is the correct printer driver installed and selected as the default printer? (You may need to contact Microsoft, the software manufacturer, or even your printer manufacturer to obtain the correct driver for your printer.)

_____ Press the Setup button in the Printer dialog box. Are the correct paper size and type selected?

_____ Check the printer manual. Does your printer have any switches that control the page size or line length?

_____ Make sure that your printer is not sending an extra line feed at the end of each line. Most software will advance to the next line correctly without additional help from the printer. Does your printer have any switches that cause your printer to send an automatic line feed at the end of each line?

_____ In your document, make sure that the font and other formatting selections are correct. Have you chosen a font that is too large to print, or tried to put too many lines on a page?

Output is Garbage

If the printer works but prints garbage, use this checklist:

_____ Check the Installed Printers box. Is the correct printer driver installed and selected as the default printer? (You may need to contact Microsoft, the software manufacturer, or even your printer manufacturer to obtain the correct driver for your printer.)

_____ Press the Setup button in the Printer dialog box. Are the correct paper size and type selected?

_____ Check the printer's connection cable. Is it snug on both ends?

_____ If you are printing to a network printer, contact the network administrator. Ask if anything has been changed or if something is wrong with the network.

_____ If you are using a laser printer, check the front panel. Is the printer set up to match the selections in the Installed Printers box? (You may need to consult the laser printer's documentation to find out.)

_____ If you are using a laser printer, are the correct font cartridges loaded and selected? (Also, make sure that the cartridges are pushed all the way in.)

_____ If you are using a serial printer, check the baud rate that is selected in the Ports-Settings dialog box. Is it set too high or too low? (Often, a lower baud rate will solve the problem.)

_____ Has your printer retained some artifacts from a previous print job? (Try resetting your printer or clearing it's memory.)

_____ Many printers can emulate another brand of printer. For example, many dot-matrix printers can pretend to be an Epson or IBM printer. Is there another printer driver that is compatible with your printer?

If your printer still does not work correctly, try using the first checklist as if your printer was not printing at all.

Output from Two Jobs Mixed

If you are running in real or standard mode and instruct a Windows application and a DOS application to print at the same time, you could get some interesting results. Print Manager only handles print tasks from Windows applications. If a DOS application tries to print, it will be sent to the printer without Window's permission.

_____ Do you have a Windows application and a DOS application assigned to the same port? Are both applications trying to print?

_____ Are two DOS applications assigned to the same port and trying to print?

If you are running in enhanced mode, Windows will display a message warning you of a device contention problem.

Laser Printer Does Not Use the Correct Fonts

If your laser printer has font cartridges or uses soft fonts but the output is not in the form that you expect, try checking the following items:

_____ Check the Installed Printers box. Is the correct printer driver installed and selected as the default printer? (You may need to contact Microsoft, the software manufacturer, or even your printer manufacturer to obtain the correct driver for your printer.)

_____ Check the printer's connection cable. Is it snug on both ends?

_____ If you are printing to a network printer, contact the network administrator. Ask if anything has changed, or if something is wrong with the network.

_____ Check the front panel on your printer. Is the printer set up to match the selections in the Installed Printers box? (You may need to consult the laser printer's documentation to find out.)

_____ Are the correct font cartridges loaded and selected? (Also, make sure that the cartridges are pushed all the way in.)

_____ In your document, make sure that the font selections are correct. For example, if you are using Write, you cannot use more than twelve different fonts in a single document. Have you chosen a font that is too large, or have you used more fonts than the application will allow?

_____ If you are using soft fonts, check the documentation that comes with them. Are the soft fonts installed correctly?

_____ If you are using fonts that need to be downloaded and your printer has been reset or turned off, the fonts will be lost. Do you need to download the soft fonts again?

_____ Downloaded soft fonts need to live in your printer's memory. If you try to load too many fonts, there may not be enough room for them. Has your laser printer run out of memory? (Try installing fewer fonts or installing them as temporary fonts.)

Only Part of Page Prints

If the printer only prints part of your document, use this checklist:

_____ Check the Installed Printers box. Is the correct printer driver installed and selected as the default printer? (You may need to contact Microsoft or your printer manufacturer to obtain the correct driver for your printer.)

_____ Press the Setup button in the Printer dialog box. Are the correct paper size and type selected?

_____ If you are using a laser printer, you may have run out of memory. This will often occur when you are printing graphics or a page with several different large fonts. Try printing your graphics at a lower resolution, or using fewer fonts. Does your laser printer have enough memory?

Exiting Print Manager

If Print Manager is running as an icon, it will automatically close and release all the memory it was using as soon as all of your print jobs are finished. You don't have to do anything.

If the Print Manager window is open, it must be closed manually. As with all Windows applications, you can always double-click the control button in the upper left corner of the title bar. You can also open the Options menu and choose Exit from the menu.

Figure 19.9

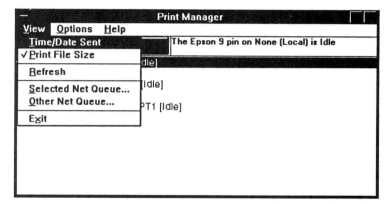

The Print Manager File menu showing the Exit command

Summary Points

1. Data from Windows applications is printed through an application called Print Manager.

2. To use Print Manager, open the Print menu from any Windows application and select Print.

3. When you are printing from a DOS application that is running under Windows, Print Manager is not used.

4. Print Manager is actually only a print queue. A print queue is simply a list that indicates which file is currently printing and which files are waiting to be printed.

5. When Print Manager starts a job, Print Manager icon will appear on the desktop at the bottom of your screen.

6. To change the order of the files in the Print queue, open the Print Manager window and drag the files to a new location in the list.

7. When Print Manager window is open, you can cause the current job to pause (or Resume) as necessary by pressing the appropriate button. When a job is paused, it can be deleted if you press the Delete button.

8. If a job has not started printing, it can be deleted if you select it and press the Delete button. You can also delete a job if you press ⎇+D from the keyboard.

9. You can change the speed of background print operations if you change the priority. High priority prints fastest, and the foreground operations run slowest. Low priority prints slowest, but the foreground operations run fastest.

10. You can control the display of Print Manager messages if you open the Options menu and select (or deselect) Alert Always, Flash If Inactive, or Ignore If Inactive. These choices do not affect the display of System messages.

11. If a printing problem does occur, don't give up. First check the printer's documentation. Next, follow the necessary checklist and track the problem down. If necessary, contact your printer manufacturer or dealer.

12. Normally, when all print jobs are finished, Print Manager will terminate automatically. If the Print Manager window is open, double-click the Control button or open the Options menu and select Exit.

Practice Exercises

Perform the following exercises at your computer:

1. Open the Write word processor and load the file named PRINTERS.WRI. Open the Print menu and send it to Print Manager. This file contains additional information about printers and Windows. (You may want to keep it with your Windows documentation for future reference.)

2. For additional practice (and documentation), you may also want to print the following files:

    README.WRI   SYSINI.WRI

    WININI.WRI   NETWORKS.WRI

■ **Note** Some of these files are rather long. You may want to check with your instructor before you print any of these files.

Comprehension Questions

1. Describe the main function of Print Manager.

2. What do you need to do to use Print Manager when printing from a Windows application?

3. What do you need to do to use Print manager to print directly from a DOS application?

4. List at least two reasons to print your data to a file.

5. What is a print queue?

6. List the steps to examine the print jobs that are loaded into Print Manager.

7. Actually, there are two types of print queues. What are they?

8. What do you need to do to change the order of the jobs that have not started printing?

9. How do you pause a print job that is already processing?

10. List the steps needed to delete a print job that has already started printing.

11. If you open the Options menu and choose Alert Always, how is the display of Print Manager messages affected? How is the display of system messages affected?

12. When you are troubleshooting a printer problem, at what point are you supposed to give up?

13. When Print Manager is finished, what do you need to do to close Print Manager application? (Assume Print Manager is displayed as an icon on your desktop.)

Completion Questions

1. Print Manager performs its job as a _____ operation.

2. When you choose High Priority from the Options menu, the _____ runs faster and the _____ runs slower.

3. When you choose Low Priority from the Options menu, the _____ runs faster and the _____ runs slower.

4. When Print Manager is displayed as a window, open the _____ menu and select _____ to close Print Manager window.

20

Installing a Printer in Windows

Learning Objectives

1. Define printer driver.

2. Define default printer.

3. List the information needed to install a printer in Windows.

Performance Objectives

1. Install a printer using the Windows Setup program.

2. Install a printer from Windows Control Panel.

3. Set the basic configuration options for an installed printer.

4. Remove an installed printer.

**Default
Printer**

If you do not tell Windows which printer to use, it will use the Default Printer.

**Graphics
Resolution**

In general, the higher the resolution of a graphic, the higher the print quality. High resolution printing can take much more time than low resolution.

**Landscape
Orientation**

Landscape Orientation means that the paper in the printer is wider than it is tall. In other words, the text is printed sideways on the page.

**Portrait
Orientation**

Portrait Orientation means that the paper in the printer is taller than it is wide. When you think of Portrait Orientation, think of how a portrait of a person would appear on a piece of paper.

Printer Driver

The Printer Driver is a special file that contains the information that Windows needs so that it can use your printer correctly. The Printer Driver includes important details about your printer's features, fonts, and any special commands (called control sequences) that Windows may need.

Chapter Overview

Before you use Print Manager, you need to provide Windows with a little bit of information about your printer. This information is supplied by a file called a printer driver. It provides important details about your printer's features, fonts, and any special commands (called control sequences) that Windows may need to use your printer.

Windows comes with many printer drivers, and chances are good that your printer is included. To install your printer, choose your printer from the list, make a couple of default selections, and you are ready to go.

■ **Note**

If you cannot find a driver for your printer in Windows, check with the printer manufacturer or your dealer. Also, many software packages include special drivers as part of the package.

Getting Started

Before you begin to install your printer, you should complete the following checklist:

_____ Printer manufacturer and model number

_____ Printer port being used (LPT1, LPT2, or other)

_____ Paper source (tractor feed, sheet feed, letter tray, etc.)

_____ Paper size and format

_____ How much memory is installed in printer

_____ Printer cartridges available (if any)

_____ Desired graphics resolution

Installing a Printer Driver from Control Panel

Use this procedure to add a printer driver to Windows.

What to Do   **What Happens**

1. Open the Main Group and   The Printers dialog box
launch Control Panel. When   will appear as shown in
Control Panel opens,   Figure 20.1.
double-click on the Printers
icon.

Figure 20.1

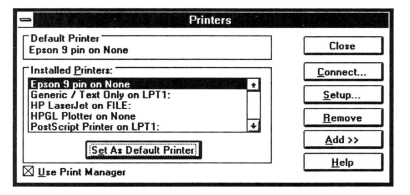

2. Press the Add >> button.   The Printers dialog box will change as shown in Figure 20.2.

Figure 20.2

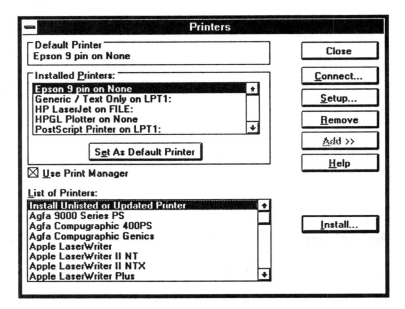

3. Select (highlight) the name of the printer that you want to install from the displayed list, and press the Install button.   A dialog box will appear similar to the one shown in Figure 20.3.

Figure 20.3

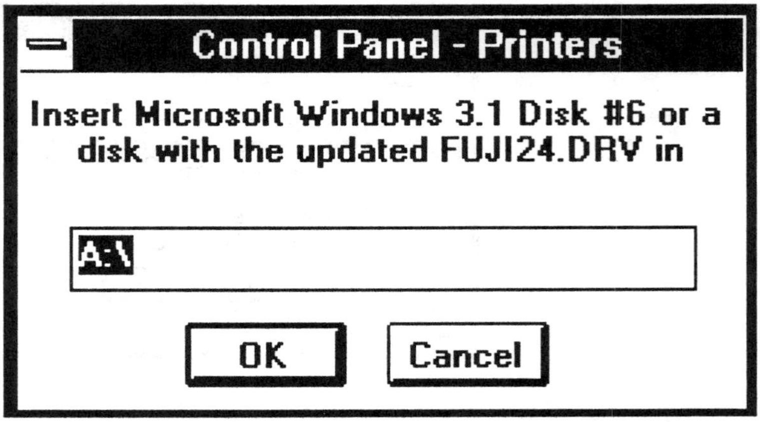

4.	Put the requested disk into drive A: and press the OK button.	Windows will read the printer driver from the disk and add the printer to the Installed Printers list.
5.	Press the Connect button and select a printer port. Press the OK button when you are finished.	The printer driver is now ready.
6.	In the Status box, select the Active radio button and press the OK button to close the Printers dialog box.	The dialog box will close.

Selecting a Printer Port

Use this procedure to assign an output port to your printer.

	What to Do	**What Happens**
1.	Open the Main group and launch Control Panel. When Control Panel opens, double-click on the Printers icon.	The Printers dialog box will appear.
2.	Look at the Installed Printers list and select (single-click) name of the printer that is to be assigned to a port.	The name of the selected printer will be highlighted.
3.	Press the Connect button and a dialog box will appear.	See Figure 20.4.

Figure 20.4

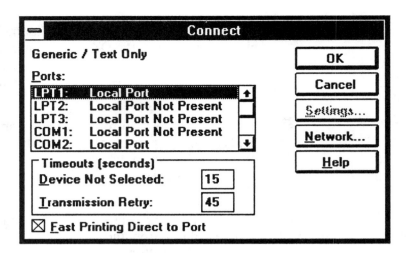

4. This box will list the ports that are available. LPT ports are used with parallel printers and COM ports are for serial printers. EPT is a special port used with some printers such as the IBM Personal Pageprinter and it requires a special interface card. The File port is used to transfer the output from your application to a disk file.

Select the correct port for your system. (If necessary, check the documentation for your printer.)

The selected port will be highlighted.

5. Press OK. The selected port will appear in the Installed Printers box next to the name of your printer.

The printer port is now assigned.

Choosing the Default Printer

When Print Manager prints, it sends its data to the printer that is selected as the default printer. If the wrong printer is selected, Print Manager can't do it's job. Use the following procedure to choose the correct printer:

What to Do	**What Happens**

1. Open the Main group and launch Control Panel. When Control Panel opens, double-click on the Printers icon.

The Printers dialog box will appear.

2. Look at the Installed Printers list and press the button marked Set as Default Printer.

The printer's name will be displayed in the Default Printer box.

■ **Note** You may also select the default printer with a double-click.

3. Choose OK to return to Control Panel.

The default printer is now selected (see Figure 20.5).

Figure 20.5

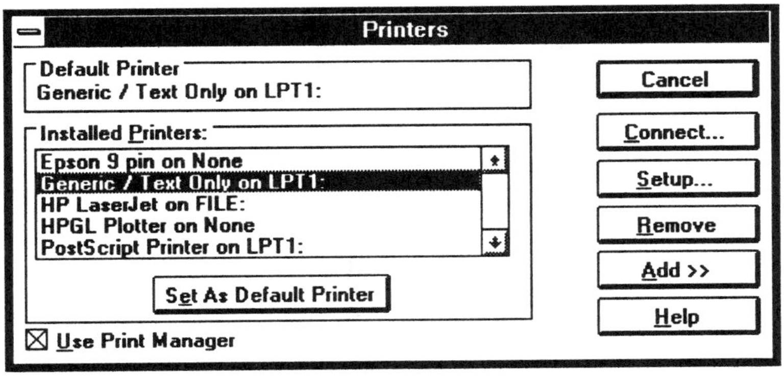

Setting the Configuration of Your Printer

We are almost finished. At this point you need to provide Windows with very specific information about your printer. Different kinds (or brands) of printers can use the same printer-driver file, so it is necessary to tell Windows exactly which printer you will be using and how it is set up.

■ Note Actually, Windows can probably use your printer correctly at this point. Unless you are using your printer in a special way, you usually don't need to change any of these settings.

Setting the Print Options

What to Do	What Happens
1. Once again, open the Main Group and launch Control Panel. When Control Panel opens, double-click on the Printers icon.	The Printers dialog box will appear.
2. Look at the Installed Printers list and select (single-click) the name of the printer that you are installing.	The name of the selected printer will be highlighted.
3. Press the Setup button.	A box will appear similar to the one in Figure 20.6.

Figure 20.6

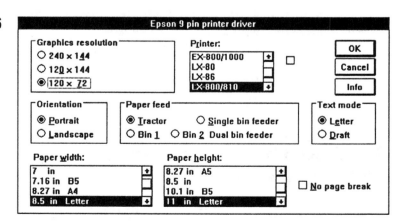

4. Change, as necessary, any (or all) of the options in the box. Most of the options are explained in the section that follows. Press OK when you are done and proceed to the next section.

When you are finished, most of the important settings will be correct.

■ **Note** Different printers will have different Configure boxes.

Use This Option

To Do This

1. Printer

This selection allows you to choose the specific printer attached to your system. As mentioned earlier, different types (or brands) of printers may use the same printer driver. If the name of your printer is not displayed in the selection box, press the arrow to the right of the box to display the full list. Use the scroll arrows until you find the correct name and select it.

2. Paper Source (or Feed)

Many printers will let you feed paper into them from more than one source. For example, your dot-matrix printer may let you use continuous paper (tractor feed) or single sheets (sheet feed). Use this option to tell Windows which paper source is being used. To see the available choices, press the arrow to the right of the box, and make your selection.

3. Paper Size (Paper Format)

Use these boxes to tell Windows what size paper you intend to use. Select the correct size and continue.

4. Memory

In this box, you can tell Windows how much memory your printer contains. This information can usually be found in your printer manual. If necessary, contact your dealer or the printer manufacturer. If you can't find this information, use the default setting.

5. Orientation

Portrait orientation means that the paper is taller than it is wide. (Think of how a portrait of a person would appear.) Landscape orientation means that the paper is wider than it is tall. (In other words, the text is printed sideways on the page.)

6. Graphics Resolution

Many printers will allow you to print your graphics at several resolutions. In general, the higher the resolution, the higher the print quality, but you don't get something for nothing. High resolution printing can take much longer to print than low resolution. If you are using a dot-matrix printer, low-resolution printing will make your printer ribbons last longer.

7. Cartridges

If your printer can use add-on print cartridges, use this box to select which ones (if any) are available. The choices listed here will vary according to the printer that is selected.

Selecting the Timeout Options

Timeout options are used to control the length of time that Windows will wait before it reports a printer problem. If you cannot locate a Timeout setting, it means that is not necessary to set Timeout for your printer.

Figure 20.7

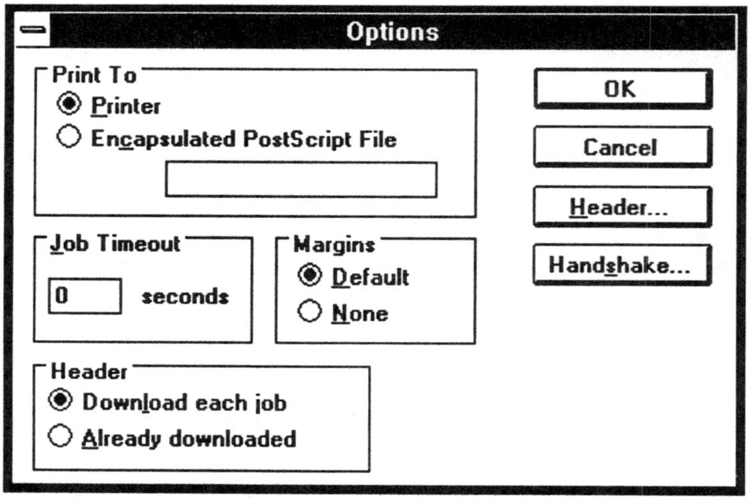

A typical Options box for a PostScript Printer

Some PostScript printers will need some extra time. This is especially true of PostScript printers that are using PostScript on a plug-in cartridge.

To change the Timeout options, open Control Panel, choose Printers and press the Configure button. Select your printer and press Setup. When the next dialog box appears, press Options and enter a value into the Job Timeout box (see Figure 20.7).

■ **Note**   The default settings for the Timeout options should work with most printers. This is another case of "if it ain't broke, don't fix it." Unless you are having trouble printing, you should leave these options alone.

Removing an Installed Printer

If you change printers or have selected the wrong printer accidently, you may want to "clean up" the list of installed printers by removing one or more of the printer definitions.

The following procedure explains how to delete a printer from the list:

What to Do	**What Happens**

1. Open the Main Group and launch Control Panel. When Control Panel opens, double-click on the Printers icon.

The Printers dialog box will appear.

2. Look at the Installed Printers list and select (single-click) name of the printer that you want to delete.

The name of the selected printer will highlight.

3. Press Remove button.

See Figure 20.8.

Figure 20.8

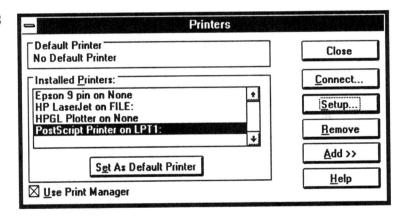

4. Press OK.

The printer will be removed from the list (see Figure 20.9).

Figure 20.9

Summary Points

1. Before you use Print Manager, you need to provide Windows with specific information about your printer. You should probably make a list of information about your printer and any options that you want to select before you begin.

2. To add a printer driver to Windows, open Control Panel, double-click on the Printers icon and press the Add Printers button.

3. Before you can print, you must select a printer port. To select a printer port, open Control Panel, double-click on the Printers icon, select the correct printer from the list, press Configure, and select a port from the list.

4. If you install more than one printer, you must tell Windows which printer to use. When using Windows, more than one printer can be installed but only one printer can be active at any one time.

5. To activate a printer, press the radio button marked Active in the Printer dialog box.

6. When Print Manager prints, it sends it's data to the default printer. To select a default printer, double-click on the name of the correct printer in the list of installed printers. You can also select the printer (with a single-click) and press ⌘+D.

7. Before a printer can be selected as the default, it must be the active printer.

8. To set the print options, open Control Panel, double-click the Printers icon, select (from the list) the printer to be configured, press the Configure button, and select Setup. Make any necessary changes and press OK when you are finished.

9. Timeout options should only be changed if there is a problem printing.

10. To remove a printer from the list of installed printers, open Control Panel, double-click on the Printers icon, select the printer to be removed, press the Configure button, and select Remove. When the dialog box appears, press OK, and the name of the printer will disappear from the list.

It is a good idea to have a printer driver installed for the generic printer. The generic printer driver can be used to "print" a file to disk. A file that is printed to disk can be easily transferred to other applications, sent over a modem, or printed later on a different computer or printer.

To install the generic driver, follow this procedure:

1. Open Control Panel and double-click on the Printers icon.

2. Press the Add Printers button.

3. When the list of printers appears at the bottom of the screen, scroll through the list until you find the Generic/Text Only printer.

4. Press the Install button.

5. Windows will ask you to insert one of the numbered disks from the set of original Windows disks into a floppy disk drive. Insert the requested disk and press OK.

6. When the system finishes reading the driver information, press the Configure button.

7. Scroll through the Ports box, select File: as the port for the generic printer, and press the OK button.

8. If you want to use the generic printer driver now, press the Active radio button and press OK to finish. If you don't need the generic driver until later, just press OK. The new printer driver will remain on file until you need it.

Comprehension Questions

1. What is a printer driver?

2. Before you install a printer, you should know several things about it. List these important items of information.

3. Where is the Printers icon normally found?

4. How many printers can be active at the same time?

5. List the steps needed to activate a selected printer.

6. When you are specifying printer options, what is the difference between Portrait orientation and Landscape orientation?

7. Under what conditions should the Timeout options be changed?

8. List the steps to remove a printer from the list of installed printers.

Completion Questions

1. When you are installing a parallel printer, you should choose one of the _____ ports from the Port Selection list.

2. To install a serial printer, you choose one of the _____ ports from the list.

3. To transfer the output from your application to a disk, you should select the _____ port.

4. When High Resolution is selected, the graphics quality will be _____ and the printer will take _____ time to finish.

5. When Low Resolution is selected, the graphics quality will be _____ and the printer will take _____ time to finish.

6. Before a printer can be selected as the default, it must be _____.

21

Fonts and Printers

Learning Objectives

1. Define font and typeface.

2. Identify serif and sans-serif fonts.

3. Explain the difference between a raster font and a vector font.

4. Define True-Type fonts.

5. Identify a True-Type font.

Performance Objectives

1. Select a font style (typeface) and appropriate type size.

2. Add a font to Windows.

3. Delete a font from Windows.

Chapter Terms

Decorative Typeface Decorative Typefaces are sometimes called display typefaces and are usually used only for special emphasis. For example, you may choose to use a large, decorative type as an introduction to a paragraph, or as a headline at the top of a newsletter.

Font The mechanism that is used to transfer the details of a typeface to the finished page is called a Font.

Point There are almost, but not quite exactly, 72 points in an inch. In other words, 72-point lettering would be about 1 inch tall. Standard type is usually about 12 points tall.

Raster Font Raster Fonts are also called Screen Fonts. See the definition for Screen Fonts below.

Sans Serif If a typeface does not have serifs, it is referred to as *sans serif* type. *Sans serif* means without serifs.

Scalable Font If a font is Scalable, that means that it can be displayed (and printed) in almost any point size. When you specify a scalable font, you must also specify its size.

Screen Font Screen Fonts are little graphic pictures (bit maps) of each letter in a fixed size. Screen fonts are used mostly to display information on your display screen but they are also used by some dot-matrix printers and are built into some laser printers. Screen fonts cannot be scaled.

Serif A serif is a little flag or counter stroke that is added to the tops and bottoms each letter stroke. Serifs are not merely decorations, but are functional design elements that make a block of text easier to read.

Text Font Most of the text that you read is set in a text fonts because they tend to be highly readable when set as a passage of running text. Typically, text fonts have serifs but their basic design tends to stay rather simple.

True-Type Font True-Type fonts eliminate the need to have both screen fonts and vector fonts. In other words, a True Type font is used on both the screen and the printer. In a list of fonts, True Type fonts will be preceded by a special symbol to help you identify them.

Typeface	A Typeface is a design or pattern that is applied to all of the letters, numbers, and characters of the alphabet. Typefaces have names to identify them — such as Times Roman, Helvetica, or Bookman — and are used to create a harmonious appearance within a block of text.
Vector Font	Vector fonts are scalable fonts and can be printed (and displayed) in almost any point size. When you specify a Vector Font, you must also specify its size.

Chapter Overview

When you install Windows, the Setup program copies information to your hard disk which can be used to control the appearance of the text on your screen (and printer). This information, called typefaces (and fonts), can be used to create a mood that is business-like or silly, serious or even amusing. There is magic in words. What you say is important, but how you say it can have even greater impact.

What is a Font?

A typeface is a design or pattern that is applied to all of the letters, numbers, and characters of the alphabet. Typefaces have names to identify them — such as Times Roman, Helvetica, or Bookman — and are used to create a harmonious appearance within a block of text. The mechanism that is used to transfer the details of each letter to the finished page is called a font.

In the early days of printing, each letter was cast into a small metal block. A typesetter would select the necessary letters, arrange them in rows and columns, cover them with ink and press them against a piece of paper. When a printer needed a font, it would be necessary to make (or purchase) a collection of little letters, all cast in the same typeface.

Figure 21.1

This is Times Roman in 12 point.

This is Times Roman in 16 point.

This is Times Roman in 22 point.

A single typeface in several point sizes

In other words, a typeface is a collection of letters that have a specific design applied to their appearance, and a font is a set of instructions a system uses to produce that typeface in various sizes.

■ Note   In the old days of typesetting, the cast letters were stored in trays or drawers that would help the printer to quickly locate the letters that were needed. There would often be two trays, one stacked on top of the other. The capital letters and punctuation would be stored in the case on top (the upper-case) and the small letters and numbers would be stored on the bottom (or lower-case).

Fonts and   Fonts are sized with a unique set of measurements called points,
Font Sizes   and are measured from the top of the tallest upper-case letter to the bottom of the lowest descender — plus a little bit. The extra little bit is added so that letters will not touch each other from one line to the next. When you choose a font, in addition to the typeface, you must also specify a point size.

There are almost, but not quite exactly, 72 points in an inch. In other words, 72-point lettering would be about 1 inch tall. Standard type is usually about 12 points tall. With these sizes in mind, you should have very little trouble choosing the correct size type for your applications.

▲ Hint   Rule of thumb: "If it looks OK, and fits in the space allowed, then it is OK." ▲

As we have already discussed, a typeface is a general design applied to all the letters, numbers, and other characters in the alphabet. The actual appearance of each letter can be modified by changing the thickness of the strokes in the letters, the width of each character, and adding (or omitting) decorations.

One of the decorations that may be added to letters are referred to as *serifs*. A serif is a little flag or counter stroke that is added to the tops and bottoms each letter stroke. Actually, serifs are not merely decorations, but are functional design elements that make a block of text easier to read.

If a typeface does not have serifs, it is referred to as *sans serif* type. Typefaces in this group have a very clean and modern appearance. Usually, sans-serif typefaces are constructed with uniform line thicknesses. Because sans-serif type tends to have a very uniform appearance, proofreading can be difficult. You should probably avoid using sans serif type faces for long blocks of text.

■ **Note**   *Sans serif* means without serifs.

Another way to classify typefaces is by use. From this viewpoint, typefaces can be divided into two very general groups: text faces and decorative faces (see Figure 21.2).

Figure 21.2   This is an example of a typical text font.

This is an example of a decorative font.

An example of a text font compared to a decorative font

Most of the text that you read is set in a text face because they tend to be highly readable when set as a passage of running text. Typically, text faces have serifs but their basic design tends to stay rather simple.

Decorative typefaces (sometimes called display typefaces) are usually used only for special emphasis. For example, you may choose to use a large, decorative type as an introduction to a paragraph, or as a headline at the top of a newsletter. Decorative typefaces tend to be difficult to read when arranged in continuous blocks of text.

▲ **Hint**   In general, you should stick to the conservative (or text) faces. Conservative typefaces encourage the reader to take the content more seriously. ▲

Where Do Fonts Come From?   An artist designs a typeface by specifying the curves and lines of each letter. Typefaces have been designed in this way for more than five hundred years (ever since Gutenberg), but as you can see, the technology used to transfer the shapes of the letters to the finished page has changed a great deal.

■ **Note**   Actually, when you obtain a letter design, you purchase a font, not a typeface. The design of the typeface remains the property of the designer.

It is no longer necessary to create little cast letters for each different typeface and font size. In Windows, fonts are stored electronically on your disk drives in the form of instructions used by your printer (or other display device) to create the finished letter designs. Before you can use any of these fonts, they must be installed.

When you run the Windows Setup program, you can automatically install the fonts that are shipped in the Windows package. If you want to add additional fonts later, they must be installed manually.

Screen Fonts and Vector Fonts

The Windows package comes with two types of fonts: screen (or raster) fonts and vector (or stroke) fonts. In general, screen fonts are little graphic pictures (bit maps) of each letter in a fixed size. Screen fonts (as their name implies) are used mostly to display information on your display screen but they are also used by some dot-matrix printers and are built into some laser printers. Screen fonts cannot be scaled. When you look at a list of available fonts, screen fonts will display a series of point sizes next to the name of each typeface. This list shows the sizes available for each particular font. If the typeface does not have a list of sizes next to its name, then the font is probably a vector font.

Vector fonts are scalable fonts. If you choose a vector font it can be printed (and displayed) in almost any point size (within practical limits, of course). That means when you specify a vector font, you must also specify its size.

■ Note

If you select a vector font and Windows does not have (or cannot display) a matching screen font, Windows will select a font that matches as closely as possible. In any case, the formatting on the screen (lines per page, length of lines, etc.) will be the same as the formatting on the printer.

True Type Fonts

Windows version 3.1 adds a third type of font. At first, you may think that a third type of font will just make things more complicated, but actually this new type of font makes things easier. The new font is called True Type and it eliminates the need to have both screen fonts and vector fonts. In other words, a True Type font is used on both the screen and the printer.

A True Type font is used in the same way that you use a vector font (that is, you select the font and choose a point size). The font that you choose will display on your screen the same as it will print on your printer. In a list of fonts, True Type fonts will be preceded by a special symbol to help you identify them.

Selecting a Font While in an Application

As you know, one of the major advantages of using Windows is its consistency from one application to another. Once you know how to perform an operation in one application, then you know how to perform the same application in almost all Windows applications. For example, if you know how to select a font in Windows Write, then you also know how to select a font in Paintbrush, and in most other Windows applications.

Selecting a Font

■ **Note**   The following example shows how to select a new font in the Windows Write application. Other applications may be slightly different.

What to Do	**What Happens**
1. Start by selecting the text that you want the font change to affect.	The selected text will be highlighted.
2. Open the Character menu and choose Fonts.	See Figure 21.3.

Figure 21.3

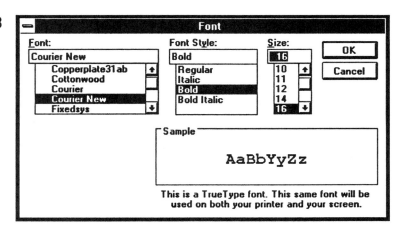

3.	Select the name of the font that you want to use. If necessary, also select the font style and point size.	The font you choose will be selected.
4.	Press OK.	The selected text will change to the font you choose.

Adding Fonts to Windows

When you install a Windows printer driver, the fonts that come with Windows (and can be used by your printer) are installed automatically. If you purchase additional fonts or want to add fonts supplied by the printer manufacturer, you can use Windows Control Panel to install them.

■ **Note**   Usually, fonts purchased from a third party manufacturer will come with their own installation program. In these cases, follow the manufacturer's instructions rather than using the Control Panel.

How to Add a Font	**What to Do**	**What Happens**
1.	Open the Main Group and launch Control Panel.	The Control Panel selections will appear (see Figure 21.4).

Figure 21.4

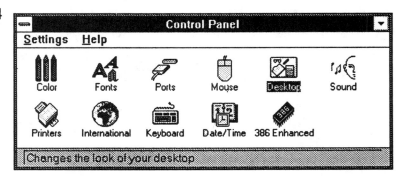

2. Launch the Fonts icon from Control Panel.

The Fonts dialog box will display as shown in Figure 21.5.

Figure 21.5

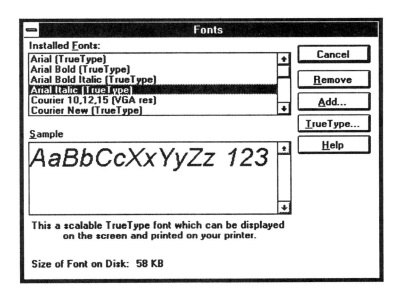

■ **Note**   Inside the Fonts dialog box you will see a list of fonts that have been already installed. A sample of the selected (highlighted) font will be displayed in the box marked Sample. If the selected font is a screen font, a sample of each available size will be displayed. If the selected font is a vector font, the only size that will display is the one that was used to design the font. (But remember, a vector font can be scaled to almost any size you need.)

3. Press the Add button.

Control Panel will display a text box as shown in Figure 21.6.

Figure 21.6

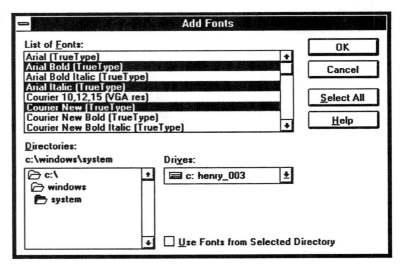

4. Select the fonts to be installed. If necessary, change the path and directory (in the Drives box) until the correct list of fonts is displayed.

The selected fonts will be highlighted.

5. When all fonts have been selected, press the OK button.

The selected fonts will be installed.

Removing Fonts from Windows

Every font that you install uses memory. If you don't use certain fonts, or if you just need additional memory for any reason, you can remove one (or more) of the fonts that are installed.

Removing Fonts from Windows

What to Do	**What Happens**
1. Open the Main Group and launch Control Panel.	The Control Panel selections will appear (see Figure 21.7).

Figure 21.7

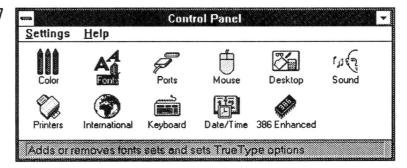

2. Launch the Fonts icon from Control Panel.	The Fonts dialog box will display.
3. Select (highlight) the fonts to be removed.	See Figure 21.8.

Figure 21.8

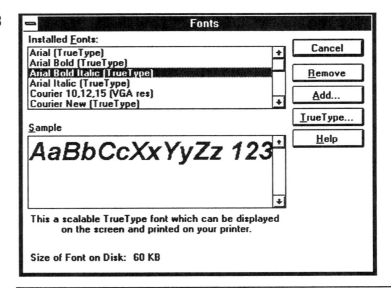

4. Press the Remove button. A dialog box will appear as shown in Figure 21.9.

Figure 21.9

5. Press OK to finish. The selected fonts will be removed.

Summary Points

1. When you install Windows, the Setup program copies information to your hard disk that can be used to control the appearance of the text on your screen (and printer).

2. A typeface is a design or pattern that is applied to all of the letters, numbers, and characters of the alphabet.

3. Fonts are measured in points, from the top of the tallest upper-case letter to the bottom of the lowest descender plus a little bit.

4. A serif is a little flag or counter stroke that is added to the tops and bottoms of each letter stroke.

5. If a typeface does not have serifs, it is referred to as *sans serif* type.

6. Typefaces can be divided into two very general groups: text faces and decorative faces.

7. The Windows package comes with three types of fonts: screen (or raster) fonts, vector (or stroke) fonts, and True Type fonts.

8. Screen fonts cannot be scaled. They are only available in the sizes that are displayed next to their names.

9. Vector fonts and True Type fonts are scalable fonts. If you choose a scalable font, it can be printed (and displayed) in almost any point size.

10. If you purchase additional fonts, or want to add fonts supplied by the printer manufacturer, you can use Windows Control Panel to install them.

11. If you don't use certain fonts, or if you just need additional memory for any reason, you can remove one (or more) of the fonts that are installed.

Comprehension Questions

1. How are fonts usually measured?

2. Why is a little extra space added to the size of a font?

3. What is the difference between a serif typeface and a sans serif typeface?

4. There are two very general groups of typefaces. What are they?

5. What is the difference between a screen font and a vector font?

6. If Windows does not have a screen font to match the vector font that is selected, what will happen?

7. Why is it sometimes necessary to add fonts to Windows?

8. If you purchase a third party font and it comes with its own Install program, what should you do to add that font to Windows?

9. Why would you want to remove a font from Windows?

10. In the Fonts dialog box, how can you tell a screen font from a vector font?

11. How can you identify a True Type font in the fonts dialog box?

Completion Questions

1. A _____ is a collection of letters that have a specific design applied to their appearance.

2. The mechanism that is used to transfer the details of each letter to the finished page is called a _____.

3. There are approximately _____ points in an inch.

4. Fonts are measured from _____ to _____ plus a little bit extra.

5. _____ fonts can be scaled to almost any size you need.

6. In a block of continuous text a _____ typeface is usually the easiest to read.

7. A _____ font is usually used only for headlines or special emphasis.

8. To add fonts to Windows, first open the _____ Group and launch the _____ _____.

9. Vector fonts and True Type fonts are both _____ fonts and can be displayed in almost any point size.

Changing the Appearance of Windows

Learning Objectives

1. Define hue, saturation, and luminosity in relation to custom colors.

2. Define wallpaper.

3. Identify the desktop pattern.

Performance Objectives

1. Change the screen colors.

2. Create a custom color.

3. Select a wallpaper display.

4. Change the width of window borders.

5. Edit (and change) the desktop pattern.

Custom Color A custom color is a new color that is created by changing the values of the settings in the custom color palette. Once a custom color is created, it can be used to change the color of any of your desktop elements.

Hue Hue is the position of a color along the color spectrum. Hue can be changed by moving the indicator horizontally in the color refiner box.

Saturation Saturation is the purity of a color ranging from grey to pure color. Saturation can be changed by moving the indicator vertically in the color refiner box.

Luminosity Luminosity of a color is a measure of a color's brightness ranging from pure white to complete black. You can control the luminosity of a color by moving the little arrow indicator up or down on the Vertical Luminosity Bar located to the right of the color refiner box.

Wallpaper Wallpaper is an optional bitmap image that can be displayed in the desktop area. When a Wallpaper image is displayed, it can cover the entire desktop and hide the normal bland grey surface.

Screen Element Each item that goes into the display of a window is called a screen element. For example, the title bar at the top of a window, the lettering in the title bar, and the window borders are all separate elements. The color of each element can be changed from Control Panel.

Color Refiner Box The main part of the custom color selector is a large colorful box called the Color Refiner. After a base color is selected, you can use the other controls in the custom color selector to create new colors.

Color Sample Box The small box below the Color Refiner (in the custom color selector) is called the Color Sample Box. The right side of the Color Sample box is marked Solid, and displays a pure color that is directly supported by your display screen. The left side of the Color Sample Box (marked Color) will show a nonsolid color produced by a pattern of tiny colored dots.

Chapter Overview

Staring at the same old boring computer screen every day can get real old, real fast. The plain grey background, the conservative blue title blocks, and the bland grey borders certainly don't do much to brighten your work day. Wouldn't it be nice to see some brighter screen colors or to display an attractive background design? All you need to do is open Windows Control Panel and make your choices (see Figure 22.1).

Figure 22.1

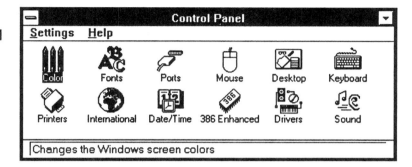

The Control Panel window

Changing the Screen Colors

When you install Windows on a color monitor, the colors it uses (by default) are perfectly acceptable. But, if you want your display to have a little more personality, you can change almost everything.

The Windows display screen contains many individual elements. For example, the lettering in the title bar is separate from the title bar itself. The window borders may display one color and the work area another. You can use Windows Control Panel to change the color of each individual element to any color you like — even if some of the color choices are worthless. For example, you may want to change the color of the tile bar and borders to dark blue. If the lettering in the title bar is also dark blue, it makes the lettering impossible to read.

To change the screen colors, start by opening the Main Group. Next, launch Control Panel, choose the Color application, and you will see a dialog box similar to the one shown in Figure 22.2.

Figure 22.2

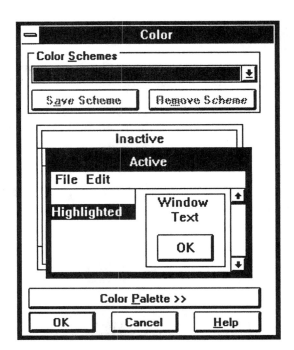

The Change Colors dialog box

At the top of the window you will find a box marked Color Schemes. Press the Down arrow next to the box and a list (with scroll bars) will open. This list contains the names of the color schemes that are already defined. Click on any of these predefined color schemes and a sample of the color selections will display in the main part of the Color Schemes window. If you find a predefined color scheme that you want to use, just press the OK button at the bottom of the window. Unless you make new selections, every time you run the Windows program it will use these colors to display your data.

▲ **Hint**   If you choose a group of colors and then decide that you don't like your choices, press the Cancel button at the bottom of the Color Scheme window. The window will close and no changes will take place. ▲

Selecting   If you don't find an acceptable scheme in the predefined selec-
Colors   tions, you can specify each element of the screen individually. Press the Color Palette button near the bottom of the window and the Color Scheme will expand to resemble Figure 22.3.

Figure 22.3

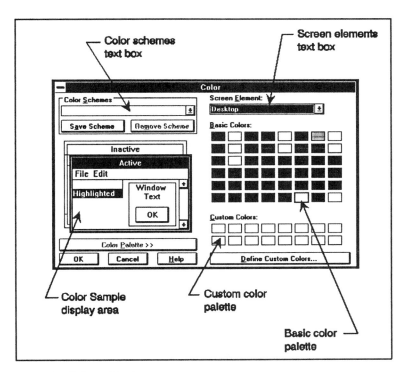

The Color Palette Display

Near the top of the expanded section, you will see a new text box labeled Screen Element. Press the Down arrow and a list of the screen elements that can be changed will display. To change the color of an element, select it from the list, click on the desired color in the Basic Colors area, and the sample display area will change to show your choice.

■ **Note**   Some window elements will only use the solid color closest to the nonsolid color you select. These elements include the Window Frame, Window Text, Menu bar, Menu Text, Title Bar Text, and the Window Background.

For example, to change the color of the work area, open the list box and select Work Area from the displayed choices. Now, move the mouse pointer into the basic color palette area, click on the color that you want to use, and the sample display area will change to show your selection. Continue selecting different elements and choosing new colors until you are pleased with all of your changes. When you are finished, remember to press the OK button or your changes will be lost.

▲ **Hint**
You may also select a screen element if you click on it in the sample display area. For example, if you click on the window border in the sample area, the Screen Element text box will change to say "window border." Once the name of the element is displayed, all you need to do is choose new colors as desired.

▲

Creating Custom Colors

For many people, the choices offered by the basic color palette are not enough. If the colors are not quite right, you can press the Custom Colors button at the bottom of your window and

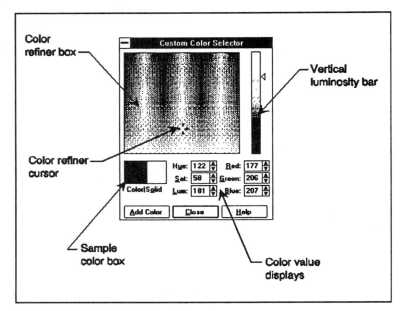

the screen will change to look like Figure 22.4.

Figure 22.4

The Custom Colors palette

The new window is called the Custom Color Selector, and the main part of the new window is the *color refiner box*. Inside the color refiner box you will see a small crosshair style cursor called the color refiner cursor. Drag the color refiner cursor around inside the color refiner box to select a base color. Once you have selected a base color, you can use the other controls in the Custom Color Selector to create new colors.

The color refiner cursor allows you to define a color's hue and saturation. Hue is the position of a color along the color spectrum, and saturation is the purity of the color ranging from grey to the pure color.

■ **Note**   If you move the color refiner cursor horizontally in the color refiner box, you are changing the hue of the color.

If you move the color refiner cursor vertically, you are modifying the saturation.

To the right of the color refiner box, you will see the vertical luminosity bar. Next to the bar is a little indicator arrow. You can drag this arrow up and down the scale to control the luminosity of a color. The luminosity is a measure of a color's brightness ranging from pure white to complete black.

The numerical values for hue, saturation, and luminosity are displayed in the labeled boxes near the bottom of the window. If desired, you can type a number directly into each box or use the Up/Down arrows to change the displayed values. In any case, as you move the color refiner cursor (or enter values into the boxes) a sample of the new color will be displayed in the Color Sample box near the bottom of the window.

▲ **Hint**   When creating a custom color, luminosity takes precedent over saturation and saturation takes precedent over hue. ▲

Creating a Custom Color

Start by opening the Main Group, launching Control Panel, and selecting the Color feature. When the Color window opens (as in Figure 22.2), use this procedure to create custom colors.

What to Do	What Happens
1. Press the Color Palette button.	The box will expand to display the color palette area.
2. At the bottom of the color palette area, press the Define Custom Colors button.	The Custom Color Selector window will open.

3. Drag the color refiner cursor to the area of the box that contains the color that you want. You may also enter a number directly into one or more of the color value boxes below the color refiner box.

The Color Sample box will change to reflect your selections.

■ **Note** You have probably noticed by now that the Color Sample box is divided into two parts. One part is marked Color and the other is marked Solid. The right side of the box will display a pure color that is directly supported by your display screen. The left side will display a nonsolid color produced by a pattern of small colored dots that simulates (as closely as possible) the color that you have created. If you want to use the solid color rather than the simulated color, double-click on the right side of the box or press Ⓐⅼⅼ+O.

4. Select an empty box in the Custom Colors palette area. In other words, move the mouse pointer to an empty box and click.

The selected box will be highlighted.

5. Press the Add Color button.

The new color is placed in the Custom Colors palette.

▲ **Hint** If you do not select a box, windows will automatically select the next empty one for you. If you select a box that already contains a custom color, the new color will replace the old one. ▲

6. Press the Close button to return to the man Color dialog box.

The Custom Color Selector window will close.

Saving Your Color Set
Once you have made all of your color selections, Windows will continue to use them until you change them again. If you want to save your choices, you can name them and add them to the Color Schemes selection list.

What to Do	**What Happens**

1. Make all your color choices until you are satisfied with the arrangement.

The sample display area will reflect your choices.

2. Press the Save Scheme button.

A dialog box will open as shown in Figure 22.5. The dialog box will display the same name as the currently selected color scheme.

Figure 22.5

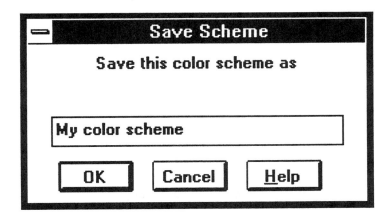

3. If you want to change the colors in the selected color scheme, just press OK (or [Enter◄─]). To create a new color scheme, type a name into the dialog box and then press OK.

The new (or modified) color scheme will be placed on the list.

4. Press the OK button in the Color window to finish.

The Control Panel window will be displayed.

Wallpaper

The main background of your display screen is called the desktop. By default, the desktop area will be colored a rather bland grey. However, if you wish, you can place a picture called wallpaper in the desktop area. You could display a pleasant picture of a sunset at the beach or a dramatic mountain scene. In fact, if you get tired of looking at one picture, you can put up a new one. Wallpaper can be almost as nice as having a window in your office.

Using Images Provided by Windows

The Windows program is shipped with several ready-made wallpaper images. These images are easily identified by their .BMP extensions. To place wallpaper on your desktop, use the procedure described here.

What to Do	**What Happens**
1. From the Main Group, locate and launch Control Panel.	The Control Panel will display.
2. From Control Panel, double-click on the Desktop icon.	The Desktop window will display as shown in Figure 22.6.
3. Click the Down arrow to the right of the Wallpaper text box.	A list of the available images will appear.
4. Select an image from the list, or if necessary, type the entire pathname that points to the image that you want to use.	The name of the image that you select will display in the Wallpaper box.

Figure 22.6

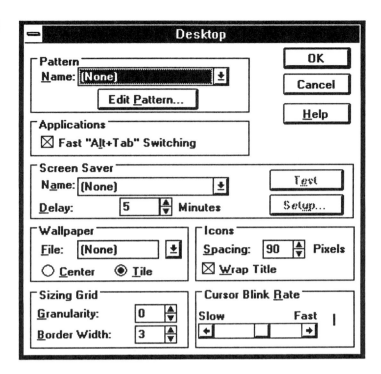

5. Select Center or Tile. If the image is large and intended to cover the entire screen, choose Center. If the image is small, choose Tile. A small image that is tiled will repeat all over the screen in a mosaic pattern.

Nothing yet.

■ **Note** If the image covers the entire screen, it doesn't really matter if you choose Center or Tile. The selected image will still cover the entire screen.

If you select Center and the image does not cover the entire screen, you will be able to see the desktop surface around the outside of the image.

If the file is too large or takes up too much memory, Windows will not display the image at all.

6. Press OK to finish. The selected wallpaper will be displayed.

Obtaining (or Creating) Custom Wallpaper

Actually, wallpaper is nothing more than a bitmap image stored on a disk. To use a bitmap image as wallpaper, copy (or move) it into the Windows subdirectory and it will automatically display in the Wallpaper list box. As already mentioned, Windows is shipped with several ready made wallpaper files but you can use any bitmap you can find (or create) as wallpaper on your system.

■ Note

A bitmap is one of several file formats used to store graphics. Other formats include .TIF, .GIF, .PCX, .WPG, and .MSP. If you want to use an image that is stored in a different format as wallpaper, you must first convert it to a bitmap (or .BMP) file.

One good source of bitmap files is the Windows Paintbrush application. In other words, open the Accessories group, launch Paintbrush and use it to create your own original wallpaper. When you are finished drawing, save your work and move the new file into the Windows subdirectory. Finally, launch Desktop and select your new wallpaper.

If you don't feel like an artist, another source of wallpaper is public domain and Shareware libraries. You can usually find these libraries through a local computer club or even at your computer dealer. You may also want to use a MODEM and check with any small local (or large commercial) bulletin board systems. Often large collections of .BMP files (and many other types of files) are just a phone call away. Many of these images are created by professional artists and are very high quality. Again, to use these images all you need to do is copy the .BMP files into the Windows subdirectory.

Maintaining Your Wallpaper File Collection

Have you ever noticed that when you need a paper clip all you can find are rubber bands, but when you need a rubber band all you can find are paper clips? It seems that sometimes inanimate objects take on a magical life of their own. Once your begin to collect wallpaper images, they will begin to pop up everywhere. In fact, if you leave a stack of disks lying around long enough, wallpaper pictures seem to multiply all by themselves.

Probably the easiest way to control your wallpaper collection is to store most of it on a series of floppy disks. Wallpaper files often require a large slice of disk space and if your hard disk space is limited, it is probably a good idea to delete all of your wallpaper files except for the one that is currently in use. Floppy disks are inexpensive and if you fill one up, just start a new one. Besides, it is easier to find a specific image if it is stored on a floppy disk with other related images.

Another simple way to organize your wallpaper images is to create a subdirectory on your hard disk and move all the files that are not in use into their own directory. This method has some advantages and some disadvantages.

The major advantage of this method is that all of your wallpaper files are in one convenient location. Any time you want to change your wallpaper, you can use File Manager to move the old file back into the Wallpaper subdirectory and the new one into the Windows subdirectory.

The major disadvantage of this method is that wallpaper files tend to be large, and as mentioned before, if you have limited hard disk space there could be problems. In any case, the best way to keep track of your files is the method that works best for you. As long as you don't violate any of the basic computer rules, and remember to make frequent backups, everything should be OK.

▲ **Hint** To quickly locate all of the .BMP files on your hard disk, you can launch File Manager, open the File menu, and use the Search feature to locate all of the files that end with a .BMP extension. ▲

Other Convenient Features

The intention of this entire chapter is to make the Windows environment more pleasant. If your work area is attractive, and any inconvenient aspects of the program have been eliminated (or at least minimized), you will get more work done in less time.

Changing the Border Width By now you have probably noticed that it is sometimes difficult to position the mouse pointer in exactly the right place when you want to move a window border. You can easily solve this problem if you make the borders wider. As before, begin by opening the Main Group and launching Control Panel.

What to Do	**What Happens**

1. When Control Panel opens, select the Desktop feature.

The Desktop box will display as in Figure 22.7.

Figure 22.7

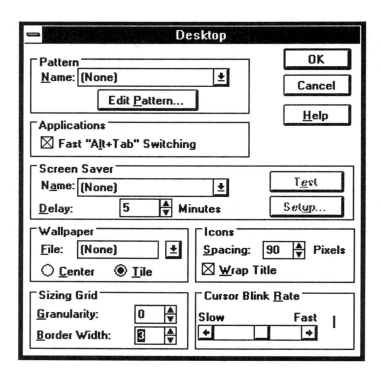

2. Move to the Border Width box (in the bottom left corner) and click the Up or Down arrow to change the displayed value. If desired, you can simply type a number between 1 and 49 into the box.

The displayed value will change to show your choice.

■ **Note** A border width of 1 is the smallest possible. Many people find that a border width of around 8 is both attractive and functional.

3. Press OK to finish

When you return to the Windows work area, the border width will be changed.

Editing the Desktop Pattern

Before you add wallpaper or make any other changes, your desktop will be a continuous solid color. The most flexible way to brighten your desktop is to add wallpaper, but like everything else, you don't get something for nothing. To display wallpaper on your desktop, you have to give up some of the memory that would normally go to applications. If you computer's memory is limited, it might be better to do without wallpaper.

However, this doesn't mean that you are stuck with a bland single-color desktop. Windows provides another tool, called Desktop Pattern, that can be used to break up the monotony.

■ **Note**

The background color of the desktop pattern will be the same as the desktop itself. The lines and dots that make up the actual pattern (the foreground color) will be the same as the Window text. You can change these colors, along with the other screen elements, as discussed earlier.

How to Change the Desktop Pattern

To add (or change) the pattern on the desktop, start by opening the Main Group, launching Control Panel, and choosing the Desktop icon.

What to Do

What Happens

1. When the Desktop window displays, locate the box marked Pattern.

Nothing yet.

2. To select a predefined pattern, press the Down arrow on the left of the text box.

The list of predefined patterns will be displayed.

3. Select a pattern from the list

The name of the pattern will be entered into the text box.

4. To preview or edit the pattern, press the button marked Edit Pattern.

The Desktop-Edit Pattern window will open as shown in Figure 22.8.

Figure 22.8

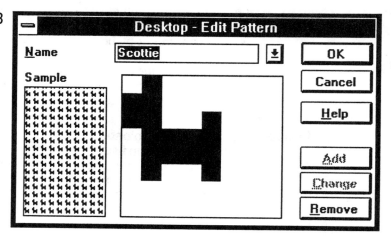

5. If necessary, modify the pattern by turning its dots on or off. If a dot is on, click it to turn it off. If it is off, click to turn it on.

The Preview Pattern box will change to display the desktop pattern.

■ **Note** If you do not have a mouse, you cannot edit patterns.

6. When you are satisfied with the changes, select (highlight) the text in the box at the top left of the Edit Pattern window and enter a name for the pattern.

The name will be displayed.

7. Press the Add button and the press OK. Caution: if you press [Enter⏎] at this point, your new pattern will be lost!

The name of the new pattern will be added to the list of patterns.

8. Press OK to select the pattern.

The desktop will display the selected pattern.

■ **Note** Most of the patterns make the titles of the icons on your desktop difficult to read.

Summary Points

1. The Windows display screen contains many individual elements and you can use Windows Control Panel to change the color of each element to any color you like.

2. To change screen color, open the Main Group, launch Control Panel, and select the Color icon.

3. If you don't find an acceptable scheme in the predefined selections, you can change the color of each element of the screen individually. Press the Color Palette button near the bottom of the Color window, and the Color Scheme window will open.

4. If the choices offered by the basic color palette are not enough, you can press the Custom Colors button at the bottom of your screen and create your own colors.

5. Hue is a color's position along the color spectrum.

6. The saturation of a color is its purity ranging from grey to the pure color.

7. A color's luminosity is defined as its brightness. Luminosity ranges from pure white to complete black.

8. When defining a custom color, Luminosity takes precedence over saturation, and saturation takes precedence over hue.

9. The main background area of the display screen is called the desktop. You can display a picture called wallpaper in the desktop area.

10. To change the width of the window borders, launch Control Panel and select the Desktop icon. Finally, enter a value between 1 and 49 into the Border Width box and press OK to finish.

11. Windows provides a second tool called the Desktop Pattern that can be used to break up the monotony of the desktop.

12. To add (or change) the pattern on the desktop, open the Main Group, launch Control Panel, and select the Desktop icon. At this point you can select a predefined pattern from the list or create a new one.

Practice Exercises

Project One

Change the colors on your screen. You can start with one of the predefined color sets or create a new set of colors from scratch. When you are finished save your new color scheme using the name My Color Set.

Project Two

Add wallpaper to your desktop. You can use one of the patterns supplied with the Windows program, or any pattern obtained from another source (such as from your instructor).

Project Three

Experiment with the desktop pattern. Observe where the pattern does and does not appear. Remember, it is a good idea to keep the pattern simple. On many displays, complex patterns can make some of the screen elements difficult (or even impossible) to read.

Comprehension Questions

1. List the steps to change the color of the lettering in the title bars of all windows.

2. What is a custom color?

3. Some screen elements can only display using pure colors. List these elements.

4. List the steps to save a color scheme once it is created.

5. Why would you want to place wallpaper on your desktop?

6. List several sources of wallpaper files other than the ones that come with Windows.

7. If a wall paper image covers the entire screen and the Tile option is selected, what will happen?

8. If a wallpaper file is too large or if it takes up too much memory, what will happen?

9. Why would you want to change the width of a window's borders?

10. Under what conditions might you choose to display a desktop pattern rather than use wallpaper?

11. List the steps to save a newly created desktop pattern.

Completion Questions

1. _____ of a color is a measure of a color's brightness ranging from pure white to complete black.

2. _____ is the position of a color along the color spectrum.

3. _____ is the purity of a color ranging from grey to pure color.

4. Each item that goes into the display of a window is called a _____ _____.

5. The main part of the custom color selector is a large colorful box called the _____ _____.

6. To the right of the color refiner box, you will see the _____ _____ bar.

7. Once you have made all of your color selections, Windows will continue to use them until _____ _____ _____.

8. Wallpaper is nothing more than a _____ _____ stored on a disk.

Match the following terms to their definitions

_____ Luminosity

A. The area of the screen that is outside of all window borders. By default, this area is a single uniform color.

_____ Hue

B. A picture, stored in the form of a bitmap, that can be displayed on the desktop.

_____ Saturation

C. The measure of a color's brightness, ranging from pure white to complete black.

_____ Desktop

D. A file format that is used to store graphic images.

_____ Screen Element

E. The purity of a color ranging from the pure color to grey.

_____ Wallpaper

F. Any part of a window such as a window border, title bar, or title bar text. The colors of these items can be changed from Control Panel.

_____ Bitmap

G. The position of a color along the color spectrum.

Making Windows Work with You

[Not Against You]

Learning Objectives

1. List three ways to automatically launch an application when starting Windows.

2. Define Screen Saver.

Performance Objectives

1. Launch Windows and automatically load an application from the DOS prompt.

2. Automatically load an application by moving it (or copying it) to the Startup Group.

3. Automatically load an application by modifying the WIN.INI file.

4. Set the system time and date from Control Panel.

5. Activate Windows Screen Saver.

6. Adjust the ways that the mouse responds in Windows.

7. Adjust how the keyboard responds in Windows.

Chapter Terms

Mouse Trails   When this option is selected, the mouse pointer will leave little visual "echoes" of itself as you move the mouse across the screen.

Password   Windows version 3.1 lets you assign a password to your screen saver. If a password is assigned, anytime your screen saver activates you must enter the correct password before you can continue to work.

Screen Saver   A Screen Saver lurks in the background, waiting. If you do not move the mouse, press a key, or perform some other computer operation for five minutes, the Screen Saver "wakes up," takes over your screen, and displays some sort of animated pattern.

Startup Group   Any program item placed in the Startup group will launch automatically every time you start Windows.

Chapter Overview

When you start Windows, it is often convenient to launch several applications, minimize them, and leave their icons on the desktop to be used later. To make your work easier (and faster), Windows provides "a byte in shining armor," ready to rescue you from repetitive tasks. If you provide the correct instructions, any application can be loaded automatically and ready to use at the beginning of every Windows work session.

More Ways to Launch Applications

Different people like to do things different ways. With that in mind, Windows provides several tools to automatically launch applications. You can choose to automatically launch applications for a single work session, or load a series of applications every time you start Windows. In fact, when using Windows 3.1, there are two ways to launch applications that are used in every session.

Automatically Launch a Windows Application from the DOS Command Line

As you know, to start Windows at the DOS command line, you type WIN and press [Enter←]. Windows will load and you can begin work. However, if you know ahead of time that you will need to work with a specific application, you can start Windows with the standard WIN command followed by the name of the application you want to use.

For example, to start Windows and automatically launch Excel, you would type(at the DOS command line) WIN EXCEL and press [Enter←]. The combination command will cause Windows to load and launch Excel immediately.

■ **Note** When you are finished using an application that was launched in this way you can close it normally and continue working with Windows.

If you want to work with a specific application and know the name of the data file you want to work on, you can use a similar technique to load Windows, launch your application, and load the data file with one short instruction from the DOS command line. To load the data file, just add the name of the data file to the end of the instruction. With this in mind, you would now type WIN EXCEL datafile (and press [Enter←]). As you would expect, this command will cause Windows to run and Excel to launch. When Excel is ready, the data file that you specify will be loaded and ready to go.

▲ **Hint** If you have a data file that is associated to its application, it is not necessary to include the name of the application in the startup command. For example, to automatically load the SYSINI.TXT file into the Notepad application as you start Windows, you could type WIN SYSINI.TXT. In this case, the name of the application (Notepad) is optional. ▲

Using the Startup Group to Launch Applications

Windows 3.1 adds a new feature called the Startup Group. (When you install Windows 3.1, the Startup Group is created automatically.) Any program item placed in this group will launch automatically, in the order it is displayed, every time you start Windows.

Figure 23.1

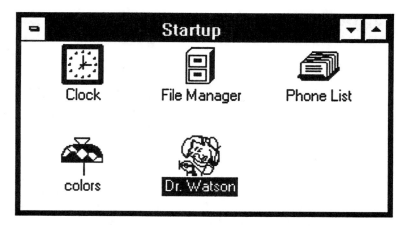

A typical Startup Group

Many users find it convenient to load Calculator and File Manager at the beginning of a work session. To make Windows load these applications automatically, just move (or copy) the Calculator icon (from the Accessories Group) and File Manager icon (from the Main Group) into the Startup Group (see Figure 23.1). Of course, you can put anything you want to into the group, but don't ignore the limits of your system. If you try to automatically launch every application that you own, you will run out of system resources.

▲ **Hint** You can also place an item in the Startup Group that refers to the name of an associated document file. For example, to launch the Notepad application and automatically load a file called TIMELOG.TXT, create a new program item that refers to the filename. The new item will adopt the icon from the parent application (in this case, Notepad) and will launch automatically with the specified file in place ready to go. ▲

Modifying the WIN.INI File to Automatically Load Applications

If you want to automatically launch applications when using Windows 3.0, you must change a file called WIN.INI. This file is created by the Setup program when you install Windows, and is nothing more than a data file that stores information needed when Windows in launched. To change WIN.INI, all you need to do is load it into an editor (such as Notepad or Sysedit), and type.

How to Add Applications to the WIN.INI File

What to Do	**What Happens**

Warning: Do not skip this step.

1. Launch File Manager. Locate the WIN.INI file and click on it.

The WIN.INI will be selected (highlighted).

2. Open the File menu and choose Copy. Type a new file name, such as WIN.BAK, into the To box.

Windows will make a backup copy of the WIN.INI file called WIN.BAK.

Warning: Do not skip this step.

3. Close (or minimize) File Manager.

File Manager will move out of the way.

4. Open the Accessories Group and double-click on Notepad.

The Notepad application will launch.

5. In Notepad, open the File menu and select Open.

See Figure 23.2.

Figure 23.2

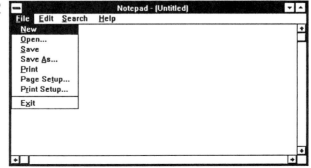

6. When the text box appears, locate the WIN.INI file and double-click to load it into Notepad.

See Figure 23.3.

Figure 23.3

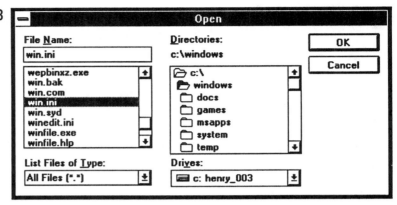

7. Near the top of the WIN.INI file you will find a line that reads LOAD= and a line that reads RUN=. Move the mouse pointer to the end of the LOAD= or RUN= line and click.

The insertion point will move to where you click.

8. Type the name of the applications that you want to load automatically. Type a space between each filename. For example, to automatically launch Clock and Calculator, you would type CLOCK.EXE CALC.EXE.

See Figure 23.4.

■ **Note** When you restart Windows, applications that are entered on the Load line will launch as icons on the desktop. Applications that are entered on the Run line will launch full size.

Figure 23.4

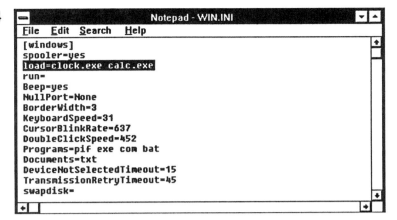

9. When you are finished, open the File Menu and choose Save.

The modified file will be saved (see Figure 23.5).

Figure 23.5

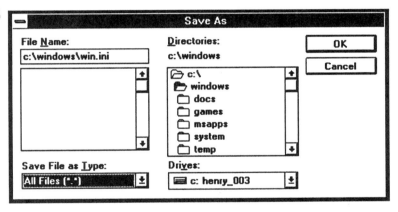

10. Close the Notepad application, and exit Windows.

The DOS prompt will return to the screen.

11. Restart Windows.

When Windows restarts, the applications that you specify will launch automatically

If you make a mistake during this procedure, don't panic. Close the Notepad application and do not save your work. Restart the procedure beginning at Step Five and everything will be fine.

If you make a mistake and have already saved the file, open File Manager and delete the defective WIN.INI file. Locate WIN.BAK (created in Step Two) and rename it to WIN.INI. Now you can go back to Step One and try again.

▲ **Hint**   You can also use the WIN.INI file to automatically launch applications in Windows 3.1. If you modify the WIN.INI file, it is more inconvenient for someone to make changes. For example, if you are setting up a system used by several different people, anyone can accidently add or delete items in the Startup Group. If you modify the WIN.INI file, you can force specific applications to launch in addition to the items that may (or may not) be in the Startup Group. ▲

Using the Windows Screen Saver

If you leave the same image on your display screen for a long time, eventually you will be able to see this image even when the monitor is turned off. This problem is called screen burn and can be prevented very easily. All you really need to do is turn the monitor off or to turn the brightness control down. However, you can also use the Screen Saver program to protect your monitor automatically.

Technically, Screen Saver is a little program that is loaded automatically at the beginning of a Windows work session and lurks in the background waiting to do its job. If you do not move the mouse, press a key, or perform some other computer operation for about five minutes, the Screen Saver application "wakes up," takes over your screen, and displays some sort of animated pattern. Because the pattern moves continuously, nothing stays in the same place on your screen long enough to cause any damage. When you need to resume your work, move the mouse or press anything and your display will return to normal.

How to Activate the Windows Screen Saver

What to Do	**What Happens**
1. Open the Main Group, launch Control Panel, and double-click the Desktop icon.	A dialog box similar to the one in Figure 23.6 will be displayed.

Figure 23.6

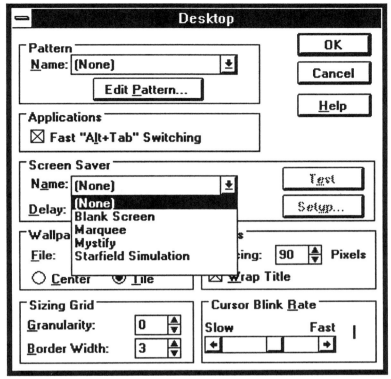

2. Locate the box marked Screen Saver and click the Down arrow to list the Screen Saver pattern choices.

The list of choices will display.

■ **Note** If you choose None as a pattern, Windows Screen Saver will be disabled.

3. Choose a pattern from the following choices:

The pattern that you choose will be displayed in the text box.

- Default: blank screen.

- Flying Windows: A flock of Microsoft Windows logos fly out of the screen.

- Marquee: displays a line of text across the screen.

- Mystify: moving multicolored polygons made from a series of lines.

- Starfield simulation: stars appear to move past as from the deck of a starship.

4. Press the Setup button to set the special options for the screen saver that you have selected. When all the options have been set, press OK.

The options dialog box will close.

■ **Note** Each Screen Saver has its own unique Options dialog box.

Figure 23.7

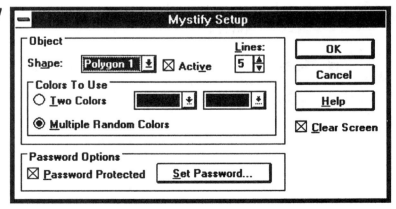

5. To preview the Screen Saver you have selected, press the Test button.

Your Screen Saver will be displayed.

6. Set the delay time for your Screen Saver. The default is five minutes. That means if there is no activity at your computer for five minutes, the Screen Saver will activate.

The selected delay time will be displayed.

■ **Note** After the Screen Saver pattern is selected, you can specify a password that must be used to return to Windows after the Screen Saver has activated.

7. If you want to add password protection to your Screen Saver, press the Setup button and click the box marked Password Protected. Finally, press the Set Password button.

The Change Password dialog box will appear as shown in Figure 23.8.

Figure 23.8

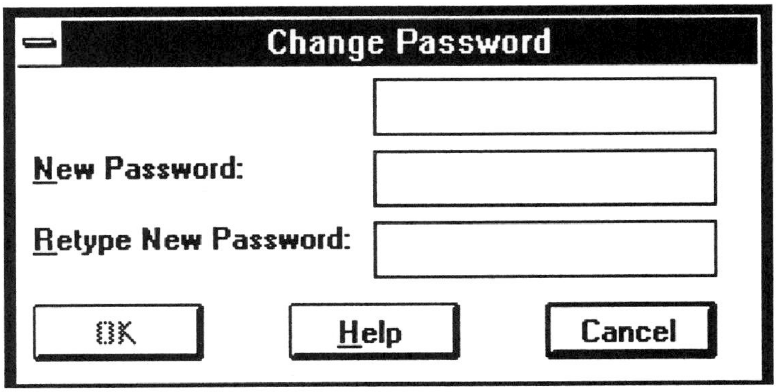

8. Type your password into the box. When you are finished, press ⌷Tab⌷.

The password will not appear as you type. You will see a line of asterisks instead.

■ **Note** A password can be up to 20 characters long.

9. Type the same password into the text box marked Retype New Password. When you are finished, press the OK button.

A line of asterisks will appear in the text box.

■ **Note** If you are changing your password, you must first type your old password into the top dialog box. Next, type the new password into the box in the center and finally type the new password a second time into the Retype New Password box.

10. Press the OK button to finish.

Your Screen Saver is now installed.

■ **Note** If you are using another Screen Saver program, do not use Windows Screen Saver. They might conflict with each other and cause system problems.

Changing System Information

Windows Control Panel is also used to control the settings of all the system information such as the language being used, the ways the system responds to input, and the time and date.

Figure 23.9

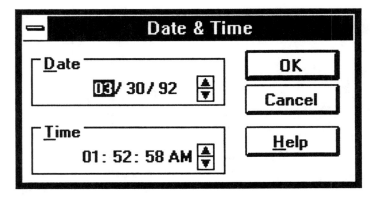

The Date/Time dialog box

Correcting the System Date and Time

If Windows displays the date and/or time incorrectly, you can use Control Panel to correct it. Open the Main Group, launch Control Panel, and choose the icon for Date/Time. The dialog box shown in Figure 23.9 will display. Use the Up/Down arrows (or just type) to correct time and/or date. Press the OK button when you are finished.

Mouse Adjustments

The Mouse icon will let you control the way that the mouse pointer responds to actual movements of your mouse and to the speed of your double-click (see Figure 23.10). To make any changes, click on the Left/Right arrow (for small changes), or just drag the scroll boxes to a new position on the scroll bar. You may need to change these settings several times until everything feels right. Start by making small changes, testing, and making additional small changes until you are satisfied.

Figure 23.10

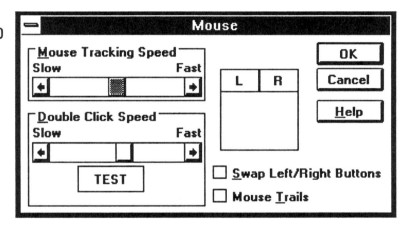

The Mouse dialog box

■ Note

While your are here, you may want to make sure that the left and right mouse buttons are working correctly. When you press a mouse button, one of the boxes in the small mouse diagram reacts. For example, if you press the left mouse button, the box marked L should highlight as long as you hold the button.

The scroll bar for the Mouse Tracking Speed controls how far the mouse moves on the screen when you move the mouse on your desk. If the Mouse Tracking Speed is set high, a small movement of the mouse will cause a large movement of the pointer on the screen. If it is set low, a small movement of the mouse will result in a small movement of the mouse pointer.

The double-click speed can be modified by moving the scroll box or clicking the Left/Right arrow in the next area. To test the setting, double-click in the box marked Test. If the speed is OK, the test box will highlight.

If you are left handed, you may want to place your mouse on the left side of your work area. To switch the buttons for left handed use, check the box marked Swap Left/Right Buttons.

Finally, if you like screen clutter, you may want to check the Mouse Trails box. When this box is checked, the mouse pointer will leave little visual "echoes" of itself as you move the mouse. Try it and see what you think.

■ **Note**   Actually, the mouse trails option make the mouse pointer easier to see if you are running Windows on a laptop computer or if you are using an overhead display device.

Keyboard Adjustments   Selecting the Keyboard icon will let you adjust the repeat rate and the keyboard typing delay. Move the scroll boxes (or press the Left/Right arrows) to make changes. To test your selections, press (and hold) the letter T. At the bottom of the dialog box as shown in Figure 23.11, a series of Ts will appear so you can see how your changes affect the keyboard. If you press any other key, a tone will sound. For some people, it may be easier to test the settings by listening to the delay and rate of the tone.

Figure 23.11

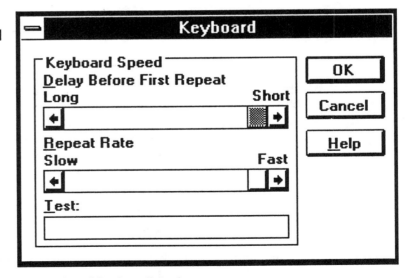

The Keyboard Settings dialog box

Summary Points

1. To automatically launch an application when Windows boots, include the name of the application on the command line when you start Windows. For example, to start Windows and load the Excel spreadsheet, you would type WIN EXCEL.

2. Any applications that are copied or moved into the Startup Group will launch automatically each time Windows is launched.

3. You can also modify the WIN.INI file to automatically launch applications. Any applications placed on the RUN= or the LOAD= line will automatically run.

4. You can activate the Windows Screen Saver to protect your display screen from damage. There are four different Screen Saver patterns to choose from.

5. When you choose a Screen Saver, you can also specify a password to protect your system from unauthorized access.

6. Windows Control Panel is used to adjust the way the system responds to input and to control the system settings such as Time and Date.

7. The Time/Date icon is used to set the system time and date. The system time/date is used to date stamp your files, among other things.

8. The Mouse icon is used to control the way the mouse responds to input from the user.

9. The Mouse icon can also be used to swap the left and right buttons for use by a left-handed user.

10. The Keyboard icon is used to adjust the keyboard delay and repeat rate.

Practice Exercises

1. Open the Main Group, launch Control Panel, and make adjustments to the mouse and keyboard until you are satisfied with the way Windows operates.

■ **Note** By default, the Control Panel is set up in a way that is perfectly acceptable to many people. It may not be necessary to make any changes at all.

2. Open the Main Group and launch Control Panel. Click the Desktop icon and activate a screen saver. Choose a pattern and enter a delay time according to your requirements.

3. Copy the Clock, Notepad, and Cardfile applications into the Startup Group. Arrange the icons so that the Clock appears in the lower left corner of the desktop. Now, close Windows and restart it to make sure that these applications load automatically.

■ **Note** You may want to experiment with the location of the applications inside the Startup Group window. Remember, the applications will launch from left to right across the rows.

Comprehension Questions

1. To start Windows and automatically load an application named Utility, what command would you need to type at the DOS command line?

2. What command would you need to type to launch Windows and automatically load a Notepad file called SYSINI.txt?

3. The Startup Group has a special function. What is it?

4. In the WIN.INI file, what is the difference between the LOAD= line and the RUN= line?

5. What is a Screen Saver?

6. Windows provides five Screen Saver patterns. What are they?

7. List the steps to activate Windows Screen Saver.

8. In general, what is Windows Control Panel used for?

9. What adjustments can be made to the way that they keyboard responds while in Windows?

10. What adjustments can be made to the way that the mouse responds in Windows?

11. To set the mouse up for use by a left-handed person, what can you do?

12. List the steps to change the system time and date in Windows.

24

PIF Editor

Learning Objectives

1. Define program information file.

2. Identify the display mode of a DOS application.

3. Define shortcut key.

4. List the keys that cannot be used in shortcut-key combinations.

Performance Objectives

1. Install an existing PIF.

2. Create a PIF for a DOS application.

3. Edit an existing PIF.

4. Use a PIF to launch a DOS application.

5. Assign a shortcut key from Program Manager.

6. Assign a shortcut key from PIF Editor.

7. Fine tune the _DEFAULT.PIF file.

Chapter Terms

Conventional Memory In general, the first 640k of memory in your computer is called Conventional Memory.

Expanded Memory Expanded Memory is a block of memory (usually 64K) that is "switched" into another area of memory so that the computer thinks that it has more memory available. To access Expanded memory, use an *Expanded Memory Manager* such as EMM-386.SYS. This program is shipped as part of the Windows package and can be installed according to the instructions in the Windows User's Guide. Expanded memory is often referred to as EMS.

Expanded Memory Manager An Expanded Memory Manager is a program that is used to access (and manage) Expanded Memory. Windows is shipped with an Expanded Memory Manager called EMM386.SYS.

Extended Memory On most 80286 and 80386 computers, Extended Memory is basically an extension of conventional memory above 1MB. In order to use Extended Memory efficiently, you must use an *Extended Memory Manager* such as the HIMEM.SYS program that ships with Windows. Extended memory is often referred to as XMS.

Extended Memory Manager An Extended Memory Manager is a program that optimizes the way that your computer uses Extended Memory. Windows is shipped with an Extended Memory Manager called HIMEM.SYS and it is automatically installed when you set up Windows.

High Memory Area The High Memory Area (or HMA) is the first 64K of extended memory and is often used by memory-resident utilities such as network drivers.

High Graphics If your application runs in EGA or VGA mode then it is using High Graphics.

Low Graphics If your application runs in CGA mode then it is using Low Graphics.

PIF A PIF (or Program Information File) contains information about memory requirements, video modes, and several other items that Windows will need to run a specific DOS application.

Start-up Directory	When you are defining a PIF, the Start-up directory is the name of the directory that is used to store the application's primary working files.
Text Mode	If your DOS application does not use any graphics at all, then it is probably running in Text Mode.

Chapter Overview

When you launch an application that is written for Windows, any special information such as the amount and type of memory needed, the video display modes, and any other technical specifications are built in to the application itself. In other words, Window knows how to do Windows, but does not know how to do DOS.

When you run a DOS application under Windows, the technical specifications are not built in. One of the major weaknesses of DOS applications is that there are no standards. This critical information must come from an outside source and in Windows, this outside source is a *program information file*.

What are PIFs Used For?

A program information file (or PIF) contains information about memory requirements, video modes, and several other items that Windows will need to run a specific DOS application. If a PIF does not exist, you must obtain one from another source or create it from scratch using PIF Editor. Each DOS application should have its own PIF.

If you try to run a DOS application that does not have a custom-made PIF, Windows will use a PIF called _DEFAULT.PIF (the underscore at the beginning is a part of the filename). This file contains enough information to run most DOS applications but they may not run very efficiently. To make sure that every DOS application can take full advantage of what Windows can offer, each DOS application should have its own custom PIF.

■ Note	You can always identify a PIF by its extension (.PIF). As you will remember, Windows thinks that PIFs are executable files.

Ready-made PIFs

Many DOS program manufacturers realize that people are using Windows. In fact, when you purchase a DOS program, the package may include a ready-made PIF. Any time you create a program item for a DOS application, make sure that you check its documentation. If the manufacturer provides a PIF, the documentation will most likely tell you what it is named and explain how to install it.

Some DOS applications include a PIF but don't mention it or provide any instructions about installation. After you have copied a DOS application onto your hard disk, use the Search feature (in File Manager) and look for any files with the extension .PIF. If you find a PIF that has a name similar to your application's name, use File Manager and copy this file into the Windows subdirectory. Once a PIF is copied into the correct location, Windows will use it automatically.

▲ Hint

It is a good idea to *copy* the PIF into the Windows subdirectory rather than *move* it. That way, if something happens, you can copy the original file into the Windows subdirectory again. ▲

Using a Ready-made PIF

What to Do

What Happens

1. Locate the PIF. Use File Manager to search your hard disk or to search the actual application disks.

The name of the PIF will display as shown in Figure 24.1.

Figure 24.1

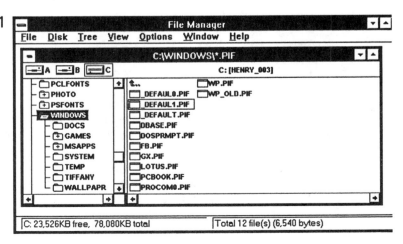

	2.	Click on the file to be copied.	The selected file will highlight.
	3.	Press (and hold) the [Ctrl] key (so that the file will be copied rather than moved) and drag the file into the Windows subdirectory.	The selected file will be copied.

Creating a Custom-made PIF

Remember, a PIF contains the missing information that Windows needs to run a DOS application correctly.

▲ Hint Most of the information you will need to complete a PIF can be found in the application's documentation. ▲

How to Create a PIF	**What to Do**	**What Happens**
	1. Open the Accessories Group and launch the PIF Editor application.	See Figure 24.2.

Figure 24.2

PIF Editor - [Untitled]

File   Mode   Help

Program Filename:
Window Title:
Optional Parameters:
Start-up Directory:

Video Memory: ● Text   ○ Low Graphics   ○ High Graphics
Memory Requirements: KB Required   128   KB Desired   640
EMS Memory: KB Required   0   KB Limit   1024
XMS Memory: KB Required   0   KB Limit   1024
Display Usage: ● Full Screen   Execution: ☐ Background
                 ○ Windowed   ☐ Exclusive
☒ Close Window on Exit   Advanced...

Press F1 for Help on Program Filename

▲ Hint While you are filling in a PIF, you can get help about a specific area if you select that area and press the F1 key. ▲

2. Type the name of the DOS application into the box marked Program Filename. When you are finished, press ⌷Tab⌷.

The name of the executable file will be displayed.

■ Note Use the name of the executable file used to start the application from the DOS command line. In other words, if you type C:\UTILITY.EXE to run your applications, type C:\UTILITY.EXE into the first box. (Be sure to specify the entire path.)

3. Type the title of the program into the second box and press ⌷Tab⌷ when you are finished. This title will be displayed in the title bar any time your application is run in a window. (The title can be up to 30 characters long.)

The title will be displayed in the second box.

4. Type any necessary optional parameters into the third box and press ⌷Tab⌷.

The option parameters will display.

■ Note Optional parameters are any switches or other information needed to run your applications. For example, if you type UTILITY /W at the DOS command line, the /W would be placed in the Optional Parameters box.

5. Enter the name of the Start-up Directory into the fourth box.

The name of the Start-up Directory will be displayed.

■ Note Start-up Directory is the name of the directory that is used to store the application's working files. For example, if the application's files are stored in a directory named UTILITY, you would type UTILITY into the fourth box.

6. Select a video mode.

The Radio button will indicate which mode is selected.

■ **Note** If your DOS application uses only text, select Text mode. If it uses text and CGA graphics, then select Low Graphics. Use High Graphics only if your application runs in EGA or VGA mode. Check your documentation for more information.

7. Specify the memory requirements.

The entries will display as entered.

■ **Note** This information can usually be found in the application's documentation. If in doubt, start at 128K required and 640K desired. Increase the desired number in increments of 64K until your application will launch. If your application uses (or requires) extended (XMS) or expanded (EMS) memory, be sure to place appropriate values in these boxes. (As usual, check your documentation.)

8. Set the Radio button to select the way your application will display when it launches.

The Radio button will show your choice.

■ **Note** If you choose Full Screen, your DOS applications will display exactly the same way it runs from the DOS prompt. If you select Windowed, when the application launches, it will be displayed in a sizable window with a title bar at the top. Warning: Many DOS applications will not run in a window.

9. Make your selection to control how the DOS application will execute.

The selections you choose will display an X in the appropriate boxes.

■ **Note** If you choose Background, when the DOS application is switched into the background, it will continue to run.

If you choose Exclusive, when the DOS application is in the foreground, the operation of all other applications will be suspended.

10. If you want the application to return to Windows when it closes, leave the Close Windows on Exit box checked.

The Close Window on Exit check box will reflect your choice.

■ **Note** If the Close Window on Exit box is not checked, the DOS prompt will display when the application terminates. To return to Windows, you will need to type EXIT and press ⌊Enter↵⌋.

Your DOS application will now run correctly. It is usually not necessary to set any advanced options. Your application may not run at it's very best, but it will run. If the way it runs is acceptable, you may want to leave the advanced settings the way they are. Remember, if it ain't broke, don't fix it.

Using a PIF to Launch a DOS Application

After a PIF is defined, as far as Windows is concerned it is an executable file. In other words, it can be entered at the Run line, launched from File Manager with a double-click, or used as the filename when you create a program item.

If the PIF has a filename that is similar to the main application, no additional action is required. For example, to launch a DOS application named SPELLS.EXE, open the File menu, select Run, and when the dialogue box appears type SPELLS.EXE as the filename. Windows will automatically search for a file named SPELLS.PIF and use the information it finds to actually launch the application. Again, if Windows can't find a match, it will use the _DEFAULT.PIF and try to launch the application anyway.

Using a PIF to Launch an Application	Remember, as far as Windows is concerned, a PIF is an executable file. That means that anything you can do with the filename of an executable program you can also do to a PIF. For example, you already know how to create a new program item using an executable file and that means you know how to create a new program item using a PIF. The only difference is, rather than specifying the file that has an extension of .EXE, refer to the file that has extension of PIF.
■ **Note**	Just as a review, to create a new program item, open the group that is to receive the item, access the File menu and choose New. When the dialogue box appears, type a descriptive title for the application and press ⌨Tab. Then type the executable name of the application, along with it's path, and press OK.
	You can also launch a PIF if you enter its name into the Run box from File Manager or Program Manager. In these cases, open the File menu and type the name of the PIF into the dialogue box.
▲ **Hint**	Don't forget, when you are in File Manager, you can launch an application if you double-click on it's filename. That means that a PIF can also be launched with a double-click. ▲

Using a PIF to Launch an Application and Load a Data File

The first line of the PIF Editor dialog box is used to store the name of the executable file that is to be launched. If you have a frequently used document that is associated to an application, you can enter the name of this data file into the Program Filename box. The application will launch and the data file will load using the PIF information that you specify.

For example, if you have a spreadsheet data file that you use often, make sure that it is properly "associated" to it's parent application, and type the name of the data file (not the application) into the Program Filename box. Now, when you launch the PIF, the specified data file will automatically load and be ready to go (see Figure 24.3).

■ **Note**   Remember, for this technique to work correctly, your DOS application must be able to accept the name of a data file as part of the startup command.

Figure 24.3

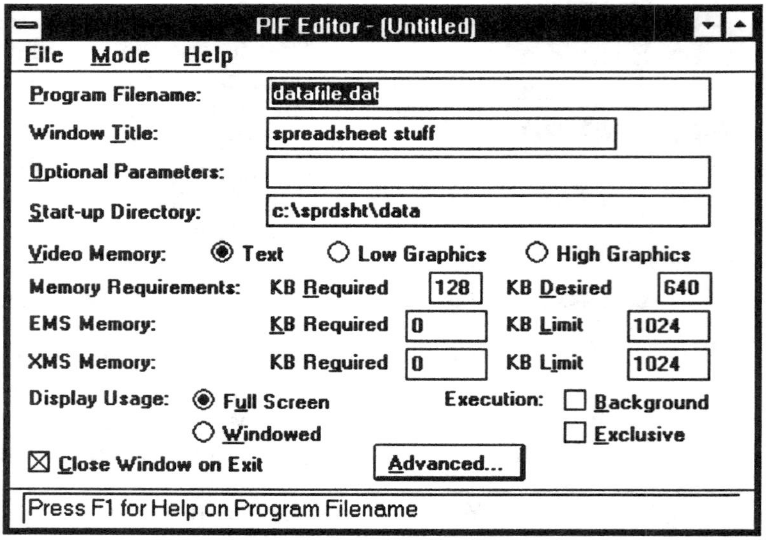

PIF Editor - (Untitled)

File   Mode   Help

Program Filename: `datafile.dat`

Window Title: `spreadsheet stuff`

Optional Parameters:

Start-up Directory: `c:\sprdsht\data`

Video Memory: ● Text   ○ Low Graphics   ○ High Graphics

Memory Requirements: KB Required `128`   KB Desired `640`

EMS Memory: KB Required `0`   KB Limit `1024`

XMS Memory: KB Required `0`   KB Limit `1024`

Display Usage: ● Full Screen   Execution: ☐ Background
                   ○ Windowed   ☐ Exclusive

☒ Close Window on Exit   [Advanced...]

Press F1 for Help on Program Filename

The main PIF editor screen

Advanced PIF Settings

Figure 24.4

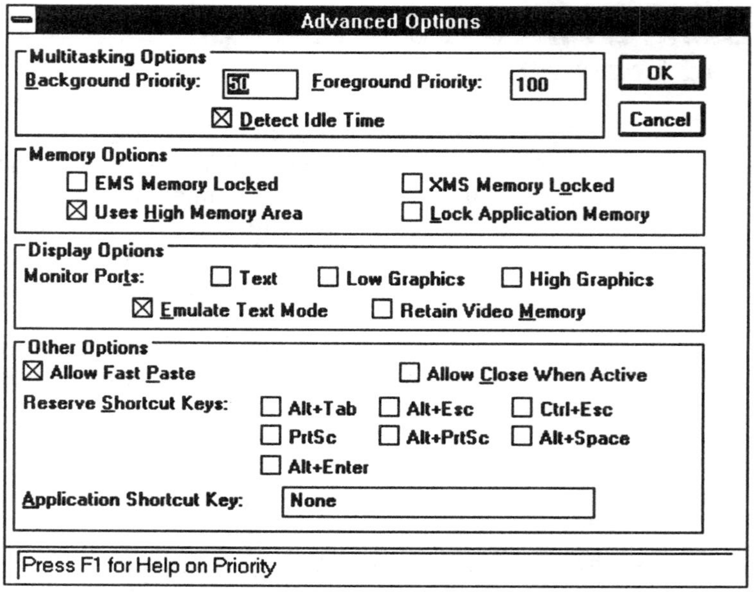

Advanced Options

Multitasking Options
Background Priority: `50`   Foreground Priority: `100`   [OK]

☒ Detect Idle Time   [Cancel]

Memory Options
☐ EMS Memory Locked   ☐ XMS Memory Locked
☒ Uses High Memory Area   ☐ Lock Application Memory

Display Options
Monitor Ports: ☐ Text   ☐ Low Graphics   ☐ High Graphics
☒ Emulate Text Mode   ☐ Retain Video Memory

Other Options
☒ Allow Fast Paste   ☐ Allow Close When Active

Reserve Shortcut Keys: ☐ Alt+Tab   ☐ Alt+Esc   ☐ Ctrl+Esc
                           ☐ PrtSc   ☐ Alt+PrtSc   ☐ Alt+Space
                           ☐ Alt+Enter

Application Shortcut Key: `None`

Press F1 for Help on Priority

The Advanced Options dialog box

When you are running Windows in 386 enhanced mode, you will find a button at the bottom of the PIF Editor window marked Advanced. If you press this button, another dialog box will appear (see Figure 24.4). Don't panic. It's not as complicated as it appears to be. In fact, unless your DOS application is not behaving properly, you won't need to change these settings at all.

Multitasking Options

Figure 24.5

Application number **1**:	**800 (running in foreground)**
Application number **2**:	**100 (running in background)**
Application number **3**:	**100 (running in background)**
Total time available:	**1000**
Summary:	

Application number **1** will get **80%** of the total time
Application number **2** will get **10%** of the total time
Application number **3** will get **10%** of the total time

The first set of options deals with the amount of time Windows will spend on each task. Windows appears to do several things at the same time, but actually your computer spends a little bit of time on one application, suspends what it is doing, goes on to the next task, spends a little time there, then returns to the first task, and so on. The amount of time that Windows will spend on a DOS task is controlled by the values entered into the Background and Foreground Priority boxes.

Each of these boxes will accept a value between 0 and 10,000, but these values only have meaning if you compare them to the background and foreground priorities of all active applications. Examine the chart in Figure 24.5 for an example of how the available computer time is shared when three applications are running.

■ **Note**   It is not necessary to calculate the exact percentage of time Windows is going to spend on each task. In general, if a DOS application running in the foreground seems to be running too slow, increase the value in the Foreground Priorities box.

At the bottom of the Multitasking Options area, you will find a check box marked Detect Idle Time. A background application is idle anytime it is waiting for input from the user (from you, in other words). If Windows sees that an application is idle, it will not get its full share of processor time. Rather than wasting this time on an application that isn't doing anything, Windows will automatically give this time to the applications that are actually busy. Normally you will want to leave this box checked. If you have a DOS application that seems to run abnormally slow, it may mean that for some reason Windows thinks this application is idle all of the time. In this case, try clearing the Detect Idle Time box to see if it helps.

Memory Options

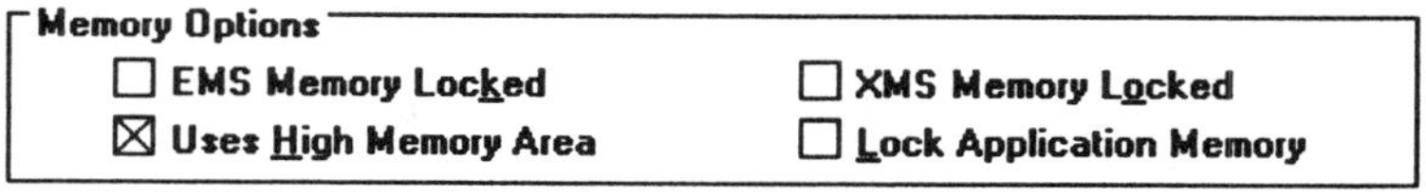

Figure 24.6

The Memory Options area of the Advanced Options dialog box

In the next area of the Advanced Options dialogue box, you will find four check boxes that deal with the way Windows manages conventional, expanded (or EMS), and extended (or XMS) memory (see Figure 24.6). Some DOS applications will use only conventional memory, and others will use various combinations of conventional, expanded, and extended memory. You should be able to find information about the type of memory your application uses in its documentation.

The first two boxes (marked EMS Memory Locked and XMS Memory Locked) should be checked if you don't want Windows to swap an application's memory to hard disk. Locking the memory of an application can improve it's performance, but all other applications will slow down and the total amount of memory available to the system will be reduced.

The next box is marked Uses High Memory Area. In general, leave this box checked. If the high memory area (HMA) is available (and your application can use it), more memory is made available to the application. If your application does not use the HMA, nothing is wasted. If this box is cleared, your application will not use HMA, even if it is available.

■ Note The high memory area (or HMA) is the first 64K of extended memory and is often used by memory-resident utilities such as network drivers. If an application "grabs" the HMA when Windows starts, it will not be available to any other applications.

The last box is marked Lock Application Memory. If this box is checked, Windows will not swap an application's conventional memory to the hard disk. This choice can make some DOS applications run faster, but it will make all other applications run slower. As before, it will reduce the total amount of memory available to the system.

Display Options

Figure 24.7

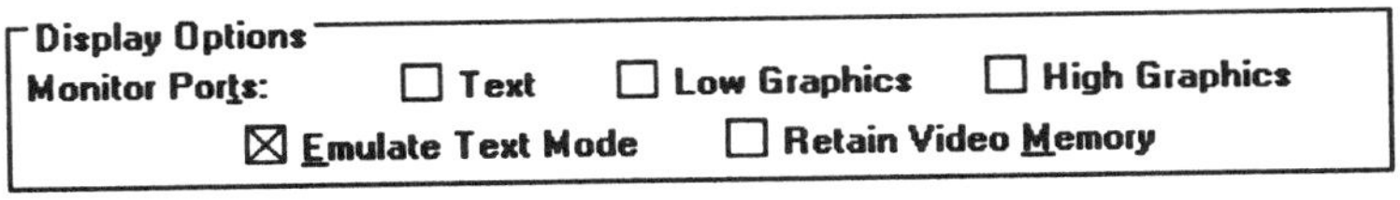

The Display Options

The next section of the Advanced Options dialog box is Display Options (see Figure 24.7). It controls how your DOS application will appear on the display screen and how Windows will allocate the video memory. DOS applications can display your work as text, low-resolution graphics, or high-resolution graphics. Some applications will use only one of these methods, but others may switch from one mode to another. For example, your DOS word processor will probably spend most of its time in text mode, but when you preview the finished page, it may switch to High Graphics. Each of these modes has different properties (and memory requirements) and if Windows is going to run everything correctly, it may need some additional information.

Setting the Monitor Ports Options

Many DOS applications will control the display adapter by transferring information directly to an input or output port. When an application of this type is running, Windows needs to keep track of (or monitor) these transfers. If an application does not display correctly, you will need to select the port option that matches the mode that was being used when the problem occurred. In other words, if the DOS application was running in text mode, then check the Text box. If it was running in high graphics, then check the High Graphics box, and so on.

If Your Application Uses	Then select this box
Text	This option sets aside enough memory to display the application in text mode. Text mode uses the least amount of memory (usually less than 16K).
Low Graphics	If you select this check box, Windows will reserve enough memory to display your application in low graphics mode. Usually, low graphics mode is used for a CGA monitor and adapter card. About 32K of memory is used.
High Graphics	If you have a EGA or VGA adapter/display, click the High Graphics box. High graphics mode uses about 128K of memory.
■ Note	Most applications need to have the High Graphics box checked, and most applications do not need to have Text or Low Graphics boxes checked.

| Emulate Text Mode | In general, you leave this box checked and most applications will be able to display text a little faster. If your application displays garbled text, or if text is displayed in the wrong location, try running it with this box cleared. |

Retain Video Memory

Figure 24.8

┌─ Display Options ───┐
│ Monitor Ports: ☐ Text   ☐ Low Graphics   ☐ High Graphics │
│   ☒ Emulate Text Mode   ☐ Retain Video Memory   │
└───┘

Check the box in this area to retain video memory as explained in the text.

Windows will do everything it can to use your system as efficiently as possible. For example, if you are running a DOS application in High Graphics mode and switch that application to Text mode, less memory is needed. Windows will detect the switch and release the additional memory to be used by other applications. However, if you are running an application in Text mode and need to switch to High Graphics, there may not be enough memory available and your application will disappear.

To eliminate this problem, check the Retain Video Memory box and the Video Memory option (on the basic setup page) that matches the mode where the problem occurred. For example, if your application disappears in the High Graphics mode, check the Retain Video Memory box and click the Radio button for High Graphics on the basic setup page as shown in Figure 24.8. The Video Memory option guarantees that there will be enough memory available, and the Retain Video Memory option makes sure that Windows does not release any of that memory for use by other programs. However, any time both selections are checked, the video memory cannot be used by other applications even when it is available.

▲ **Hint**   If your application does disappear, you can usually make it reappear by releasing memory from somewhere else. One way to do this would be to close any applications that are open but not in use. ▲

Other Options

Figure 24.9

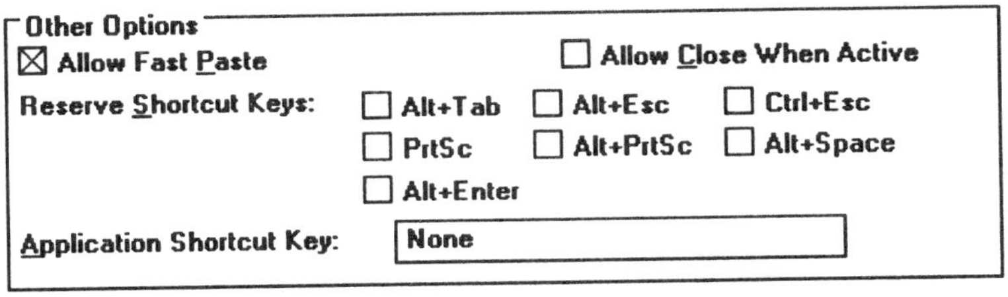

The Other Options section

The last section of the Advances Options dialog box is used to customize the way your DOS application runs in the enhanced mode. (See Other Options box in Figure 24.9.)

Allow Fast Paste   For the most part, when you transfer information from one application to another, Windows will automatically handle all of the necessary data translation. All you need to do is open the Edit menu in the source application, choose Copy (or Cut), move to the target application, open its Edit menu, and choose Paste. Windows will transfer the information from the original application to Clipboard, and from Clipboard to the target application. If your DOS application lets you perform this operation without any trouble, leave the Allow Fast Paste box checked.

If you try to paste data into a DOS application and nothing happens, it might mean that your application cannot accept data using the Fast Paste method. To Fix this problem, use the following procedure:

What to Do	What Happens
1. Press the [Esc] key.	The Paste operation will be canceled.
2. Open the appropriate PIF and press the Advanced Options button.	The Advanced Options dialog box will appear.
3. Clear the Allow Fast Paste box.	The X will disappear from the check box.
4. Save your changes and close PIF Editor.	The updated PIF will be saved to your hard disk.
5. Restart your DOS application and try again.	The Paste operation should work correctly.

Allow Close When Active If you check this box, you give Windows permission to close a DOS application without using its Exit command. Setting this option allows you to exit Windows without having to close each application separately.

■ Note Selecting this option can be dangerous. If Windows exits a DOS application before it has closed all of its files, you might lose any changes that were made.

Reserve Shortcut Keys

Figure 24.10

Reserve Shortcut Keys:	☐ Alt+Tab	☐ Alt+Esc	☐ Ctrl+Esc
	☐ PrtSc	☐ Alt+PrtSc	☐ Alt+Space
	☐ Alt+Enter		

Reserve Shortcut Keys area

Windows uses several special key combinations to perform certain actions. For example, you can display the Task List by pressing $Ctrl+Esc$, or if you press $Alt+Esc$ you can cycle through the active applications in the order that they were started.

On occasion, a DOS application will use a key combination that is the same as a Windows key combination. Any time Windows is running, it will "grab" the key combination, perform an action, and your DOS application will never receive the instruction. In fact, it may be impossible to use you DOS application because Windows insists on intercepting important commands.

The check boxes in the Reserve Shortcut Keys area solve this problem (see Figure 24.10). If you check any of the boxes in this area, Windows will ignore the specified key combination any time your DOS application is running.

How to Assign an Application Shortcut Key

The last part of the Advanced Options allows you to assign a shortcut key to your DOS application. Shortcut keys can be used to switch quickly to any active application from anywhere in Windows, no matter what application is in the foreground, and without using the mouse. When you press a shortcut key, the application that is assigned to it will instantly become the foreground application.

The key combinations that you choose must include the Alt or the $Ctrl$ key. For example, $Ctrl+C$, $Alt+R$, $Alt+Shift+T$, and $Ctrl+Shift+F1$ are all valid shortcut-key combinations. However, once you assign a shortcut key, the combination will work only when the application is loaded. If the application is not loaded, no other application, including Windows, will be able to use that combination for any other purpose. In other words, choose your shortcut-key combinations carefully.

■ **Note** Shortcut-key combinations cannot include the Esc, $Enter$, $Space$, Tab, $Print Screen$, or $BkSp$ keys.

There are two ways to assign a shortcut key to an application. If you are in Program Manager and have already created an icon for the application, you can select it, open the File menu, choose Properties, and enter a key combination into the dialog box.

▲ **Hint**   You can also use this method to assign a shortcut key to a Windows application. ▲

If you are editing (or creating) a PIF, you can enter a shortcut-key combination into the dialog box at the bottom of the Other Options area. Shortcut keys assigned from Program Manager (from the File Menu) always override keys assigned from a PIF.

▲ **Hint**   Keep a record of the shortcut keys you assign. You might want to write them on a filing card or in a small notebook stored near your computer. ▲

How to Assign a Shortcut Key from Program Manager

What to Do	**What Happens**
1. Open Program Manager (if it is not already open).	The Program Manager window will display.
2. Select the application that is to have a shortcut key.	The title of the application will be highlighted.
3. Open the File menu and choose Properties.	See Figure 24.11.

Figure 24.11

Program Item Properties	
Description:	File Manager
Command Line:	WINFILE.EXE
Working Directory:	
Shortcut Key:	None
	☐ **R**un Minimized

OK
Cancel
Browse...
Change **I**con...
Help

	What to Do	What Happens
4.	Use the mouse (or press the ⌨Tab key) to move the insertion point into the Shortcut Key box.	The insertion point will move.
5.	Press the key combination that you want to assign to this application. Remember, the shortcut-key combination must include the ⌨Ctrl or ⌨Alt key as part of the definition.	The key combination will appear in the Shortcut Key box.

▲ **Hint**   To delete a shortcut-key combination, press ⌨⇧Shift + ⌨←BkSp . ▲

6.	Press OK to finish.	The dialogue box will close.

■ **Note**   If you try to specify a key combination that Windows cannot accept, you will see an error message. Windows will then reset the shortcut key to its previous definition (if any).

How to Assign a Shortcut Key from PIF Editor

	What to Do	**What Happens**
7.	Open the Main Group and launch PIF Editor.	See Figure 24.12.
8.	Use the mouse (or press the ⌨Tab key) to move the insertion point into the Shortcut Key box.	The insertion point will move.

Figure 24.12

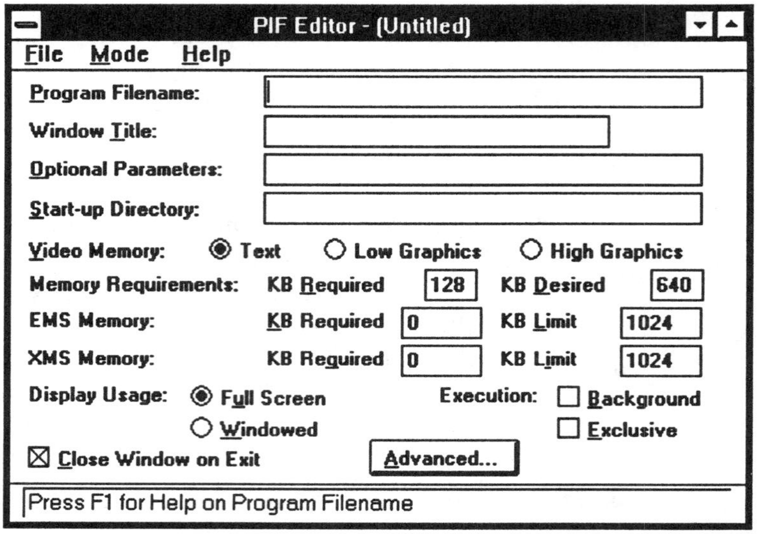

```
┌─────────────────────────────────────────────────────────────┐
│ ━          PIF Editor - (Untitled)                    ▼ ▲   │
├─────────────────────────────────────────────────────────────┤
│ File   Mode   Help                                            │
├─────────────────────────────────────────────────────────────┤
│ Program Filename:      [│                              ]      │
│ Window Title:          [                          ]           │
│ Optional Parameters:   [                              ]       │
│ Start-up Directory:    [                              ]       │
│                                                               │
│ Video Memory:     ◉ Text    ○ Low Graphics   ○ High Graphics │
│ Memory Requirements:  KB Required  [128]  KB Desired  [640]   │
│ EMS Memory:           KB Required  [0]    KB Limit    [1024]  │
│ XMS Memory:           KB Required  [0]    KB Limit    [1024]  │
│ Display Usage: ◉ Full Screen         Execution: ☐ Background  │
│                ○ Windowed                       ☐ Exclusive   │
│ ☒ Close Window on Exit      [ Advanced... ]                   │
├─────────────────────────────────────────────────────────────┤
│ Press F1 for Help on Program Filename                         │
└─────────────────────────────────────────────────────────────┘
```

9. Press the key combination that you want to assign to this application. Remember, the shortcut-key combination must include the [Ctrl] or [Alt] key as part of the definition.

The key combination will appear in the Shortcut Key box.

10. Press the OK button to finish.

The dialog box will close.

■ **Note** Remember, shortcut-key assignments made in Program Manager override any shortcut keys specified in PIF Editor.

Fine Tuning _DEFAULT.PIF

As you will remember, when you launch a non-Windows application, Windows will look for a PIF that has a name similar to the executable file name. If Windows cannot find a match, it will use a file called _DEFAULT.PIF. You should actually create a custom PIF for each DOS application that you use, but if you have a new program or a program that is only going to be used one time, creating a custom PIF may not be practical.

The _DEFAULT.PIF file contains enough information to run your DOS application, but it may not run it at its best. However, you can make a few changes (and improvements).

How to Fine Tune _DEFAULT.PIF

What to Do   What Happens

1. Launch PIF Editor, open the File menu and select Open.   See Figure 24.13.

Figure 24.13

2. When the dialogue box appears, type the filename into it. Remember to type the underline character at the beginning. The underline character is a shifted dash on most keyboards. You can also double-click on the correct filename from the list and it will load.   See Figure 24.14.

Figure 24.14

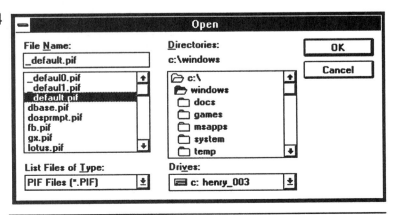

3. Make sure that the Exclusive box is set to OFF. That is, if the box is checked, click on it to clear it. The Exclusive box is near the bottom right of the PIF Editor window.

The selected option will clear.

4. Make sure that the expanded and extended memory requirements are set to 0.

The text box will reflect your choices.

5. Press the Advanced button.

The Advanced Options dialog box will appear as shown in Figure 24.15.

Figure 24.15

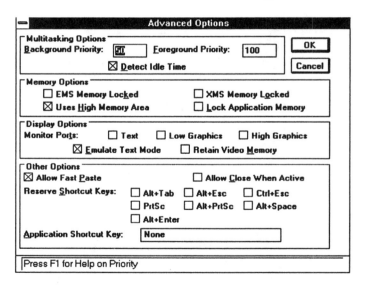

6. Set the value in the Foreground Priority box to 10,000.

The text box will display your entry.

■ **Note** This change tells Windows to give your DOS application the maximum amount of the CPU's attention. If this setting does not work, then a custom PIF is required.

| 7. | Turn all memory options off. | The boxes in the Memory Options area should be cleared. |

| 8. | Turn all Monitor Ports options off. | The boxes on the Monitor Ports line should be clear. |

■ **Note**   These options are intended to be used if you have an EGA or VGA DOS application that is acting up. Again, in these cases, a custom PIF is required.

| 9. | Check the Emulate Text Mode box. | This box should be checked. |

| 10. | Press the OK button to return to the standard settings page. | The opening screen of PIF Editor will reappear. |

| 11. | Open the File menu and choose Exit. When the dialog box appears, press the button marked YES to save your file and leave PIF Editor (see Figure 24.16). | Your updated file will be saved and PIF Editor will close. |

Figure 24.16

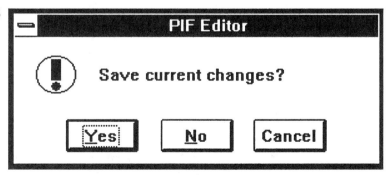

1. A PIF (or Program Information File) provides the technical specifications that Windows needs to run a DOS application correctly.

2. If you try to run a DOS application that does not have a custom-made PIF, Windows will use a PIF called _DEFAULT.PIF.

3. You can always identify a PIF by its extension (.PIF). Windows thinks that .PIF files are executable files.

4. To use a ready-made PIF, all you need to do is locate it and copy it into the Windows subdirectory.

5. Most of the information that you will need to complete a PIF can be found in the DOS application's documentation.

6. In general, to create a PIF, open the Accessories Group, launch PIF Editor, and fill in the blanks.

7. After a PIF is defined, it can be used to launch a DOS application just as if it were an executable file. In other words, you can enter its name at the Run line or launch it with a double-click in File Manager or Program Manager.

8. It often is not necessary to set any of the Advanced Options. In general, these options are used to control the way a DOS application behaves while it is multitasking.

9. DOS applications can display your work as text, low-resolution graphics, or high-resolution graphics.

10. Text mode (as the name implies) is used to display text on your screen. Many DOS-based work processors use the text mode.

11. Low-graphics mode is used if your computer is equipped with a CGA display.

12. High-Graphics mode is used by computers with an EGA or VGA display.

13. Shortcut keys can be used to switch quickly to any active application from anywhere in Windows, no matter what application is in the foreground and without using the mouse.

14. Shortcut-key combinations must include the [Alt] or the [Ctrl] key.

15. Once you assign a shortcut key, the combination will work only when the application is loaded. If the application is not loaded, no other application (including Windows) will be able to use that shortcut key combination for any other purpose.

16. You can assign a shortcut key from Program Manager (using the Properties box) or from PIF Editor. Shortcut keys assigned from Program Manger always override any shortcut keys assigned from PIF Editor.

Comprehension Questions

1. In general, what information does a PIF contain?

2. Why do Windows applications not need PIFs?

3. List two sources of PIFs.

4. How can you identify a PIF in a list of files?

5. To complete a PIF, you need technical information about the program such as memory requirements and video modes. Where can this information usually be found?

6. What kind of information goes in the Optional Parameters box?

7. If you choose the Full Screen option, how will your DOS application be affected when it runs?

8. If your PIF has a filename that is similar to the main application's filename, what additional action is necessary before Windows will use that PIF to launch your application?

9. If Windows can't find a matching PIF, what will happen?

10. If a DOS application seems to be running too slowly, there are several things that you can do to speed it up. What are they?

11. What is a shortcut key?

12. If you have an application that does not use the High Memory (HMA) and the High Memory Area box is checked, what will happen?

13. What is the difference between reserving a shortcut key and assigning a shortcut key?

14. List the keys that cannot be used as part of a shortcut-key combination.

Completion Questions

1. The letters PIF stand for _____ _____ _____.

2. If a DOS application does not have a custom-made PIF, then Windows will use a PIF called _____.

3. While you are filling in a PIF, you can get help about a specific area if you select the area and press the _____ key.

4. As far as Windows is concerned, a PIF is an _____ file.

5. If your DOS application uses text and CGA graphics, you should select the _____ _____ mode.

6. The amount of time that Windows will spend on a DOS task is controlled by the values entered into the _____ and the _____ priority boxes.

7. Each of the Priority boxes will accept a value between _____ and _____.

8. If you want a DOS application to return to Windows when it closes, then the _____ _____ _____ _____ box should be checked.

9. A shortcut key must use either the _____ or the _____ key as part of its definition.

25

Recorder

Learning Objectives

1. Define macro.

2. Identify operations that could be recorded as macros.

3. Identify operations that would not make good macros.

Performance Objectives

1. Start and stop the macro Recorder

2. Create a macro that will play back in any application.

3. Create a macro for a specific application.

4. Run a macro after it is recorded.

5. Retrieve a macro file.

Looping
Macro

A Looping Macro is a macro that runs continuously. In other words, when a Looping Macro ends, it starts over again from the beginning. The only way to stop a Looping Macro is to press Ctrl + Break.

Macro

A Macro is a recording of your keystrokes and mouse actions. You can think of a macro as a little magical helper that watches over your shoulder and keeps track of everything that you do.

Chapter Overview

One of the best reasons to use a computer is to help eliminate repetitive jobs. When you are using Windows and you find that you are performing the same task again and again, you can use Recorder to "teach" the computer how to do that job for you. For example, rather than typing your return address at the beginning of every letter you write, Recorder can be used to capture your keystrokes and then replay them the next time they are needed.

You can think of Recorder as a little magical helper that watches over your shoulder and keeps track of everything that you do. Any time your little magical helper is awake, it will memorize every keystroke and every mouse motion that you make. You only need to perform an operation once and Recorder will quickly play it back as often as necessary and without any errors.

Macro Recorder

Figure 25.1

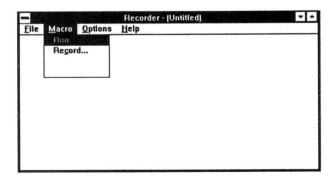

Main Recorder window

A macro is simply a recording of your keystrokes and mouse actions. To "wake up" your magical helper, open the Accessories group and launch the Recorder application. (The icon for Recorder looks like a little video camera.) When the Recorder window opens, you will see that it looks just like any other Windows application (see Figure 25.1). In other words, Recorder has a title bar with standard buttons, a menu bar, and a work area.

Your First Macro

Figure 25.2

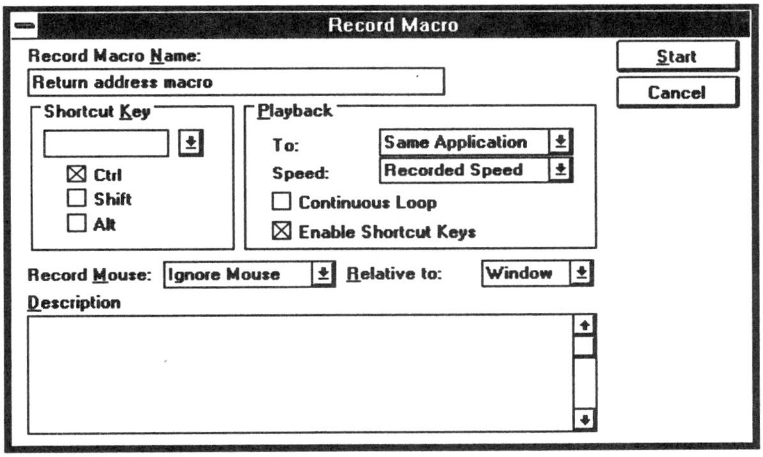

Record Macro window

To begin recording a macro, open the Macro menu, choose Record, and a new window will open (see Figure 25.2). The insertion point will be in the first box which is labeled Record Macro Name. Type a descriptive name (up to 40 characters long) and then use the mouse (or press [Tab]) to move to the Description box. (Skip all of the choices in between for now.)

When you get to the Description box, type a few sentences that explain what the macro will do. You can make the description as long as you want, but it is a good idea to keep it rather short. Always provide a good description for your macros. If you take the time to record a macro, you should take a few extra seconds to enter a description that will help you remember what each of your macros are used for.

Now you are ready to record. Press the Start button and the Record Macro window will minimize, but your magical helper will lurk in the background and memorize everything that you do. When you are finished with the operation you want to record, reopen Recorder and a dialog box will appear. Select one of the options in the box and your magical helper will go back to sleep.

Recorder will also let you specify a shortcut key that can be used to play back your macro. A shortcut key is a single keystroke and must include some combination of the [Ctrl], [Alt], and/or [⇧ Shift] key.

To assign a shortcut key, start by moving the insertion point into the Shortcut Key box and typing a single letter. Then, check one or more of the boxes (marked [Ctrl], [⇧ Shift], and [Alt]) to select a key to be used with that letter. For example, to assign the combination [Alt]+D to your macro, type a letter D into the box and make sure that only the [Alt] box is checked. To play back your macro, just press (and hold) the [Alt] key and press the letter D.

If you want to use a key other than a letter or number as a shortcut key for your macro, press the Down arrow next to the Shortcut Key box. This will cause a list of other keys, including the function keys, to display. To use one of these keys, open the list, click on the name of the key that you want to use, and it will be displayed in the Shortcut Key box.

■ **Note**   You must name your macro. That name can be in the form of a shortcut key, a descriptive name, or both.

When you are ready to play back your macro, open the Recorder window, locate the name of the macro you need, and double-click on it. Or, if you have assigned a shortcut key to your macro, just press the correct key combination. In any case, Windows will then play back your keystrokes (and mouse motions) exactly the same way they were entered.

■ **Note**   To play back your macros, first launch Recorder (if it is not already active) and load the file that contains your macro information.

How to Record a Macro

What to Do	**What Happens**

1. Open the Accessories Group and launch the Recorder application.

The Recorder window will appear.

2. Open the Macro menu and choose Record.

The Record Macro window will open as shown in Figure 25.3.

Figure 25.3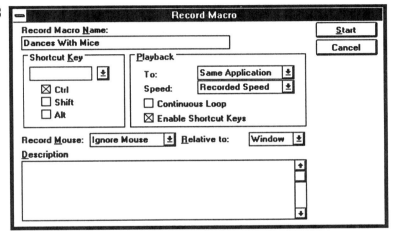

3. Type a name for the macro to be recorded into the Record Macro Name box. For this example, use the name DANCES WITH MICE. Make certain that the Record Mouse box reads: Everything.

The name will appear in the box as typed.

■ **Note** If you want to use a shortcut key to run your macro, type a key combination into the Shortcut Key box.

4. Press the START button.

Recorder will minimize to a flashing icon.

5. Perform the following operations:

Recorder will "memorize" your actions.

- Open the Main Group.
- Launch Control Panel.
- Close Control Panel.
- Open the Games Group.
- Close the Games Group.

Figure 25.4

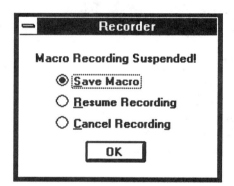

6. Double-click the Recorder icon (or press [Ctrl]+[Break]).

A dialog box will appear as shown in Figure 25.4.

7. Make sure that the Save Macro button is checked, and press the OK button.

Recording will stop.

8. Save your macro file. Open the Recorder window (if it is not already open), select the File menu, and choose Save. When the Save box appears, (as shown in Figure 25.5), assign a filename and press OK.

Your macro file will be saved.

Figure 25.5

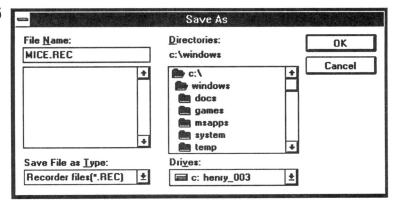

▲ Hint When you specify a filename for a macro file, Windows will automatically assign an .REC extension. You can use a different extension if you want, but if your macro files all end with .REC, they will be easier to find later.

How to Play Back Your Macro

What to Do   **What Happens**

1. Open the Recorder window   See Figure 25.6.

Figure 25.6

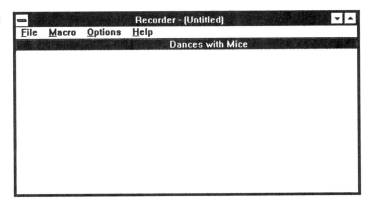

2. Double-click the name of   The macro will run.
the macro you want to use.

■ Note If you assigned a shortcut key to your macro, all you need to do is press the shortcut key combination and your macro will run.

Macros and Your Mouse

Recorder can log all keystrokes and every mouse movement. Unfortunately, that means that if you rearrange your work area, Recorder might not be able to find what it is looking for, and the next time you run your macro it will probably crash.

Windows Recorder has two tools that you can use to help control this problem. Near the center of the Record Macro window, you will find text boxes marked Record Mouse and Relative To. These boxes can be used to control the way that Recorder uses the mouse.

▲ Hint Incidentally, if you have a problem while your macro is running, you can stop it if you press the [Ctrl]+[Break] key combination. ▲

The first box (Record Mouse) has three choices. (Press the Down arrow next to the text box and a list of these choices will display). By default, Recorder will remember mouse actions only when you press (or hold) a mouse button. For example, if you want to close a window, you can double-click its Control Menu button. When Recorder is active, the mouse pointer will move to the correct location, and the double-click will occur, however, Recorder will not remember how the mouse pointer moved from its original location to the location of the Control Menu button.

If you need Recorder to remember the details of every mouse trail, activate the Everything option. When this selection is active, every motion the mouse makes will become part of the macro. It's fun to watch a macro run when this option has been used, but in general, it makes your macros run more slowly.

■ Note If you are recording a macro and choose the Everything option, you must press [Ctrl]+[Break] to stop recording. If you use the mouse to stop recording, your macro may not play back correctly.

Macros from the Keyboard You may have noticed that the problem related to rearranging your Windows screen has not been solved. Even if you choose one of the options described in the preceding paragraphs, your macro still may stop working. There is only one way to completely eliminate this problem, and that is not to use the mouse at all.

The third option in this list is Ignore Mouse. When this option is selected, Recorder will only remember keystrokes. It can take a little more time and be a little more troublesome to record a macro in this way, but when you are finished your macro will almost always work. The exact screen location of your windows and groups is no longer a problem.

Controlling Mouse Movements

The second text box in this part of the Record Macro window is labeled Relative To. If you click the Down arrow, two choices — Relative to Window and Relative to Screen — will appear. If you choose Relative to Windows, all mouse actions will be recorded in relationship to the window where you start recording. If you move the window, the mouse motions will follow it, but if you resize the window, the macro will probably crash.

The other option, Relative to Screen, will record the absolute position of the mouse as it moves around the entire screen. For example, if you want to create a macro that uses the mouse to move something from one application to another, the Relative to Screen option would be your best choice. Remember, your macro will only work as long as nothing is moved.

Controlling the Playback of a Macro

Figure 25.7

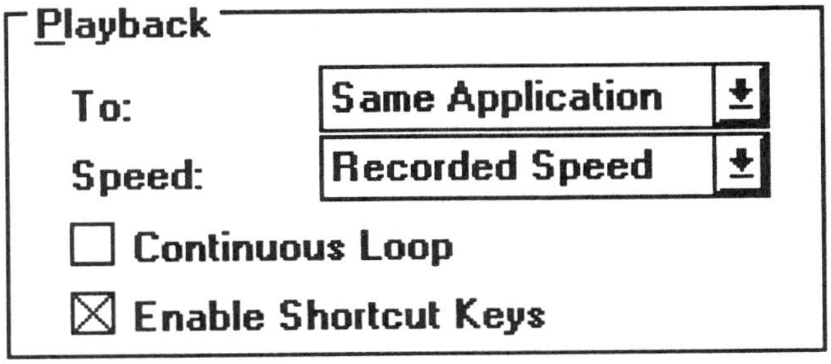

┌─ **Playback** ─────────────────────┐
│   │
│ **To:**   │ **Same Application** │±│ │
│   │
│ **Speed:**   │ **Recorded Speed**   │±│ │
│   │
│ ☐ **Continuous Loop**   │
│   │
│ ☒ **Enable Shortcut Keys**   │
│   │
└──────────────────────────────────────┘

The Playback options

Before you begin to record a macro, think about what you need it to do. For example, if you have a macro that will automatically type your return address, what will happen if that macro is accidently played back while the Paintbrush program is active?

Any time you record a macro that is specifically designed to be used with only a single application, make sure that the To: text box in the Record Macro window displays the Same Application option (see Figure 25.7). For example, when you record your return-address macro, your word processing program should be active. If the Same Application option is chosen, the return-address macro will not play back outside of your word processor. In other words, if the Paintbrush program is running and you try to play thee return-address macro, nothing will happen.

You will probably find that most of your macros will be recorded for use in a single application. However, if you want to use the same macro in several applications, or if your macro is generic and will run at any time in any application, then choose the Any Application option. For example, if you want to use the return-address macro in more than one word processing program, select the Any Application option. Remember, your macro can cause some very interesting problems if it is played back at the wrong time.

▲ **Hint**   After a macro is recorded, you can change the mouse-action and the playback options if you open the Macro menu and choose Properties. ▲

Looping (or Repeating) Macros   If you run into a situation where you need to perform the same operation over and over, you can record a macro to complete the operation once, and then start over and do the operation again. A macro of this type is called a Continuous Loop macro and it will continue to do its job until you press [Ctrl]+[Break].

Suppose you are working in your word processor and are typing a list that contains one hundred items. When you are finished, you notice that each item should have a Tab in front of it. You could manually place a Tab character at the beginning of each line, or you could start Recorder, place a Tab at the beginning of the first line, move to the next line, and stop recording. Make sure the Continuous Loop option is selected and play back your macro. If everything was recorded correctly, the macro will place a Tab, move to the next line and start over, placing a Tab on the next line, moving to the next line, and so on. It will continue to put Tabs at the beginning of each line until you press [Ctrl]+[Break] to tell it to stop.

■ **Note**   If you open the Options menu, deselect the [Ctrl]+[Break] Checking option, and then run a Continuous Loop macro, the only way to stop the macro is shut off the computer.

To create a looping macro, all you need to do is make sure that the Continuous Loop box is checked in the Record Macro window. You can check this box before you begin to record your macro, or if your macro has already been recorded, open the Macro menu and choose Properties.

Combining Macros

If you assign shortcut keys to your macros and check the box in the Playback area marked Enable Shortcut Keys, you can cause one macro to automatically run another macro. For example, if you have one macro called ⌥+D, and a second macro called ⌥+E, you could easily record a third macro that contains the keystrokes ⌥+D and ⌥+E. When you play back the third macro, the recorder will first run the ⌥+D macro, and when it is finished, it will run the ⌥+E macro.

If you are recording a large, complex macro and you make a mistake, the only way to correct your mistake is to start over. You may want to use this "nesting" technique to record a large macro as a series of small, manageable macros rather than trying to record the entire macro all at one time. Now, if you make a mistake, you only need to rerecord a short segment rather than rerecording the entire macro. When all of the separate parts have been recorded (and assigned to a shortcut key), record a master macro that refers to each of the short macros in the correct order.

▲ Hint

You may want to begin creating a library of short macros that can be combined in various ways to create new, larger macros. Just remember to assign a shortcut key to each macro and to check the Enable Shortcut Keys box. ▲

Managing Your Macro Files

Figure 25.8

The File menu for Recorder

Unless you save your collection of macros, when the Recorder application is closed, all of your work is lost. Actually, saving your work in Recorder is no different from saving your work anywhere in Windows. At the top of the Recorder work area, just below the title bar, you will find a very familiar menu bar. To save your macro collection, open the File menu (as shown in Figure 25.8) and select Save or Save As. Provide a filename and press ⌜Enter←⌟ to finish.

How to Create a Library of Macros

You will probably find that most of the macros that you create will only work inside of a single application. For example, you might have a group of macros that run inside of Write, or another group that will only work when Paintbrush is active. Before long, it might be difficult to keep track of which macro goes with which application. Fortunately, Recorder makes it easy to create convenient, logical groups and keep them together.

To create a group of macros for a specific application, start with a new, empty macro file. After you record one or two macros, save that file using a name that relates to the application that will use the macros. For example, if you are starting a set of macros to be used with Write, first launch Write, and then launch Recorder. Record one or two macros and then save the macro file under the filename WRITE with no extension. Windows will automatically add an extension of .REC which makes it easy to find your macro files later.

Figure 25.9

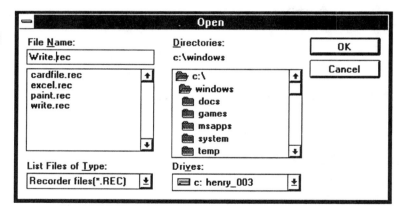

The Open dialog box for Recorder

The next time you use Write, remember to also launch Recorder. When Recorder is ready, open its File menu and you will see a dialog box similar to Figure 25.9. Load the file named WRITE.REC and all of your Write macros will be ready for use.

Is This Macro Worth the Trouble?

By this time you might begin to think that recording macros can be more time consuming and troublesome than it is worth. Actually, in some cases, this is true. Sometimes it can take longer to record a macro than to perform the same operation manually. As a general rule, if you are only going to perform an operation one or two times, even if the operation is very complex, a macro is probably not a good idea. If you are performing a task over and over, you need a macro.

▲ **Hint**   If you are not sure whether a job should be recorded as a macro, then don't record it. Only record a macro when you are certain it will be of use. ▲

Unfortunately there is no simple rule that can be used to help you decide when to record a macro. Sometimes it is impossible to make a decision about a macro until after it is recorded. Someone once said, "When you have a hammer, everything starts to look like a nail." Once you know how to use Recorder, everything could start to look like a macro. Recorder is a powerful tool when used correctly, but it cannot do everything.

Guidelines for Creating Successful Macros

1. Avoid using the mouse. If anything on your screen or in your work area is moved, your macro will no longer work.

2. Be sure to select the correct mode. If the macro is only to be used with a specific application, select the Same Application option. If the macro is to be used in more than one application (or if it is generic), then choose Any Application.

3. In general, select Fast Speed for playback. The purpose of a macro is to speed up your work. If you are creating a macro that demonstrates a particular feature of Windows (or if you just like to watch the computer work), then choose Recorded Speed for playback.

4. Any time you need to choose a group window, use the Window menu in Program Manager. For example, to choose the Main Group, open the Windows menu and type the hot-key letter (or number) that corresponds to the group you need.

5. Use Task Manager to switch between applications. Remember, you can open Task Manager at any time if your press ⌈Ctrl⌉ + ⌈Esc⌉.

6. Assign a descriptive name to each macro even if the macro is already assigned to a hot key. Descriptive names make it easier to remember what a macro does.

7. Write complete notes about the macro in the description box. There is no limit to the size of the description that can be attached to a macro. Include any details that you think might be important later.

8. Store related macros in a single Recorder file. For example, keep all of your macros that are used with Write in one file, and all of the macros for Paintbrush in another.

9. Plan ahead! Make sure you know what your macro is supposed to do before you record a single keystroke. In fact, you might want to create a pencil and paper "script" before you begin.

10. Keep your macros simple. Remember, it is very easy to change the Windows environment, but if you do, your macros may stop working.

Summary Points

1. A macro is simply a recording of your keystrokes and mouse actions. To launch Recorder, open the Accessories Group and double-click the Recorder icon.

2. To begin recording a macro, open the Macro menu and choose Record.

3. Recorder will also let you specify a shortcut key that can be used to play back your macro. A shortcut key is a single keystroke and must include some combination of the ⌈Ctrl⌉, ⌈Alt⌉, and/or ⌈⇧ Shift⌉ keys.

4. To play back a macro, open the Recorder window, locate the name of the macro you need and double-click on it. If you have assigned a shortcut key to your macro, just press the correct key combinations.

5. By default, Recorder will remember mouse actions only when you press (or hold) a mouse button.

6. If you need Recorder to remember the details of every mouse trail, activate the Everything option. This option can be selected when you begin recording a macro.

7. If you need to perform the same operation over and over, you can record a macro to complete the operation once, and then start over and do the operation again. A macro of this type is called a Continuous Loop macro.

8. If you assign shortcut keys to your macros and check the box in the Playback area that is marked Enable Shortcut Keys, you can cause one macro to automatically run another macro.

9. To save your macro collection, open the File menu and select Save or Save As. Provide a filename and press [Enter←] to finish.

10. When you begin to create a group of macros for a specific application, start with a new, empty macro file. After you record one or two macros, save that file using a name that relates to the application that will use those macros.

11. If you are not sure whether or not a job should be recorded as a macro, then don't record it. Only record a macro when you are certain that it will be of use.

Practice Exercises

Record a macro that will automatically type your return address into a Write document.

1. Open the Accessories Group and launch Write. Note: After Write is running, you may need to move or size the Write window so that you can see the Recorder icon.

2. Start the Recorder application, open the Macro menu and choose Record.

3. When the Record Macro window appears, assign a descriptive filename of TYPE RETURN ADDRESS.

4. Move to the Shortcut Key box and assign the key combination of [Ctrl]+R to the macro.

5. Move to the Playback options box. Set the options so that the macro will only play back in Same Application, and set the playback speed to Fast.

6. Move to the Record Mouse text box and set this option so that the mouse will be ignored.

7. Type a few short commands into the Description box. Remember, the information in this box can be used later to help you remember what the macro is used for.

8. Press the Start button. Recorder will minimize and flash.

9. Type your return address. When you are finished, make sure that everything is spelled correctly and it appears exactly the way you want it to appear.

10. Double-click the Recorder icon (or press [Ctrl]+[Break]) and select Save Macro. Press the OK button to finish.

To run your macro, press [Ctrl]+R or open Recorder and choose Run from the Macro menu.

Comprehension Questions

1. What is a macro?

2. What is the Description box used for?

3. A macro can be named in two ways. What are they?

4. When you are ready to play a macro back, what must you do?

5. If you need to stop a macro for any reason, what keys do you press?

6. When you are recording a macro, why should you avoid using the mouse?

7. What is a looping macro?

8. If you check the box labeled Enable Shortcut Keys (in the Record Macro window), you can cause one macro to run another separate macro. Why would you want to do this?

9. Not every Windows operation will make a good macro. How do you decide when to record a macro and when not to record a macro?

Completion Questions

1. To begin recording a macro, open the _____ menu, choose _____ , and press the _____ button.

2. A shortcut key is a single keystroke and must include some combination of the _____, _____ , and/or _____ key.

3. When you assign a name to a macro file, Windows automatically supplies an extension of _____ .

4. After a macro is recorded, you can change the mouse-action options and the playback options if you open the _____ menu and choose _____ .

5. To create a looping macro, check the _____ _____ box in the _____ area of the Record Macro window.

6. To save your macro file, open the _____ menu and choose _____ or _____ _____ .

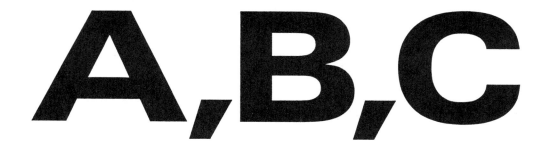

Appendices

A: Installing Windows

B: Summary of Scientific Calculator Functions

C: Summary of Keyboard Functions

Appendix A

Installing Windows

Before you can use Windows, it must be installed on your computer. In other words, you need to copy the files that your system needs from the Windows disks to your hard disk or network. Most of the installation process is handled by the Setup program that is found on Disk One of the Windows package.

To install Windows, place Disk One in an appropriate drive (usually drive A:), set that drive as the default, and type SETUP.

Running the SETUP Program

Once the Setup program starts, all you need to do is insert the correct disk at the correct time, type your name, and answer a few questions about your printer. If you try to install Windows 3.1 on the wrong type of computer (such as an XT or 8088), or on a computer that does not meet Windows minimum requirements, you may receive a warning message. In general, Setup does most of its work automatically. Just respond to the prompts and everything will be fine.

■ **Note**   You may want to boot your system from a "clean" floppy disk before you install Windows. Booting from a clean disk ensures that no memory-resident or other special programs remain in your computer's memory. Some resident programs can interfere with the Windows installation process.

How to Install Windows on Your Computer

What to Do	What Happens
1. Boot your computer and if necessary, exit from your menu program. In other words, to install Windows properly, you must start from the DOS prompt.	The DOS prompt should display. If you boot your computer from a hard disk, it should read: **C>** or **C:\>**.
2. Place the Windows Disk One in an appropriate drive and close the drive door (if necessary).	Nothing yet.
3. Type the name of the drive that you are using (followed by a colon) and press [Enter←]. For example, if you are installing Windows from drive A: you would need to type A: and press [Enter←].	The selected disk drive will display as the prompt.
4. Type SETUP and press [Enter←]. After a few seconds, the Windows Setup Welcome Screen will appear.	The Setup process will begin.

5. At the next screen, choose Express Setup or Custom Setup. To choose Express Setup, just press ⌨Enter◄──⌐.

The Express Setup process will begin.

■ **Note** For most people, the Express Setup will work best. If you are not sure which to choose, use the Express Setup.

6. Read the screen. Change disks as prompted by the Setup program.

The Setup process will continue.

7. When the Printer Installation box appears, scroll through the list and select the name of your printer.

After you have selected your printer from the list, the Setup process will continue.

■ **Note** If the name of your printer is not in the list, check your printer manual for an equivalent printer that can be used. Most uncommon printers can emulate a common printer and everything will work correctly.

8. Windows will now search your hard disk for applications. If Setup finds an executable file it recognizes, it will create an icon and place it in the Applications Group. If the filename could belong to more than one application, you may need to select the correct name from a list that will be displayed.

The Applications Group will be created.

9.	When Setup is finished, it will ask you if you want to run through the tutorial program. You can run the tutorial now or run it later by choosing Windows Tutorial from the Help menu.	If you choose Tutorial, it will run.
10.	Windows Setup will now ask if you want to restart your system. Press the appropriate button.	Windows will restart or your system will return to DOS, based on the choice you make.

Upgrading from 3.0 to 3.1

Many of the differences between Windows 3.0 and 3.1 are subtle, but upgrading to 3.1 is highly recommended. Windows 3.1 has many new features and enhancements that won't be available to you unless you upgrade.

When you upgrade from 3.0 to 3.1, you can still use the procedure described above. The new version will install on top of the old version, but your existing program groups will be maintained and all of your system information settings will be preserved. Upgrading will also update any existing device drivers (if necessary), but will not disturb any device drivers that Windows did not install.

■ Note If you are using DOS 5.0 (or greater), the Windows upgrade will also preserve any "optimization" statements in your AUTOEXEC.BAT and CONFIG.SYS files such as DEVICEHIGH= or DOS=HIGH.

Two Ways to Install Windows Actually, there are two ways to install Windows 3.1, but most users can use the Express Setup as described in the previous procedure. To perform the Express Setup, all you need to know is the name of the disk drive used to read the original Windows disks, the name of the drive and subdirectory that you want to use to store the Windows files, and the name of your printer and the port it uses.

▲ **Hint**   For most installations, the default choices are perfectly acceptable. The default choices usually are:

Install from:Drive a:\
Install to:C:\WINDOWS
Printer name:Get this information from your printer manual. ▲

Performing a Custom Installation

■ **Note**   **This section is for experienced users only.**
If you need (or want) to install Windows using the
Custom Setup, complete the following checklist before
you begin. Then, during the installation, provide this
information when requested by the Setup program.

_____   What directory do you want to use to store the
Windows files?

_____   What type of computer (i.e. 80286, 80386, etc.)
are you using?

_____   What type of monitor is connected to your system?

_____   What type of mouse (if any) is present?

_____   What type of keyboard are you using?

_____   What language (for example, Spanish, French,
German, etc.) are you going to use while running Windows?

_____   What network type (if any) are you connected to?

_____   What is the brand and type of your printer and
what printer port is it connected to?

_____   What applications on your hard disk do you want
to use with Windows?

_____   What changes do you need to make to your
AUTOEXEC.BAT and CONFIG.SYS files?

_____   Do you want to install any of the optional
Windows components?

_____   What virtual memory settings are required?

As you can see, some of these questions may be hard to answer. If you have trouble answering any of these questions, first check your system documentation or contact your computer's manufacturer. If you still cannot answer one (or more) of these questions completely, consider using the Express Setup instead.

■ **Note** In most cases, Express Setup will work perfectly. In fact, you should probably use Custom Setup only if Express Setup will not work. For more information about Custom Setup, check the Microsoft Windows User's Guide.

Starting Windows

After the Setup program has finished, press the Restart Windows button or, from the DOS prompt, type WIN and press [Enter←]. Finally, go to the beginning of this book and have fun!

Appendix B

Summary of Scientific Calculator Functions

Button	Key Name	**Key**	Function
Basic Operations			
+	Plus Sign	+	Adds
-	Minus Sign	-	Subtracts
*	Asterisk	*	Multiplies
/	Forward Slash	/	Divides

(	Open Parenthesis **(**		Starts a new level of parentheses. Parentheses are used to group values to ensure that the calculations are performed in the correct order. The current number of levels appears below the display up to a maximum number of 25.
)	Close Parenthesis **)**		Closes the current level of parentheses. There should be one close parenthesis to match each open parenthesis in a calculation.
Int	Semicolon	**;**	Converts the number in the display to an integer. In other words, if a number 12.345 is displayed, pressing this key will convert the number to 12. If you use the INV function with this key, it will display the decimal part of thee number only. For example, the number 12.345 would become .345.
Mod	Percent sign	**%**	Displays the modulus, or remainder, of an x/y calculation. For example, 11 Mod 3 displays 2.

Bitwise Operations

And	Ampersand	**&**	Performs a bitwise AND calculation.

Lsh	Less than	<	Performs a binary shift left. Inv+Lsh performs a binary shift right. After you press this key you must specify how many positions (in binary), to the left or right you want the number to shift and then press the equal sign (=).
Not	Tilde	~	Calculates the bitwise inverse of the number in the display.
Or	Vertical bar	|	Calculates bitwise OR of the number in the display.
Xor	Caret	^	Calculates bitwise exclusive OR of the number in the display.

Number-Base Functions

Bin	n/a	F8	Converts the number in the display to the binary equivalent.
Byte	n/a	F4	Displays only the lower 8 bits of the number in the display. The value of the number does not change.
Dec	n/a	F6	Converts the number in the display to the decimal equivalent. This is the default setting. Uses Deg, Rad, or Grad in trigonometric functions but the Dword, Word, and Byte do not apply.

Dword	n/a	F2	Displays the full 32-bit representation of the number in the display.
Hex	n/a	F5	Converts the number in the display to the hexadecimal equivalent.
Oct	n/a	F7	Converts the number in the display to the octal equivalent.
Word	n/a	F3	Displays only the lower 16 bits of the number in the display. The value of the number does not change.

Statistical Functions

Ave	n/a	Ctrl+A	Calculates the mean of the values in the Statistics Box. Inv+Ave calculates the mean of the squares of the numbers.
Dat	Insert	Ins	Places the number in the display into the Statistics Box.
s	n/a	Ctrl+D	Calculates the standard deviation with the population parameter as n-1. Inv+s calculates standard deviation with the population parameter as n.
Sta	n/a	Ctrl+S	Causes the Statistics Box to open and activates the Ave, Sum, s, and Dat buttons.

| Sum | n/a | $\boxed{\text{Ctrl}}$+T | Calculates the sum of the values in the Statistics Box. Inv+Sum calculates the sum of the squares. |

Advanced "Scientific" Functions

cos	letter o	o	Calculates the cosine of the number in the display. Inv+cos calculates the arc cosine. Hyp+cos calculates the hyperbolic cosine. Inv+hyp+cos calculates the arc hyperbolic cosine.
Deg	n/a	$\boxed{\text{F2}}$	Sets trigonometric input to degrees. For example, to calculate the cosine of 45 degrees, press $\boxed{\text{F2}}$, enter the number 45, and press the cos button. (Available in decimal mode only.)
dms	letter m	m	Converts the number in the display to degree-minute-second format assuming the number is in degrees. Inv+dms converts the number in the display to degrees assuming the number is in degree-minute-second format.
Exp	letter x	x	Allows you to enter numbers in scientific notation. The exponent has an upper limit of +307. You can continue to enter numbers as long as you only use keys 0-9. This function is only available with the decimal number system.

F-E	letter v	**v**	Causes the display to switch between scientific notation and normal (decimal) notation. The Calculator always displays numbers larger than 10^ in scientific notation. This function is used only with the decimal number system.
Grad	n/a	F4	Sets trigonometric input for gradients in decimal mode.
Hyp	letter h	**h**	Sets the hyperbolic function for sin, cos, and tan. The hyperbolic function automatically shuts off after a calculation is completed.
Inv	letter i	**i**	Sets the inverse function for sin, cos, tan, PI, x^y, x^2, x^3, ln, log, Ave, Sum, and s. The inverse function automatically shuts off after calculation is completed.
ln	letter n	**n**	Calculates the natural (base e) logarithm of the number in the display. Inv+ln calculates e raised to the xth power, where x is the number in the display.
log	letter l	**l**	Calculates the common (base 10) logarithm of the number in the display. Inv+log calculates 10 raised to the xth power.
n!	Exclamation	**!**	Calculates the factorial of the number in the display.

PI	letter p	**p**	Enters the value of PI into the display. Inv+PI displays 6.28 (or 2*pi).
Rad	n/a	F3	Sets trigonometric input for radians in decimal mode. Input can be from 0-2*pi.
sin	letter s	**s**	Calculates the sine of the number in the display. Inv+sin calculates the arc sine. Hyp+sin calculates the hyperbolic sine. Inv+hyp+sin calculates the arc hyperbolic sine.
tan	letter t	**t**	Calculates the tangent of the number in the display. Inv+tan calculates the arc tangent. Hyp+tan calculates the hyperbolic tangent. Inv+hyp+tan calculates the arc hyperbolic tangent.
x^y	letter y	**y**	Calculates the number x raised to the yth power. Inv+x^y calculates the yth root of x.
x^2	at sign	**@**	Displays the squares of the number in the display. Inv+x^2 calculates the square root of the number in the display.
x^3	octothorpe	**#**	Calculates the cube of the number in the display. Inv+x^3 calculates the cube root of the number in the display.

Summary of Keyboard Functions

The keystrokes listed here can be used to navigate in Windows without a mouse. Often, pressing one or two keys can be faster than using a mouse. Also, if your mouse is not working for some reason, you may be forced to use these key sequences.

System Keys

The keys listed here can be used anywhere in Windows regardless of the application you are using.

Press This Key
(or combination)

To perform this task

`F1`	Open the HELP window (if the application has Help).
`Ctrl` + `Esc`	Causes the Task List window to open.
`Alt` + `Esc`	Pressing this key combination will cause Windows to switch to the next active application. It doesn't matter if the application is running in a window or running as an icon.
`Alt` + `Tab`	This combination will cause Windows to switch to the next application. If you press (and hold) the `Alt` key, it will switch to the next application each time you press `Tab`. To return to the original application, hold the `Alt` key, and press `Esc`.
`⇧ Shift` + `Alt` + `Tab`	This combination is basically the opposite of the `Alt` + `Tab` combination. You can switch to the previous applications if you press (and hold) `Alt` + `⇧ Shift` while repeatedly pressing `Tab`. To return to the original application, continue to hold the `Alt` key, and press `Esc`.
`Print Screen`	This key will copy an image of the screen into the Clipboard. Note: This combination only works for non-Windows applications if they are running in text mode.

`Alt` + `Print Screen`	This combination will copy an image of the active window into Clipboard.
`Alt` + `Space`	This combination will open the Control menu for the selected application window or icon.
`Alt` + `-`	This combination will open the Control menu for a document window or icon.
`Alt` + `F4`	Use this combination to close an application or application window.
`Ctrl` + `F4`	This combination will close the active group window or document window.
`Alt` + `Enter←`	Use this combination to toggle a non-Windows application between running in a window and running full screen.
`↑` `↓` `←` `→`	The arrow keys can be used to move a window after you choose the Move command from a Control menu. If you choose the Size command from the Control menu, you can use the arrow keys to change the size of the selected window.

Menu Keys

Use the following keys to select menus and choose commands from an open menu:

**Press
This Key**
(or combination)   **To perform this task**

`Alt` **or** `F10`   You can press one of these keys to select (or cancel your selection) of the first menu on the menu bar. To select the next (or previous) menu from the menu bar, press the `→` (or `←`) arrow key. To open a menu after it is selected, press `Enter←` or the `↓`.

**A
Character
Key**   When a menu is open, you can choose the command whose underlined letter or number matches the one you type. When the menu bar is selected (by pressing `F10` or `Alt` as explained above) you can choose the menu item whose underlined character matches the one you type.

⬅ or ➡	When the menu bar is selected, you can use these keys to move between menus.
⬆ or ⬇	When a menu is open, these keys will move the cursor bar between commands. If the menu is closed, pressing the ⬇ will cause it to open.
Enter⬅	This key opens the selected menu or command.
Esc	The Esc key could be called the panic button. Press Esc to cancel the selected menu name or to close the open menu.

Dialog Box Keys

Any time you are working in a dialog box, you can use these keys rather than the mouse:

**Press
This Key**
(or combination)   **To perform this task**

Tab	Pressing this key will move the selection from option to option (left to right and top to bottom).
Shift + Tab	This combination is the opposite of the combination described above. Pressing this combination will move the selection from option to option in reverse order.
Alt + a character key	If you press this combination, the selection will move to the option or group whose underlined letter or number matches the one you type.
⬆ ⬇ ⬅ ➡	Pressing an arrow key will move the selection cursor from option to option within a group of options. You can also use the arrow keys to move the cursor within a list or text box.
Home	Pressing this key will move the selection to the first item (or character) in a list (or a text box).
End	This combination is the opposite of the combination described above. Pressing this key will move the selection to the last item (or character) in a list (or a text box).

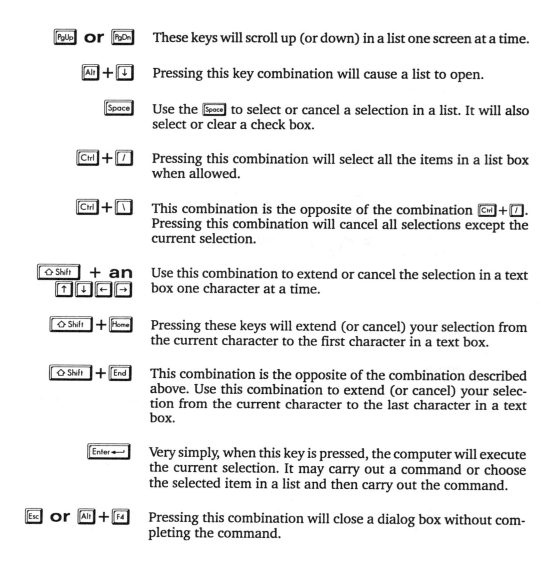

PgUp or PgDn   These keys will scroll up (or down) in a list one screen at a time.

Alt + ↓   Pressing this key combination will cause a list to open.

Space   Use the Space to select or cancel a selection in a list. It will also select or clear a check box.

Ctrl + /   Pressing this combination will select all the items in a list box when allowed.

**Ctrl + **   This combination is the opposite of the combination Ctrl + /. Pressing this combination will cancel all selections except the current selection.

Shift + an ↑ ↓ ← →   Use this combination to extend or cancel the selection in a text box one character at a time.

Shift + Home   Pressing these keys will extend (or cancel) your selection from the current character to the first character in a text box.

Shift + End   This combination is the opposite of the combination described above. Use this combination to extend (or cancel) your selection from the current character to the last character in a text box.

Enter◄┘   Very simply, when this key is pressed, the computer will execute the current selection. It may carry out a command or choose the selected item in a list and then carry out the command.

Esc or Alt + F4   Pressing this combination will close a dialog box without completing the command.

Cursor Movement Keys

The cursor movement keys are used any place you need to move the cursor or insertion point. For example, they can be used to move between text boxes, or to move any other place you can type such as in Notepad or in your word processor.

Press This Key
(or combination)

To move the insertion point

Key	Action
↑	Up one line.
↓	Down one line.
→	To the right, one character.
←	To the left, one character.
Ctrl + →	To the right, one word.
Ctrl + ←	To the left, one word.
Home	To the beginning of the current line.
End	To the end of the current line.
PgUp	Up one screen or page.
PgDn	Down one screen or page.
Ctrl + Home	To the beginning of a document.
Ctrl + End	To the end of a document.

Editing Keys

These keys can be used to help edit text while you are in a dialog box or window. They will also work in most word processing programs such as Notepad or Write.

Press This Key
(or combination)

To perform this task

`←BkSp`　　Press this key to delete the character to the left of the insertion point. If you have selected a block of text, the entire selection will be deleted.

`Del`　　This key will delete the character to the right of the insertion point. If you have selected a block of text, the entire selection will be selected. When a block of text is selected, `←BkSp` (above) and `Del` perform the same function.

`⇧Shift` + `Del` **or** `Ctrl`+X　　These combinations will delete the selected text and place it on the Clipboard.

`⇧Shift` + `Ins` **or** `Ctrl`+V　　These combinations will paste (copy) text from the Clipboard into the currently active window.

`Ctrl`+`Ins` **or** `Ctrl`+C　　Pressing one of these combinations will copy the text you have selected and place it on the Clipboard.

`Ctrl`+Z **or** `Alt`+`←BkSp`　　If you press one of these combinations, it will undo your last editing action. In other words, if you cut the wrong block of text, you can undo the cut if you press `Ctrl`+Z or `Alt`+`←BkSp`.

Text Selection Keys

The following key combinations can be used in most Windows applications. However, in some applications, some of the keys here might not work everywhere you can select text. All of the combinations listed here start at the insertion point. If you have already selected a block of text, pressing these combinations will cancel your selection.

Press This Key (or combination)	To select or cancel the selection
⟨⇧ Shift⟩ + ⟨←⟩ or ⟨→⟩	Move the selection one character at a time to the left (or right).
⟨⇧ Shift⟩ + ⟨↑⟩ or ⟨↓⟩	Move the selection one up (or down) one line of text.
⟨⇧ Shift⟩ + ⟨PgUp⟩	Select (or deselect) all text one screen up.
⟨⇧ Shift⟩ + ⟨PgDn⟩	Select (or deselect) all text one screen down.
⟨⇧ Shift⟩ + ⟨Home⟩	Select the text from the current location to the beginning of the line.
⟨⇧ Shift⟩ + ⟨End⟩	Select the text from the current location to the end of the line.
⟨Ctrl⟩ + ⟨⇧ Shift⟩ + ⟨←⟩	Add (or remove) the previous word to (or from) the selection.
⟨Ctrl⟩ + ⟨⇧ Shift⟩ + ⟨→⟩	Add (or remove) the next word to (or from) the selection.
⟨Ctrl⟩ + ⟨⇧ Shift⟩ + ⟨Home⟩	Select (or deselect) all of the text from the current location to the beginning of the document.
⟨Ctrl⟩ + ⟨⇧ Shift⟩ + ⟨End⟩	Select (or deselect) all of the text from the current location to the end of the document.

Program Manager Keys

The keys in the following table can be used to perform the operations listed when you are working in group windows in Program Manager.

Press This Key (or combination)	To perform this task
⬆️ ⬇️ ⬅️ ➡️	To move between items inside a group window.
Ctrl + F6 or Tab	To move between group windows and icons.
Enter ↵	Pressing this key will launch the selected application.
⇧ Shift + F4	This combination will arrange the open group windows as Tiles.
⇧ Shift + F5	This combination will arrange the open group windows in a Cascade pattern.
Ctrl + F4	This combination will cause the active group window to close.
Alt + F4	This combination will exit Program Manager. Remember, when you exit Program Manager, you exit Windows.

File Manager Keys

File Manager actually has several subsections that use the same key combinations in a way that may be slightly different than you expect.

Directory Tree Keys

Any time you are working with the Directory Tree, the following key combinations can be used:

Press
This Key
(or combination)

To perform this task

`Tab`	When you press this key, you can move between the Directory Tree, the contents list, and the disk- drive icons.
`←`	Pressing this key will select the directory listed above the current subdirectory.
`→`	Pressing this key will select the first subdirectory listed below the current directory (if there is another subdirectory below the current directory).
`Enter ←`	Pressing this key will display (or hide) any subdirectories.
`⇧ Shift` + `Enter ←`	When you press this key, a new window will open that displays the contents of the currently selected directory.
`↑` or `↓`	Use these keys to select a directory listed above (or below) the current directory.
`Ctrl` + `↑`	This combination will select the previous directory at the same level if it exists.
`Ctrl` + `↓`	This combination will select the next directory at the same level if it exists.
`PgUp`	Press this to select the directory one screen up from the current directory.
`PgDn`	Use this combination to select the directory one screen down from the current directory.
`Home` or `\`	When you press this combination, the root directory will be selected.
`End`	Pressing this key will select the last directory in the list.
A Character Key	Pressing a character key will select the next directory whose name begins with the specified letter or number if one exists.

⊞	Pressing this will make the current directory expand and display all sub-directories (if any exist).
⊟	This key causes the current (expanded) directory to collapse.

Contents List Keys

When you are working with a list of files in File Manager, you can use these keys to help.

Press This Key (or combination)	**To perform this task**
⌨ Tab	When you press this key, you can move between the Directory Tree, the contents list, and the disk-drive icons.
⌨ PgUp	Press this to select the directory one screen up from the current directory.
⌨ PgDn	Use this combination to select the directory one screen down from the current directory.
⌨ Home	When you press this combination, the root directory will be selected.
⌨ End	Pressing this key will select the last directory in the list.
A Character Key	Pressing a character key will select the next directory whose name begins with the specified letter or number if one exists.
⌨ Shift **+ an** 	Pressing this combination will select (or cancel the selection) of multiple items.
⌨ Ctrl + ⌨ /	Pressing this combination will select all items in a list.
⌨ Ctrl + ⌨ \	This key combination will cancel all selections in a list except for the current selection.

⇧ Shift + F8	This key combination is used to select (or unselect) nonconsecutive items. To use, press **⇧ Shift + F8** and then use the arrow keys and the **Space** to toggle your selections.
↑ ↓ ← →	These keys will move the cursor or scroll to other items in a window.
Space	Use the **Space** to toggle (select or cancel) a selection of nonconsecutive items when they are marked by a blinking cursor.
Enter←	Press this to open a directory or start an application.
⇧ Shift + Enter←	When you press this combination, a new window will open that displays the contents of the selected directory.

Drive Area Keys

Finally, when you are working in the drive area, you can use the following keys:

Press This Key (or combination)	**To perform this task**
Ctrl + a drive letter	Pressing this key combination will change to the disk-drive icon that matches the letter you specify.
← or →	Use the arrow keys to move between drive icons.
Space	Pressing the **Space** will change to a new drive.
Enter←	Pressing **Enter←** will open a new directory window.

Help Window Keys

While you are working in the HELP screens (from any application), the following keys will be useful.

**Press
This Key
(or combination)**   **To perform this task**

`Tab`   Press this key to move clockwise through the hot spots in a topic.

`Shift` + `Tab`   This combination moves counter-clockwise through the hot spots in a topic. This combination is the opposite of the combination described above.

`Ctrl` + `Tab`   Pressing this combination will select (or deselect) all of the hot spots in a topic.

`Ctrl` + `Ins`   Pressing these keys will copy the current Help topic, an entire annotation or a portion of an annotation into the Clipboard without displaying the Copy dialog box.

`Shift` + `Ins`   Press this to paste the contents of the Clipboard into the Annotation dialog box.

`Alt` + `F4`   When you press this combination, the current Help Window will close.

Write Keys

The following key combinations can be used while you are working in Write. Note: When the key combination includes a 5, it means to use the number 5 key on the numeric keypad.

Movement Keys

The following keys will help you move the insertion point while in a document.

Press This Key
(or combination)

To perform this task

5+→ This combination will move the insertion point to the next sentence.

5+← This combination will move the insertion point to the previous sentence. This combination is the opposite of the combination described above.

5+↓ Press this to move the insertion point to the next paragraph.

5+↑ Press this to move the insertion point back to the previous paragraph. This combination is the opposite of the combination described above.

5+PgDn This combination will cause the insertion point to move to the next page. Note: If your document has not been repaginated, it may not go where you expect it to go.

5+PgUp This combination will cause the insertion point to move to the previous page. Note: If your document has not been repaginated, it may not go where you expect it to go. This combination is the opposite of the combination described above.

Editing Keys

Use the following keys while you are editing text in Write:

Press This Key
(or combination)

To perform this task

`Ctrl` + `Enter⏎` Press these keys to insert a manual page break.

`Ctrl` + **Z or** `Alt` + `←BkSp` Pressing this combination will undo your last typing or editing action.

`↓` If you press this while the cursor is above the upper-left corner of a picture, the picture will be selected.

`↑` `↓` `←` `→` When a picture is selected, you can use these keys to move the Size Picture cursor. To move a selected picture, choose Move Picture from the Write Edit menu.

`Ctrl` + `⇧ Shift` + `-` This combination will insert a hyphen that will only display if the word that contains the optional hyphen is placed at the end of a line.

`Alt` + `F6` If you press this, Write will switch between the document and the Find or Replace dialog box. If you are typing a page header (or footer), it will switch between the document and the Page Header (or Page Footer) dialog box.

INDEX

open windows, arranging, 216–17
Options menu, 217–18
   Confirmation option, 261–63
   Font option, 260
   Minimize on Use option, 261, 278, 285–86
   Save Settings on Exit option, 217, 261
   Status Bar option, 261
   printing text files from, 291–92
Replace File dialog box, 242, 244
selecting files, 239–40
sending files to a specified location, 244–46
status bar, 200
subdirectories, copying/moving/deleting/renaming, 271–72
subdirectory branches, 210
Tree menu:
   controlling display with, 212–13
   expanding/collapsing subdirectory tree with, 269–70
   Indicate Expandable Branches option, 270
View menu, 202, 211–12, 214, 215, 256–61
   All File Details option, 257
   By File Type option, 202, 259–60
   Directory Only option, 214
   Partial Details option, 258
   Sort options, 258–59
   Tree Only option, 213
Window menu:
   Cascade option, 216
   New Window option, 215
   Refresh option, 290–91
   Tile option, 216–17
File menu, 11, 20
   Exit command, 11
   File Manager, 55, 239–40, 270–71, 279–80, 282–84, 291–92
   New command, 89, 91
   Properties command, 99
Filenames, 26
   DOS reserved device names, 31
   drive indicator, 30
   extension, 26, 30–31
      identifying applications by, 43
   maximum length of, 29
   parts of, 29
   special characters not used in, 29–30
Files, 26, 28–29
   application files, 26, 43–44

.BMP files, 185, 190, 354, 357
   changing attributes of, 255–56
      archive attribute, 256
      hidden attribute, 256
      read-only attribute, 256
      system attribute, 255–56
   copying, 38–40, 240–46
   data files, 26, 43, 51, 204
   displaying list of, 31–33
   macro files, managing, 417–18
   program files, 204
   retrieving, 29
   saving:
      in Paintbrush, 189–90
      in Write, 162–64
   types of, 43–44
Floppy disks, 26
   backing up, 36–38
   preparing for use (formatting), 34–36
   types of, 34
Fonts, 134, 331–44
   adding, 338–40
   decorative fonts, 332, 335
   definition of, 333
   origin of, 335–36
   point size, 332, 333–34
   removing, 340–42
   sans serifs, 334–35
   screen fonts, 332, 336
   selecting, 337–38
   serifs, 332, 334
   text fonts, 332, 335
   True-Type fonts, 332, 336–37
   vector fonts, 333, 336
   Write accessory, changing, 146–48
   See also Printer
Fonts icon (Control Panel), 339–42
   adding fonts, 338–40
   removing fonts, 340–42
Footers:
   definition of, 134
   Write accessory, 155–57
FORMAT command, DOS, 34–36
Format Diskette command, File Manager, 225–29
Formatting floppy disks, 34–36

G

Games Group, 53, 64, 72, 86
Go-To key, 134, 138
Graphics/pictures, Write accessory, 157–62
Group description, 86, 89

Group filename, 86, 89
Group icon, label, 90
Groups, 50, 52
   Accessories Group, 52, 72, 86
   Applications Group, 53
   deleting program group, 96–97
   deleting program items from, 95–96
   Games Group, 53, 64, 72, 86
   Main Group, 52, 64, 72, 86
   moving/copying icons from one group to another, 95
   See also Program Manager
Group Window, 50
GUI (Graphic User Interface), 50, 51

H

Hard disk, 26, 27
Hardware, 16, 17–18
Headers:
   definition of, 134
   Write accessory, 155–57
HELP window keys, 448
Hidden attribute, changing, 255–56
High graphics, 382, 387, 394
High Memory Area (HMA), 382, 392–93
Hue, 346, 350–51

I

I-beam pointer, 134
Icons, 3, 4, 8–9, 64
   application icons, 72, 74
   Arrange Icons command:
      Task Manager, 80, 81
      Window menu, 68, 100
   arranging, 79–81
   copying, from one groups to another, 95
   default icon, 86
      changing, 99–100
   dragging, 2, 10, 95
   identifying file type by, 204–5
   moving, 65
      from one groups to another, 95
   opening, 8
   program group icons, 72, 74
   spacing, changing, 100–102
Inactive windows, accessing, 76
Input, 16, 17, 21
Insertion point, 134

PIFs (Program Information
Files), 43, 382
  custom-made, creating, 385–88
  launching DOS applications
  with, 388–90
  purpose of, 383
  ready-made, 384–85
Playback:
  macros, 410, 413
    Continuous Loop option,
    416–17
    controlling, 415–17
    Enable Shortcut Keys option,
    417
    To: Any Application option,
    416
    To: Same Application option,
    415–16
Point size, fonts, 332, 333–34
Printer:
  checklist for identifying, 317
  configuration of, setting,
  321–26
  default printer, 316
    selecting, 320–21
  fonts and, 331–44
  installing, 315–30
  printer driver:
    definition of, 316
    installing from Control
    Panel, 317–19
  printer port, selecting, 319–20
  print options, setting, 322–25
  removing an installed printer,
  326–27
  timeout options, selecting,
  325–26
  See also Fonts
Printers icon, Control Panel,
298–300, 322
Printing:
  in Calendar, 116–17
  in Cardfile, 123
  from File Manager, 291–92
  Paintbrush drawings, 190–93
  in Write, 165
Print Manager, 52, 295–314
  DOS applications and, 297
  exiting, 311
  Options menu, 302–3
    message control options,
    303–4
    print priority options, 302–3
  pausing/resuming printing,
  301–2
  printing to a file, 297–300
  printing without, 304–5
  Print Queue, 300–303

changing job order in, 301
  deleting job from, 302
  looking at, 300–301
  print speed, changing, 302–3
  troubleshooting problems in,
  305–10
Processing, 16, 17–18, 21
Program files, 204
Program group icons, 64, 72,
74
Program groups, 60, 64,
85–104
  adding items to, 89–94
  arranging, 87
  creating a new group, 87–89
  default icon, changing, 99–100
  deleting a group, 96–97
  deleting program items from,
  95–96
  icon spacing, changing,
  100–102
  moving/copying icons from
  one group to another, 95
Program group window, 72,
73–74
  maximizing, 74
Program item icons, 74
Program Item Properties dialog
box, 99
Program Manager, 50, 51–53
  assigning application shortcut
  keys from, 398–99
  keys, 444
  launching applications from,
  53, 71–84
  program groups and, 64–65
  starting, 59–70
Prompt, 27
/P switch, DIR command, 32

Q

Quick format, 224, 228

R

RAM (Random Access
Memory), 60, 63
Raster fonts, See Screen fonts
RD (Remove Directory)
command, 43
Read-only attribute, changing,
256
Real mode, 62
.REC extension, 413
Recorder, 52, 407–23
  Record Macro window, 409–14
    Ignore Mouse button, 415

Record Mouse box, 414
Relative To box, 414, 415
uses for, 408–9
See also Macros
Regular slash, 40
Repagination, 134, 137
Root directory, 268
Ruler, Write accessory, 151–54

S

San serif fonts, 332, 334–35
Saturation, 346, 350–51
Saving:
  Calendar, 117
  color scheme, 352–53
  macros, 412–13
  Paintbrush files, 185–90
  Write files, 162–64
Scalable fonts, 332
Scientific calculator, 106,
110–11
  advanced functions, 434–36
  basic operations, 430–31
  bitwise operations, 431–32
  number-base functions, 432–33
  statistical functions, 433–34
  See also Calculator
Screen elements, 346, 349
Screen fonts, 332, 336
Screen Saver:
  activating, 366, 372–76
  adding password protection to,
  375–76
Scroll bars, 9
Scroll box, 9–10
Serif fonts, 332, 334
Setup Program, 52, 60, 61–63,
64, 72–73, 86–87, 98, 106,
425–30
  Custom Setup, 429–30
  Express Setup, 427–29
Single-click, mouse, 9
Software, 16, 19–20
Solitaire game, 5, 53
Source disk, DISKCOPY
command, 36, 37, 224
Standard calculator, 106,
107–10
  functions, summary of, 108–9
  See also Calculator
Standard Mode, 60, 62
Start-up directory, 383
Startup Group, 72, 98, 366
  launching applications from,
  367–68
Subdirectories, 26, 40–43,
203–4, 268